CONTENTS

INTRODUCTION

'Literature has an important role to play – in a variety of ways – in improving abilities in speaking and listening and in writing, as well as in reading. Children should experiment, for example, with dramatic improvisations of the stories they read and write; they should experience and take part in the performance of poetry; they should listen critically to radio plays. They should also be encouraged to **write** fiction, poetry, plays, diaries, book reviews and so on, in response to the literature they have enjoyed and shared and discussed with their teacher and classmates. Learning to read and learning to write are intimately related. By reading a wide range of literature, children become aware of new forms of discourse and modes of expression with which they may experiment in their own writing.'

Programmes of study should be so constructed as to give all pupils the opportunity:

- to enjoy work in a wide range of literary forms;
- to encounter and find pleasure in literary works written in English – particularly new works – from different parts of the world;
- to gain pleasure and critical awareness from the study of pre-20th century writing.

National Curriculum Document: English for ages 5 to 16 (DES, June 1989)

✂

The central purpose of this book is to introduce the idea of narrative and, in particular, the narrative of fiction. Our aim is to encourage the reading of fiction, the writing of fiction, the recording of fiction, its understanding and appreciation. The text can be used either **systematically** (following the sequence outlined below) or more **freely**, the units being chosen by teachers as they relate to their own particular programmes. There are four main sections.

The first section (chapters 1–6) is concerned with **the process of making narrative**. The work begins with the sources of narrative in ordinary life (chapter 1). This moves logically to autobiography (chapter 2). The scheme continues first with the process of observing and imagining (chapter 3) then with the design and construction of books (chapter 4). Finally, it turns to the importance of the spoken voice in fiction (chapter 5) and the power and place of imitation (chapter 6).

The second section (chapters 7–11) is designed to foster an appreciation of the **formal elements of literary narrative**, namely: character (chapter 7), dialogue (chapter 8), setting (chapter 9), plot (chapter 10), and symbol (chapter 11).

The third section (chapters 12–15) focuses on the **ways of telling narrative**. It thus presents, in turn, the different modes of fiction; the first person (chapter 12), letters, diaries and journals (chapter 13), dramatic monologue (chapter 14), and third-person narrative (chapter 15).

Finally, the last chapter introduces the notions of **genre**. All the main genres of fiction are referred to but the main focus is on the genre of science fiction.

At the end of each chapter the teacher will find a varied list of 'Assignments'. Some of these are simple exercises, others are major enterprises. Some are presented with considerable guidance, others are left open. Our aim has been to achieve a necessary but delicate balance between direction and freedom. We envisage teachers and students selecting from Assignments according to their own interests and needs. The various tasks are grouped under two main headings: 'Making and presenting' and 'Researching and responding'. The first group involves **expressive** work: the writing of stories, the imagining of characters and situations, the making of drama, the designing of book-jackets, the making of cassettes and videos, etc. The second group involves **analysis**: doing research, making reports, reviews, summaries, the writing of critical and appreciative essays – all of which should come out of, and further foster, sensitive reflection on the nature of fiction and the ways it works upon the human imagination. We believe that these two elements – the expressive and the analytical – should be in a continuous reciprocal relationship, and should support the creative approach advocated by the *National Curriculum Document: English for ages 5 to 16:*

> 'The "creative" response to literature . . . is two-fold in its effect. Pupils are able, through reading and responding to literature, to develop an understanding of and control over an ever-widening range of written forms. But the experience of writing creatively – of using the sonnet form, for example, or of imitating the characteristics of a particular writer's style – leads also to an increased critical awareness of literary technique in the writing of others.'

We would like to offer here a few guiding and elementary notes on the main kinds of Assignment. They will tell experienced teachers nothing which they do not already know; but they may have some value in indicating the general frame of teaching in which the book has developed.

DRAFTING AND DEVELOPING FICTION

Sometimes the students may be asked to write part of a story in a restricted length of time. That can be a valuable exercise. But generally when they work on a story they need to be given a generous span of time. Students need to have time to work on a first draft, put it away, look at it again, revise it, and so work through what might be a whole series of drafts until the story attains its final form. In writing creatively, one has to be messy before one can be tidy. In the Assignments, students will sometimes be asked to imitate a particular narrative form so that they may learn at first hand about its structure. Sometimes, stories of real worth are created in this way. At the same time, students must feel free to follow what happens as they write and to develop their own particular style. The Assignments, therefore, also offer some very open, imaginative tasks. We hope that the students will come to realise the value of moving between the two poles, now experimenting with given techniques, now freely developing their own imaginative powers. We believe that the two elements are, in fact, complementary and should always be in some kind of dynamic relationship.

RECORDING FICTION ON CASSETTE

There is, of course, no set way of reading out stories. We assume that the English teacher is not after theatrical performances. Students must find **their own speaking voice** for the fiction they are rendering. Once again, it is important to experiment with reading, to rehearse. It is vital that students are encouraged to try out different ways of reading the same story until they are happy with the reading that **most fits all the words of the narrative**. Now that the oral element in teaching has been formally recognised, particularly in the GCSE examinations, and, moreover, fully affirmed in the *National Curriculum Document: English for ages 5 to 16*, it is clear that the reading out of work (the recording of it on cassette and video) will take on a new and greater significance in the English classroom.

DISCUSSING IN GROUPS

As all English teachers know, discussing a story in small groups is in itself a fine art – or should be! It involves students attending carefully to every line, every word, and attending, at the same time, to what others have to say about it. In our view, a group works well when individuals not only talk, but talk in detail **about their responses to the story**, and also **listen to others**. In this way, a collective understanding of the story can be built up which no one individual could possibly have reached alone. At times, it can be helpful if the teacher asks each group to appoint their own chairperson to guide the proceedings, and to appoint someone to keep notes of what is said (perhaps in order to report back to another group). At other times, the structure can be left very informal, providing it is for a fairly short and prescribed period of time. If in the Assignments we have not formally specified many formal discussions, it is because we assume that the very **medium** of teaching a course on narrative is **talk**, between students and teacher and between student and student.

DOING RESEARCH

It is increasingly recognised, particularly when students have chosen their own topics, that research (both individual and collective) can be a most productive way of learning. Students, however, need to learn how to take notes, how to make summaries, and know where to look. We believe it is useful to encourage all researchers to keep a special notebook for their investigations. Also, research often needs the specific stimulus of a **context**; for this reason in the Assignments (which invariably include subjects for research) we often refer to a **classroom presentation** of what is discovered or, alternatively, a **classroom display**.

WRITING ESSAYS

There are at least two kinds of essay that students can be asked to write in relation to fiction. They can be asked to write a formal essay in which they might analyse the pattern of the story; its method of narration, say, its plot, its use of symbols and its theme. Or they can be asked to write a more informal essay, in which they are invited to explore their own personal responses: what they feel about its language or theme, and how it relates to their own experience. Both can be done well – and badly! But generally, in our view, the best kind of literary essay includes both the critical and the creative, a formal analysis of the story and a personal response to it, and brings them, tellingly, together. If in *The Forms of Narrative* we have emphasised literary structures it is because we now know that they have been seriously neglected in the last three decades of English teaching. Students need a **language** to understand and talk about the fiction they read and the feelings it engenders. There need be no division between formal understanding and living response.

⚬

We hope that this book will foster both a lively practical sense of what it is like to make good fiction and, also, a keen appreciation of some of the best fiction that has been written, by men and by women, both in our own culture and in other cultures, in our own time and in past times. Fiction matters, ultimately, because it expands imaginative experience, connects us to others, and deepens our response to living. It is hoped that in making our students more aware of the patterns of fiction, *The Forms of Narrative* will further enhance that development.

Peter Abbs and John Richardson

1 | CREATING NARRATIVE

We have a need to tell and hear stories, and through stories learn about the world we live in. Look at the following visual stories.

- What events do they narrate?
- What is their central theme?

ODE TO TINTIN

We are all narrative makers. We spend much of our lives telling our own stories and listening to the stories of others. Events happen to us, we put words around them and – depending on what we can remember, how we feel and who is listening – narrate them in different ways. These stories are our own personal stories, our own narratives. They come out of the incidents, accidents and encounters of our own lives. Often, at night, before falling asleep, we go through the story of our day's experiences and when we see our friends we exchange these stories, constantly adding to them as we grow older.

In talk, chatter, gossip we thus weave a great web of narrative: about the people we know, about our family, neighbours, teachers, acquaintances, our friends, enemies – and ourselves.

And then in daydreams we imagine other stories. We sit at dull tasks, or bored, with nothing to do, imagine other narratives for our lives. We might see ourselves rushing through the defence and scoring a spectacular goal or giving some brilliant performance and the audience clapping. We imagine ourselves defeating all opposition and gaining, at last, the recognition we feel we deserve but feel we have never had.

But not all phantasies are so positive. Quite often we can imagine ourselves being squashed by the opposition or making a speech and forgetting our lines. In our phantasies we can see ourselves defeated and humiliated. These are the stories we hope will never take place, the narratives we dread most.

Then at night in dreams we can create further imaginary narratives. These stories seem out of our control. They happen to us. We fall asleep and then find ourselves on a journey in unknown forests or strange cities. We can meet people we have never met before and experience a range of feelings, sometimes pleasurable and sometimes deeply disturbing. We can wake up screaming or with the dream story so vivid in our minds that we still feel part of it, still caught in the plot of the dream.

In the following passages three writers re-tell their dreams.

Edith Wharton's Dream

A pale demon with black hair came in, followed by four gnome-like creatures carrying a great black trunk. They set it down and opened it, and the Demon, crying out: 'Here's your year – here are all the horrors that have happened to you and that are still going to happen' dragged out a succession of limp black squirming things and threw them on the floor before me. They were not rags or creatures, not living or dead – they were Black Horrors, shapeless, and that seemed to writhe about as they fell at my feet, and yet were as inanimate as bits of stuff. But none of these comparisons occurred to me, for I *knew* what they were: the hideous, the incredible things that had happened to me in this dreadful year, or were to happen to me before its close; and I stared, horror-struck, as the Demon dragged them out, one by one, more and more, till finally, flinging down a blacker, hatefuller one, he said laughing: 'There – that's the last of them!'

The gnomes laughed too; but I, as I stared at the great black pile and the empty trunk, said to the Demon: '*Are you sure it hasn't a false bottom?*'

Edith Wharton, 1913

Katherine Mansfield's Dream

The first night I was in bed here, i.e. after my first day in bed, I went to sleep. And suddenly I felt my whole body *breaking up*. It broke up with a violent shock – an earthquake – and it broke like glass. A long terrible shiver, you understand – and the spinal cord and the bones and every bit and particle quaking. It sounded in my ears – a low, confused din, and there was a sense of flashing greenish brilliance, like broken glass. When I woke up I thought there had been a violent earthquake. But all was still. It slowly dawned upon me – the conviction that in that dream I died. I shall go on living now – it may be for months, or for weeks or days or hours. Time is not. In that dream I died.

Katherine Mansfield, *Letters and Journals*, 1919

Hugh Walpole's Dream

I was in the market-place of a town. It was filled with people, talking, buying and selling, all very happy and busy. Suddenly, as though a cloud came over the sun, the air was cold and the noise died down to the twittering of birds. Men and women looked about them. Everyone was silent. I myself felt a trembling expectant fear. I looked about me, wondering why I was so apprehensive, and found that the place was emptied like a bowl of water. It was dark and cold. Not a sound. Something told me to run for my life but I could not move. Then, from a side street, a little procession came into the square. A woman was carried on a kind of stretcher that also resembled a barrow. Two men in black carried it. They were followed by a small group of quite silent persons. And in front of the stretcher was a tall, thin man with a sallow face. But what was especially horrible about him was that his head was twisted to one side as though his neck was broken.

They advanced without a sound, their feet making no apparent contact with the pavement. There was a cold silence everywhere and great but crowded emptiness as though somewhere hundreds of people were holding their breath.

I was exactly in the path of the little procession. I knew that if the yellow-faced man touched me something appalling would follow. But I could not move.

The man and the stretcher and the followers advanced nearer and nearer. I was in an agony of terror. I woke and my pyjamas were soaked with sweat. I have never had a more horrible dream.

Hugh Walpole, 1933

These are not stories made consciously by their authors but stories which have come directly from their dreams.

Authors have often used dream as a device for telling a story or for bringing out some important feature of their story. But dreaming is something we all do. We all make narratives of some kind in our minds as we sleep.

Then surrounding our lives, on all sides, are public narratives. These are the daily news stories which tell us of public figures and public events, of political struggles, of financial scandals, scandals about sex and drugs, narratives of war and natural disasters. They are narrated constantly to us through television and radio programmes, through newspapers and magazines, through cartoons, posters, leaflets, and even comics.

QUAKE HORROR

Bridge collapses crushing drivers

Lovers 'used £25 curse in plot to kill husband'

Sad groom Garry has honeymoon with a pal

EXPOSED

The misery-guts monsieur m your holida

NEWS

Duckling 'theft' leaves caring boy distraught

There are other stories, narrated daily on commercial television, in magazines and on street hoardings, which do not refer to actual people but which are made by sophisticated publicity teams.

The characters in these stories are most often heroes or heroines who, having acquired the magical object (the right perfume, car or drink), obtain whatever they desire. The gaining of the object secures a number of transformations.

These characters stare down at us from street hoardings or look at us from television sets and magazines. They often hold up their magical object and imply that if only we too can secure it then their success will be ours. These are the fairy stories and fables of mass-persuasion. Indeed, often the advertising teams directly use, for their own purposes, the old fairy stories and myths. And many people who are not convinced by these glossy re-tellings respond by inserting their own version of the story.

All the time, then, we are making up narratives for our lives. We make these narratives out of our own direct experience, out of our phantasies, our dreams, out of the news stories of the times, and the mass-produced stories of advertising, of 'soaps', of television dramas and serials.

In their writing, storytellers and novelists work with our desire for narrative and develop it. They take us into imaginary worlds so that we can explore the meaning of human experience. In the following chapters we will consider those imaginary worlds, how they are constructed and how they relate to our own sense of life.

ASSIGNMENTS

MAKING AND PRESENTING

1 **Sharing personal narratives** In pairs or small groups, talk about those occasions from your life which you think might make good stories as personal narratives. You could select one or two of the following:

(a) *An Embarrassing Moment* Describe an occasion when you were extremely embarrassed either by your own actions or by the actions of someone in your company, consider how the incident arose, what actually happened and how it caused you embarrassment.

(b) *A Moment of Fame* Describe a time when you took the lead in some action or event which left you feeling extremely pleased with (even proud of) yourself. Try to record the event as it happened. Say how you came to act as you did and how you felt about the matter afterwards.

(c) *Bitterly Hurt* Tell the story of one occasion in your life when everything went wrong and you were left feeling hurt or upset.

2 **Recording dream narratives** Dream narratives do not always make sense to us or follow a logical pattern. Recall some of your own dreams, or fragments and snatches of dreams, and note them down exactly as you remember them. Try to let them speak for themselves, even if they appear broken or incomplete, unreal or absurd, simple or silly. The title for your written work might be *Fragments from a Dream*.

3 In pairs or small groups, try to remember any recurring dreams that you have now or may have had in the past. When you have described them to others, try to write them down as narratives, recording as you do so all the feelings and sensations that accompany them.

4 **Making stories from daydreams: 'A Perfect Day'** Write the narrative of a daydream which tells of your perfect day. Supposing you could do anything you wished for 24 hours – go anywhere you wanted, meet anyone you wanted, buy anything, eat anything. How would you get on? Write a diary entry for the day, beginning from the time you wake up.

5 **Working from fantasy** Czechoslovakian writer Franz Kafka wrote a story called *The Metamorphosis* in which the main character wakes up to find that he has turned into a large insect:

He had no difficulty in turning back the coverlet; he needed only to blow himself up a little and it fell of its own accord. But beyond that, he was impeded by his tremendous girth. To get up, he needed arms and hands, but he had only numerous little legs in perpetual vibration, over which he had no control. Before he could bend one, he had first to stretch it out, and when at last he performed the desired movement, all the others worked uncontrollably, in intensely painful agitation. 'I must not stay uselessly in bed,' said Gregor to himself . . .

The story records the horror of the realisation that the transformation is not a dream or a fantasy but a reality. Imagine a situation in which a person wakes up one morning in a different form: as an insect perhaps, or invisible, or as someone else. Write about the bizarre events of the day that follows.

6 Choose one of the illustrations in this chapter and use it as the starting-point for a piece of narrative writing.

RESEARCHING AND RESPONDING

1 A number of novels and short stories have been told through dreams or have used dreams. Here, for example, is a paragraph from the end of Lewis Carroll's *Alice's Adventures in Wonderland*:

> 'Oh, I've had such a curious dream!' said Alice. And she told her sister, as well as she could remember them, all these strange Adventures of hers that you have just been reading about; and, when she had finished, her sister kissed her, and said 'It *was* a curious dream, dear, certainly; but now run in to your tea: it's getting late.' So Alice got up and ran off, thinking while she ran, as well she might, what a wonderful dream it had been.

Discuss the strengths and weaknesses of using a dream as a way of telling a story. Find a number of examples from different authors to support your point of view.

2 Using the school and local library, do some research of your own into the life and writing of **either** Franz Kafka (titles include *The Trial*, *The Castle* and *Metamorphosis*), **or** Lewis Carroll. Prepare notes and illustrations for a classroom presentation or for a display.

3 Build up your own collection of narrative advertisements from newspapers, magazines, hoardings and television. Select one or two for close analysis.
Describe the story. What is the situation? What happens? How much is directly shown, how much suggested?
Examine the characters. How lifelike are they? What are they meant to suggest? How are we meant to respond to them? What influence do you think these narratives have on people's lives? How do you regard this influence: good? bad? neutral? mixed?

4 Working on all the material gathered in response to the last question, write an essay on 'The Narratives of Advertising'. Illustrate your argument with actual examples from the advertisements that you have selected.

5 Write a short essay on narrative based on this chapter. Outline the different ways in which we make narratives, e.g. through dreams, phantasies, conversations, through the news and advertising. In each case, give your own examples. See if you can think of other ways in which we make narratives (in jokes, for example) that are not mentioned in this chapter.

2 | TELLING OUR OWN STORIES

All the time in conversation, in phantasy and in dream, we shape a narrative for our lives from our experiences. We create a story of our lives which changes and develops as we change and develop.

One of the most common ways of recording this narrative is *The Family Album*. In the family album, photographs are arranged to tell the story of many important events – birthdays, holidays, family gatherings, excursions, weddings – and to record all the main characters taking part – grandparents, parents, relations, friends, neighbours. Taken together the photographs tell the story of the family.

Victorian family groups

Family photos from the 1950s

Yet a number of authors and photographers have recently questioned the range of the family album. Isn't it, they have asked, too restricted and too sentimental? Shouldn't it also include photographs of the members of the family at work, doing jobs in the kitchen and getting on with the ordinary tasks of life?

Shouldn't the family album capture other states of feeling – feelings of anger and frustration – and not just the happy smiles of the posed photograph? And shouldn't it also record disturbing events like those of sickness and death? Shouldn't the family album honestly narrate the whole story of the way people live together?

Other photographers wanting to make even more personal use of photography have used it to create montage images of their own life. In this way they have created in images a narrative of their own lives.

- What can you tell about the central figure in this photographic collage?
- What were her main interests?
- When do you think it was created?
- If you were to create a montage photograph from your own life, which objects would it include?
- How would you construct it?
- How much of your own life could be represented in this way?

Another way of creating an image of one's self or one's life is through the self-portrait. The pictures below present three different self-portraits by Frida Kahlo. A significant influence on her life and painting was an accident which seriously injured her spine.

From the time of St Augustine's *Confessions* (written around AD 397) onwards, writers have attempted to create the narrative of their own lives in the form of autobiography. Many autobiographies begin with the author's earliest memories and move slowly forwards through childhood and youth to the point when the author is writing.

Here are some of the very earliest memories of the French writer
Nathalie Sarraute as recorded in her recent autobiography,
Childhood, the cover of which also uses photographs taken from the
family album.

OUTSIDE that luminous, dazzling, vibrant garden, everything seems to be covered in a pall of greyness, it has a rather dismal, or rather, a sort of cramped air . . . but it is never sad. Not even what I still remember of the nursery school . . . a bare courtyard surrounded by high, sombre walls, round which we marched in Indian file, dressed in black overalls and wearing clogs.

Here, however, looming up out of that mist, is the sudden violence of terror, of horror . . . I scream, I struggle . . . what has happened? what is happening to me?

'Your grandmother is coming to see you' . . . Mama told me that . . . My grandmother? Papa's mother? Is that possible? is she really going to come? she never comes, she is so far away . . . I don't remember her at all, but I feel her presence in the affectionate little letters she sends me from over there, in the softwood boxes with pretty pictures carved in them, whose hollowed-out contours you can trace with your finger, in the painted wooden cups covered by a varnish that is soft to the touch . . . 'When will she come? when will she be here?' . . . 'Tomorrow afternoon . . . You won't go out for your walk . . .'

I wait, I watch out for her, I listen to the footsteps on the stairs, on the landing . . . there, here she is, the bell has rung, I want to rush out, I'm stopped, wait, don't move . . . the door to my room opens, a man and a woman dressed in white overalls grab hold of me, I've been put on someone's knees, I'm being held, I struggle, they press a piece of cotton wool over my mouth, over my nose, a mask, from which something atrocious, asphyxiating, emanates, suffocates me, fills my lungs, rises to my head, dying, that's what it is, I'm dying . . . And then, I am alive again, I'm in my bed, my throat is burning, my tears are flowing, Mama is wiping them away . . . 'My little kitten, you had to have an operation, you know, they took something out of your throat, it was harming you, it was bad for you . . . go to sleep now, it's all over . . .'

How long did it take you to realize that she never tried – unless very absent-mindedly and clumsily – to put herself in your place? . . .

–Yes, curiously enough that indifference, that casualness, were part of her charm, in the literal sense of the word, she charmed me . . . No word, however powerfully uttered, has ever sunk into me with the same percussive force as some of hers.

'If you touch one of those poles, you'll die . . .'
–Perhaps she didn't say it exactly in those terms . . .
–Perhaps not . . . but that was how it reached me. If you touch that, you'll die . . .

We are going for a walk somewhere in the country, I don't remember where, Mama is walking slowly, on Kolya's arm . . . I am behind, rooted to the spot in front of the wooden telegraph pole . . . 'If you touch that, you'll die,' Mama said that . . . I have an urge to touch it, I want to know, I'm very frightened, I want to see what it will be like, I stretch out my hand, I touch the wood of the telegraph pole with my finger . . . and, immediately, that's it, it's happened to me, Mama knew it, Mama knows everything, it's certain, I'm dead, I run up to them screaming, I hide my head in Mama's skirts, I shout with all my strength: I'm dead . . . they don't know it, I'm dead . . . But what's the matter with you? I'm dead, dead, dead, I touched the pole, there, it's happened, the horrible thing, the most horrible thing possible was in that pole, I touched it and it passed into me, it's in me, I roll on the ground to get it to come out, I sob, I howl, I'm dead . . . they pick me up in their arms, they shake me, kiss me . . . No, no, you're quite all right . . . I touched the pole, Mama told me . . . she laughs, they both laugh, and this calms me . . .

Nathalie Sarraute, *Childhood*

- Do you find these early memories convincing?
- What kind of language have they been written in?
- Why do you think the author has chosen this form of language?
  In the second half of the passage there seem to be two people in conversation.
- Who do you think these 'people' are?
- Why do you think the writer has shaped her earliest memories in this way?

Early memories are often very difficult to put into words.
Sometimes we are not even sure whether the events took place.
Perhaps we have constructed them from conversations or
photographs? And even if we are sure the events did take place we
are often not sure when they happened or if, in putting them into
language, we do not in some way alter them.

Here are some early memories, and later reflections on writing them, as
recorded by a young writer.

First Memories

'I'll never forget this. I'll never forget this.' The
words going through my mind for the first time –
the first time (as far as I can recall), I was making a
conscious effort to always remember an incident. I
was pre-school. I was standing outside a group of
girls. I remember the scene: they were gathered
about a table, drawing with crayons. 'There are no
crayons left for you. Go away you horrid girl.' And
I decided then and there 'I'll never forget this' –
and I never have. My first realisation – I can even
feel it now – of feeling. A surging up within of hurt
and anger. A rejection on what now may seem a
minimal scale but seemed so massive then. Such a
tight feeling in my stomach. I remember my nails
digging into my palms as I stood there. My moist
and sticky palms. I stood and stared – as I have
done so many times since – and vowed 'I'll never
forget this'. Before then, I remember nothing. Just
an image of a small, scruffy and undoubtedly
smelly girl standing in that room surveying the
scene so as never to lose its memory.

All my memories of my childhood are as such.
Recaptured emotions: rejection, embarrassment,
happiness, love, confusion and hurt. Each incident
I recall first with a feeling inside and then slowly
the image unwinds itself to a fuller picture of a
whole incident. My recollections, my autobiography, therefore, could only ever be a history of
emotions, and extremes of emotions at that.

My Commentary on the Writing of 'First Memories'

The main problem I had with recalling a memory
from the past was the speed with which I had to
write. I did not have to struggle to remember, in
fact, I remembered too much at one time. Everything seemed to come flooding back at once and I
almost forgot I was actually writing. The pen was
moving without hesitation, so it was almost as if the
memory wrote itself. I cannot say that this flood of
memory occurs for all events in my past. I do not
know what is my earliest memory. At different
times I remember different events, some of which
are earlier than others. It is as if all the memories
are there waiting for the right trigger to set them
off. (Reading different extracts of autobiography
brought past events to mind; often there seemed
no connection between the trigger and the recol-
lection.) I think I would need the help of my
parents to place many of my earliest memories in
chronological order. The memories are images, no
conversations are remembered and I don't seem to
have any picture and faces. People are just there
and I know who they are. Sometimes a smell or an
object or even a casual comment will evoke a
memory I did not know I had.

Recording memory accurately is very difficult. I
find that it rarely comes out exactly as it is remembered. It is difficult to recapture the atmosphere,
excitement, sadness and real feelings of the event
in words. How can you really capture the intense
excitement felt by a child waiting for Christmas by
using adult language and attitudes? Obviously, it
would be impossible to record all memories using
the language available at that particular age; it
would be too simplistic and basic. A child's language would not be wide enough to express how it
was feeling but it is necessary to try and recapture
the feelings of childhood to understand many
memories. Worries and anxieties experienced in
childhood may seem very trivial in an adult world
but to the child they are very important and often
influential.

Glenda Thurley

Most autobiographies narrate the author's life across a span of time.
They may well begin with early memories but they generally move
forwards, often reaching the point in time at which the writer is writing.

Autobiographies do not record all the circumstances of the author, all the experiences, but rather they make a selection from them, choosing those which strike the author as most significant.

In the following passage from the autobiographical writing of Laurie Lee, the author describes the day on which he left home at the age of 19.

THE STOOPING FIGURE of my mother, waist-deep in the grass and caught there like a piece of sheep's wool, was the last I saw of my country home as I left it to discover the world. She stood old and bent at the top of the bank, silently watching me go, one gnarled red hand raised in farewell and blessing, not questioning why I went. At the bend of the road I looked back again and saw the gold light die behind her; then I turned the corner, passed the village school, and closed that part of my life for ever.

It was a bright Sunday morning in early June, the right time to be leaving home. My three sisters and a brother had already gone before me; two other brothers had yet to make up their minds. They were still sleeping that morning, but my mother had got up early and cooked me a heavy breakfast, had stood wordlessly while I ate it, her hand on my chair, and had then helped me pack up my few belongings. There had been no fuss, no appeals, no attempts at advice or persuasion, only a long and searching look. Then, with my bags on my back, I'd gone out into the early sunshine and climbed through the long wet grass to the road.

It was 1934. I was nineteen years old, still soft at the edges, but with a confident belief in good fortune. I carried a small rolled-up tent, a violin in a blanket, a change of clothes, a tin of treacle biscuits, and some cheese. I was excited, vain-glorious, knowing I had far to go; but not, as yet, how far. As I left home that morning and walked away from the sleeping village, it never occurred to me that others had done this before me.

I was propelled, of course, by the traditional forces that had sent many generations along this road — by the small tight valley closing in around one, stifling the breath with its mossy mouth, the cottage walls narrowing like the arms of an iron maiden, the local girls whispering, 'Marry, and settle down.' Months of restless unease, leading to this inevitable moment, had been spent wandering about the hills, mournfully whistling, and watching the high open fields stepping away eastwards under gigantic clouds . . .

And now I was on my journey, in a pair of thick boots and with a hazel stick in my hand. Naturally, I was going to London, which lay a hundred miles to the east; and it seemed equally obvious that I should go on foot. But first, as I'd never yet seen the sea, I thought I'd walk to the coast and find it. This would add another hundred miles to my journey, going by way of Southampton. But I had all the summer and all time to spend.

That first day alone — and now I was really alone at last — steadily declined in excitement and vigour. As I tramped through the dust towards the Wiltshire Downs a growing reluctance weighed me down. White elder-blossom and dog-roses hung in the hedges, blank as unwritten paper, and the hot empty road — there were few motor cars then — reflected Sunday's waste and indifference. High sulky summer sucked me towards it, and I offered no resistance at all. Through the solitary morning and afternoon I found myself longing for some opposition or rescue, for the sound of hurrying footsteps coming after me and family voices calling me back.

None came. I was free. I was affronted by freedom. The day's silence said, Go where you will. It's all yours. You asked for it. It's up to you now. You're on your own, and nobody's going to stop you. As I walked, I was taunted by echoes of home, by the tinkling sounds of the kitchen, shafts of sun from the windows falling across the familiar furniture, across the bedroom and the bed I had left.

When I judged it to be tea-time I sat on an old stone wall and opened my tin of treacle biscuits. As I ate them I could hear mother banging the kettle on the hob and my brothers rattling their tea-cups. The biscuits tasted sweetly of the honeyed squalor of home — still only a dozen miles away.

I might have turned back then if it hadn't been for my brothers, but I couldn't have borne the look on their faces. So I got off the wall and went on my way. The long evening shadows pointed to folded villages, homing cows, and after-church walkers. I tramped the edge of the road, watching my dusty feet, not stopping again for a couple of hours.

When darkness came, full of moths and beetles, I was too weary to put up the tent. So I lay myself down in the middle of a field and stared up at the brilliant stars. I was oppressed by the velvety emptiness of the world and the swathes of soft grass I lay on. Then the fumes of the night finally put me to sleep — my first night without a roof or bed.

Laurie Lee, *As I Walked Out One Midsummer Morning*

In her autobiography, *I Know Why the Caged Bird Sings*, the black writer
Maya Angelou remembers what it was like to be adolescent in her
grandmother's ('Momma') and Uncle Willie's grocery shop in Arkansas,
America, and also a disturbing incident that happened to her brother
Bailey.

WEEKDAYS revolved on a sameness wheel. They
turned into themselves so steadily and inevitably that
each seemed to be the original of yesterday's rough
draft. Saturdays, however, always broke the mold and
dared to be different.

Farmers trekked into town with their children and
wives streaming around them. Their board-stiff khaki
pants and shirts revealed the painstaking care of a
dutiful daughter or wife. They often stopped at the
Store to get change for bills so they could give out
jangling coins to their children, who shook with their
eagerness to get to town. The young kids openly
resented their parents' dawdling in the Store and Uncle
Willie would call them in and spread among them bits
of sweet peanut patties that had been broken in ship-
ping. They gobbled down the candies and were out
again, kicking up the powdery dust in the road and
worrying if there was going to be time to get to town
after all.

Bailey played mumbledypeg with the older boys
around the chinaberry tree, and Momma and Uncle
Willie listened to the farmers' latest news of the
country. I thought of myself as hanging in the Store, a
mote imprisoned on a shaft of sunlight. Pushed and
pulled by the slightest shift of air, but never falling free
into the tempting darkness.

In the warm months, morning began with a quick
wash in unheated well water. The suds were dashed on
a plot of ground beside the kitchen door. It was called
the bait garden (Bailey raised worms). After prayers,
breakfast in summer was usually dry cereal and fresh
milk. Then to our chores (which on Saturday included
weekday jobs) – scrubbing the floors, raking the yards,
polishing our shoes for Sunday (Uncle Willie's had to
be shined with a biscuit) and attending to the customers
who came breathlessly, also in their Saturday hurry.

Looking through the years, I marvel that Saturday
was my favorite day in the week. What pleasures could
have been squeezed between the fan folds of unending
tasks? Children's talent to endure stems from their
ignorance of alternatives.

After our retreat from St Louis, Momma gave us a
weekly allowance. Since she seldom dealt with money,
other than to take it in and to tithe to the church, I
supposed that the weekly ten cents was to tell us that
even she realized that a change had come over us, and
that our new unfamiliarity caused her to treat us with a
strangeness.

I usually gave my money to Bailey, who went to the
movies nearly every Saturday. He brought back Street
and Smith cowboy books for me.

One Saturday Bailey was late coming back from the
Rye-al-toh. Momma had begun heating water for the
Saturday-night baths, and all the evening chores were
done. Uncle Willie sat in the twilight on the front porch
mumbling or maybe singing, and smoking a ready-
made. It was quite late. Mothers had called in their
children from the group games, and fading sounds of
'Yah . . . Yah . . . you didn't catch me' still hung and
floated into the Store.

Uncle Willie said, 'Sister, better light the light.' On
Saturdays we used the electric lights so that last-minute
Sunday shoppers could look down the hill and see if the
Store was open. Momma hadn't told me to turn them
on because she didn't want to believe that night had
fallen hard and Bailey was still out in the ungodly dark.

Her apprehension was evident in the hurried movements around the kitchen and in her lonely fearing eyes.
The Black woman in the South who raises sons,
grandsons and nephews has her heartstrings tied to a
hanging noose. Any break from routine may herald for
them unbearable news. For this reason, Southern
Blacks until the present generation could be counted
among America's arch conservatives.

Like most self-pitying people, I had very little pity for
my relatives' anxiety. If something indeed had happened
to Bailey, Uncle Willie would always have Momma, and
Momma had the Store. Then, after all, we weren't their
children. But I would be the major loser if Bailey turned
up dead. For he was all I claimed, if not all I had.

The bath water was steaming on the cooking stove,
but Momma was scrubbing the kitchen table for the
umpteenth time.

'Momma,' Uncle Willie called and she jumped.
'Momma.' I waited in the bright lights of the Store,
jealous that someone had come along and told these
strangers something about my brother and I would be
the last to know.

'Momma, why don't you and Sister walk down to
meet him?'

To my knowledge Bailey's name hadn't been mentioned for hours, but we all knew whom he meant.

Of course. Why didn't that occur to me? I wanted to
be gone. Momma said, 'Wait a minute, little lady. Go
get your sweater, and bring me my shawl.'

It was darker in the road than I'd thought it would be.
Momma swung the flashlight's arc over the path and
weeds and scary tree trunks. The night suddenly

became enemy territory, and I knew that if my brother was lost in this land he was forever lost. He was eleven and very smart, that I granted, but after all he was so small. The Bluebeards and tigers and Rippers could eat him up before he could scream for help.

Momma told me to take the light and she reached for my hand. Her voice came from a high hill above me and in the dark my hand was enclosed in hers. I loved her with a rush. She said nothing – no 'Don't worry' or 'Don't get tender-hearted.' Just the gentle pressure of her rough hand conveyed her own concern and assurance to me.

We passed houses which I knew well by daylight but couldn't recollect in the swarthy gloom.

'Evening, Miz Jenkins.' Walking and pulling me along.

'Sister Henderson? Anything wrong?' That was from an outline blacker than the night.

'No, ma'am. Not a thing. Bless the Lord.' By the time she finished speaking we had left the worried neighbors far behind.

Mr Willie Williams' Do Drop Inn was bright with furry red lights in the distance and the pond's fishy smell enveloped us. Momma's hand tightened and let go, and I saw the small figure plodding along, tired and old-mannish. Hands in his pockets and head bent, he walked like a man trudging up the hill behind a coffin.

'Bailey.' It jumped out as Momma said, 'Ju,' and I started to run, but her hand caught mine again and became a vise. I pulled, but she yanked me back to her side. 'We'll walk, just like we been walking, young lady.' There was no chance to warn Bailey that he was dangerously late, that everybody had been worried and that he should create a good lie or, better, a great one.

Momma said, 'Bailey, Junior,' and he looked up without surprise. 'You know it's night and you just now getting home?'

'Yes, ma'am.' He was empty. Where was his alibi?

'What you been doing?'

'Nothing.'

'That's all you got to say?'

'Yes, ma'am.'

'All right, young man. We'll see when you get home.'

She had turned me loose, so I made a grab for Bailey's hand, but he snatched it away. I said, 'Hey, Bailey,' hoping to remind him that I was his sister and his only friend, but he grumbled something like 'Leave me alone.'

Momma didn't turn on the flashlight on the way back, nor did she answer the questioning Good evenings that floated around us as we passed the darkened houses.

I was confused and frightened. He was going to get a whipping and maybe he had done something terrible. If he couldn't talk to me it must have been serious. But there was no air of spent revelry about him. He just seemed sad. I didn't know what to think.

Uncle Willie said, 'Getting too big for your britches, huh? You can't come home. You want to worry your grandmother to death?' Bailey was so far away he was beyond fear. Uncle Willie had a leather belt in his good hand but Bailey didn't notice or didn't care. 'I'm going to whip you this time.' Our uncle had only whipped us once before and then only with a peach-tree switch, so maybe now he was going to kill my brother. I screamed and grabbed for the belt, but Momma caught me. 'Now, don't get uppity, miss, 'less you want some of the same thing. He got a lesson coming to him. You come on and get your bath.'

From the kitchen I heard the belt fall down, dry and raspy on naked skin. Uncle Willie was gasping for breath, but Bailey made no sound. I was too afraid to splash water or even to cry and take a chance of drowning out Bailey's pleas for help, but the pleas never came and the whipping was finally over.

I lay awake an eternity, waiting for a sign, a whimper or a whisper, from the next room that he was still alive. Just before I fell exhausted into sleep, I heard Bailey: 'Now I lay me down to sleep, I pray the Lord my soul to keep, if I should die before I wake, I pray the Lord my soul to take.'

My last memory of that night was the question, Why is he saying the baby prayer? We had been saying the 'Our Father, which art in heaven' for years.

For days the Store was a strange country, and we were all newly arrived immigrants. Bailey didn't talk, smile or apologize. His eyes were so vacant, it seemed his soul had flown away, and at meals I tried to give him the best pieces of meat and the largest portion of dessert, but he turned them down.

Maya Angelou, *I Know Why the Caged Bird Sings*

There are other ways of telling one's own life and exploring its nature. Many people, including writers, keep journals or diaries, where they record the events of the day and reflect on their meaning. These too are autobiographical forms of writing.

People also write letters – and in some letters describe at length their own experiences and their own feelings. The letter written for one other person can encourage a very intimate style of writing in which the writer can reflect on his or her own behaviour and emotions.

As we shall see in chapter 13, it was partly out of the habit of writing journals, letters, diaries, confessions and autobiographies that the form of the novel grew. In the novel and the story it was possible to explore states of feeling and sequences of events not by experiencing them directly but by imagining them. The novel was an instrument for understanding life through imagining what it would be like if, for example, one was shipwrecked, if one was at war, if one was in love, if one was haunted by a ghost. Thus the novel, to appear convincing, often presented itself as if it was a form of direct autobiography.

We will return to look at these various ways of shaping narrative in chapters 12, 13 and 14.

ASSIGNMENTS

MAKING AND PRESENTING

1   With the help of careful planning and preparation (note-taking, memory aids, jottings), write the autobiography of a single day in your life. Try to include all the important aspects of the day: what happens to you, what you do, where you go, who you see, what you speak about, your honest impression of the people that you meet and, most important of all, your thoughts and feelings as the day progresses.

2   Develop one chapter in your life-story so far. Look back over some of the autobiographical pieces given earlier in this chapter and use them as possible guides to help you to structure your own chapter. Think carefully about the period in your life that you want to cover. Try to choose a self-contained episode if you can. 'School Days' or 'First Loves' or 'When I was Ten', etc., might serve as chapter headings, but you will have your own preferences. You may also wish to include photographs as part of the work.

3   **A life map**   Try to visualise your life as if it were a map; not only a map of the real places that you have been to or have been associated with, but also as a map of your feelings and experiences. It might help here if you think back to John Bunyan's famous book *The Pilgrim's Progress*, where Pilgrim travels through places with names like 'The Valley of Humiliation', 'The Delectable Mountains', 'Doubting Castle' and 'Hill Difficulty' on his life's journey. You could try to invent similar 'places' on your life map, and at each place you could write a brief passage detailing the things that happened to you at that point in your life. You will need a very large sheet of paper for this and plenty of coloured pencils or felt-tips.

4   Experiment with different autobiographical forms. Use the form of the letter, the diary or journal to create a small piece of autobiography.

5 **Designing a collage**   Get a large sheet of backing paper, a collection of old magazines and newspapers, photocopies of photographs you value, pieces of your own writing, and some glue. Now select from all these materials those words and images that reveal an important aspect of your own life.

Cut and tear out the pieces that you want to include in this collage of yourself and, without gluing, arrange them on the backing paper to create a design that you are happy with. Include as many words or passages of writing as you want.

When you are ready and satisfied with the overall effect, glue the pieces that you have chosen to the backing paper to finally complete your autobiographical collage.

6 Look through the family photograph album or collection and write about the pictures that you find. You could write a series of short passages about the events that are recorded, and your feelings.

7 Record on cassette an interview with members of your family about their childhood and early memories. Try to get them to tell you any old family stories and their memories of the past.

RESEARCHING AND RESPONDING

1 Many autobiographies have been written during the last two centuries. Using the library, make your own list of some of them. What are their titles? Who are their authors? When were they written? What are the main concerns of the autobiographies? Make some notes to report back for classroom discussion.

2 Find out more about novels which are presented as autobiographies, e.g. *Gulliver's Travels, Robinson Crusoe* and *Jane Eyre*. What are they about? Why do you think they have been presented as autobiographies? Do you think their first readers would have known that, in fact, they were works of fiction?

3 Write a short review (it could take the form of a letter) of any autobiography you have read recently. Imagine you are introducing the book to a reader who is interested in autobiography but who does not know this particular work.

4 Write an account of your own attempts at making an autobiography.
- What form did you decide to write it in?
- How did the piece develop?
- How did you select what to write about?
- How truthful is your account?
- What have you learnt about yourself and about the form of autobiography by writing an autobiography?

For an example of writing on the experience of making autobiography, see page 22 of this chapter.

5 Drawing on all the work in this chapter and on your own experience (and that of the class) of making autobiography, write an essay on the various ways in which people can tell the stories of their own lives.

Look at the following photographs.

- Who are the characters we are looking at?
- Where might the action be taking place?
- When is it taking place?
- What might the person be thinking?
- Can you re-create in words the flow of their thoughts?

Now consider this image of a group of people.

- Who are the main characters?
- What is the action?
- When and where is it taking place?

Choose any one image and work on it intensively. Describe what is taking place in the minds of two of the characters.

Simply imagine you are two of the characters and narrate their experience at the very point of the action depicted. This will give an account of the same amount from two points of view; two stories about the same event.

The storyteller, who does not rely on his or her own autobiographical experience, has to imagine all the events narrated and bring them to life through the choice of words.

In conventional stories every incident has to be re-created with the greatest care. The French 19th-century short-story writer, Maupassant, wrote:

WHATEVER you want to say, there is only one word to express it, one verb to set it in motion and only one adjective to describe it. And so you must hunt for this word, this verb and this adjective until you find them and never be content with any approximations, never fall back on verbal trickery and clownishness, however apt, in order to evade the difficulty.

In another passage Maupassant described how he had been trained to look carefully, by the novelist Flaubert. For him, close observation of the world was an essential part of the writer's task. This is what he wrote about the influence of Flaubert:

— **TALENT** is a long patience. — It involves looking at everything one wants to describe long enough, and attentively enough, to find in it some aspect that no one has yet seen or expressed. Everything contains some element of the unexplored because we are accustomed to use our eyes only with the memory of what other people before us have thought about the object we are looking at. The least thing has a bit of the unknown in it. Let us find this. In order to describe a fire burning or a tree in a field, let us stand in front of that fire and that tree until they no longer look to us like any other fire or any other tree.

That is how one becomes original.

Having stated this truth, that in the entire world there are no two grains of sand, no two flies, no two hands or noses, exactly alike — he would then make me describe, in a few sentences, a being or an object in such a way as to particularise it distinctly and to distinguish it from all other beings, or all other objects, of the same race or kind.

He would say to me, 'When you pass a grocer sitting at his door, or a concierge smoking his pipe, or a cab-stand, you must show me that grocer and that concierge, their attitude, their whole physical appearance, including as well — indicated by the aptness of your image — their entire moral nature, in such a way that I shan't confuse them with any other grocer or any other concierge; and you must make me see, with a single word, in what way one cab-horse is totally unlike fifty others that go before and after it.'

Guy de Maupassant, 'Le Roman',
Preface to *Pierre et Jean*

In a similar spirit the English novelist, John Braine, wrote the following.

LET US CONSIDER another example of how not to write. I made it up, but it's an absolutely typical passage from any unpublished novel and I have seen passages like it in more than one published novel.

'Tom walked over to the window. The sun had come out. He went upstairs and awakened Hilda.'

This is remarkable for the number of questions it doesn't answer. How did Tom walk over to the window? Slowly? Briskly? What did he see through the window? How did he go upstairs? What did he notice on the way? Or what didn't he notice on the way? How did he awaken Hilda? If he went into the bedroom, what did she look like when she was asleep?

You don't just walk over to the window in a novel. Walking is a physical action and every physical action is revealing. And the sun doesn't simply come out in novels. *Had come out* is three dead words. Nothing is seen. But what happens in real life is that the sun, in shades from pale yellow to bright orange, is reflected from water, from windows, from car reflectors; it brings out the colour of the grass and the trees and the flowers; it changes the colour of the sky; it makes new things look newer and old things older. What has happened isn't a general unremarkable fact, but a physical happening in the specific place you're writing about, seen by a specific person.

Going upstairs – running or walking, breathing easily or with effort – you notice peeling wallpaper or paint flaking, or note with satisfaction the new wallpaper and paintwork or do not notice anything. But just as the sun doesn't merely come out, so one doesn't merely go upstairs. There is no upstairs, there is a real staircase leading from the ground floor to the first floor in a real house and when you go up those stairs your eyes register your surroundings.

And how does Hilda sleep? If it doesn't matter, then

Hilda doesn't matter. Does she smile or frown when she's awakened? Or grunt? Is she easy or difficult to awaken? And what does she look like when she's asleep? What does Tom feel when he looks at her? Remember that sleeping people have no defences, their character is revealed. But let me qualify this. There are a few whose faces are perfectly composed, revealing nothing – is Hilda one of these?

We live in the physical world. We are not disembodied spirits. There are a few people to whom their physical surroundings are a matter of complete indifference; but even if you choose to write about these you'll have to show just to what they're indifferent. For most of us, what we feel about the physical world, about things, both natural and man made, is part of our character. Use all your senses to apprehend the world around you, make no judgements, forget yourself, and your novel is alive.

John Braine, *Writing a Novel*

Consider the following descriptions of dramatic events from three stories.

Lighting a Fire in Ice-cold Conditions

When all was ready, the man reached in his pocket for a piece of birch bark. He knew the bark was there, and, though he could not feel it with his fingers, he could hear its crisp rustling as he fumbled for it. Try as he would, he could not clutch hold of it. And all the time, in his consciousness, was the knowledge that each instant his feet were freezing. This thought tended to put him in a panic, but he fought against it and kept calm. He pulled on his mittens with his teeth, and threshed his arms back and forth, beating his hands with all his might against his sides.

After a time he was aware of the first far-away signals of sensation in his beaten fingers. The faint tingling grew stronger till it evolved into a stinging ache that was excruciating, but which the man hailed with satisfaction. He stripped the mitten from his right hand and fetched forth the birch bark. The exposed fingers were quickly going numb again. Next he brought out his bunch of sulphur matches. But the tremendous cold had already driven the life out of his fingers. In his effort to separate one match from the others, the whole bunch fell in the snow. He tried to pick it out of the snow, but failed. The dead fingers could neither touch nor clutch. He was very careful. He drove the thought of his freezing feet, and nose, and cheeks, out of his mind, devoting his whole soul to the matches. He watched, using the sense of vision in place of that touch, and when he saw his fingers on each side of the bunch, he closed them – that is, he willed to close them, for the wires were down, and the fingers did not obey. He pulled the mitten on the right hand, and beat it fiercely against his knee. Then with both mittened hands he scooped the bunch of matches, along with much snow, into his lap. Yet he was no better off.

After some manipulation he managed to get the bunch between the heels of his mittened hands. In this fashion he carried it to his mouth. The ice crackled and snapped when by a violent effort he opened his mouth. He drew the lower jaw in, curled the upper lip out of the way, and scraped the bunch with his upper teeth in order to separate a match. He succeeded in getting one, which he dropped on his lap. He was no better off. He could not pick it up. Then he devised a way. He picked it up in his teeth and scratched it on his leg. Twenty times he scratched before he succeeded in lighting it. As it flamed he held it with his teeth to the birch bark. But the burning brimstone went up his nostrils and into his lungs, causing him to cough spasmodically. The match fell into the snow and went out.

The old-timer on Sulphur Creek was right, he thought in the moment of controlled despair that ensued: after fifty below, a man should travel with a partner. He beat his hands, but failed in exciting any sensation. Suddenly he bared both hands, removing the mittens with his teeth. He caught the whole bunch between the heels of his hands. His arm muscles not being frozen enabled him to press the hand heels tightly against the matches. Then he scratched the bunch along his leg. It flared into flame, seventy sulphur matches at once! There was no wind to blow them out. He kept his head to one side to escape the strangling fumes, and held the blazing bunch to the birch bark. As he so held it, he became aware of sensation in his hand. His flesh was burning. He could smell it. Deep down below the surface he could feel it. The sensation developed into pain that grew acute. And still he endured it, holding the flame of the matches clumsily to the bark that would not light readily because his own burning hands were in the way, absorbing most of the flame.

At last, when he could endure no more, he jerked his hands apart. The blazing matches fell sizzling into the snow, but the birch bark was alight.

Jack London, *To Build a Fire* (short story)

The next passage comes from the work of a young writer.

A Daughter Witnesses her Mother's Funeral

The dust flew up and caught my face and hair. I walked slowly; the black veil flickered and drifted across my eyes. A wooden giant loomed before me towards a hollow, an empty hole. The sky blackened, and a fine misty drizzle was swept by the wind across the grave-yard. We still moved on, like a snake, slowly sliding towards its prey. The procession halted, and carefully the wooden box was lifted down, and lowered into the cavity, the empty cavity.

As she lay there, below me, a few flowers fell from white, shaking hands. Then it began. A shovel of earth spattered across the top of the lid. Another. She was leaving me. My face was wet with tears and rain. Farther and farther, with each shovel, smaller and smaller. I turned my head and slowly walked away, but I couldn't. I had to go back to her. I fell on my knees and my tears ran into the earth where she lay.

A hand took my arm and led me away, but I still screamed for her. How could I ever show them what she meant to me? What is she now? She was my mother. But what is she now?

Rosemary Brinton

A Man Rises from the Dead

At the same time, at the same hour before dawn, on the same morning, a man awoke from a long sleep in which he was tied up. He woke numb and cold, inside a carved hole in the rock. Through all the long sleep his body had been full of hurt, and it was still full of hurt. He did not open his eyes. Yet he knew that he was awake, and numb, and cold, and rigid, and full of hurt, and tied up. His face was banded with cold bands, his legs were bandaged together. Only his hands were loose.

He could move if he wanted: he knew that. But he had no want. Who would want to come back from the dead? A deep, deep nausea stirred in him, at the premonition of movement. He resented already the fact of the strange, incalculable moving that had already taken place in him: the moving back into consciousness. He had not wished it. He had wanted to stay outside, in the place where even memory is stone dead.

But now, something had returned to him, like a returned letter, and in that return he lay overcome with a sense of nausea. Yet suddenly his hands moved. They lifted up, cold, heavy and sore. Yet they lifted up, to drag away the cloth from his face, and push at the shoulder bands. Then they fell again, cold, heavy, numb, and

sick with having moved even so much, unspeakably unwilling to move further.

With his face cleared, and his shoulders free, he lapsed again, and lay dead, resting on the cold nullity of being dead. It was the most desirable. And almost, he had it complete: the utter cold nullity of being outside.

Yet when he was most nearly gone, suddenly, driven by an ache at the wrists, his hands rose and began pushing at the bandages of his knees, his feet began to stir, even while his breast lay cold and dead still.

And at last, the eyes opened. On to the dark. The same dark! yet perhaps there was a pale chink, of the all-disturbing night, prizing open the pure dark. He could not lift his head. The eyes closed. And again it was finished.

Then suddenly he leaned up, and the great world reeled. Bandages fell away. And narrow walls of rock closed upon him, and gave the new anguish of imprison-ment. There were chinks of light. With a wave of strength that came from revulsion, he leaned forward, in that narrow well of rock, and leaned frail hands on the rock near the chinks of light.

Strength came from somewhere, from revulsion; there

was a crash and a wave of light, and the dead man was crouching in his lair, facing the animal onrush of light. Yet it was hardly dawn, and the strange, piercing keenness of daybreak's sharp breath was on him. It meant full awakening.

Slowly, slowly he crept down from the cell of rock, with the caution of the bitterly wounded. Bandages and linen and perfume fell away, and he crouched on the ground against the wall of rock, to recover oblivion. But he saw his hurt feet touching the earth again, with unspeakable pain, the earth they had meant to touch no more, and he saw his thin legs that had died, and pain unknowable, pain like utter bodily disillusion, filled him so full that he stood up, with one torn hand on the ledge of the tomb.

To be back! To be back again, after all that! He saw the linen swathing-bands fallen round his dead feet, and stooping, he picked them up, folded them, and laid them back in the rocky cavity from which he had emerged. Then he took the perfumed linen sheet, wrapped it round him as a mantle, and turned away, to the wanness of the chill dawn.

He was alone; and having died, was even beyond loneliness.

D. H. Lawrence, *The Man Who Died* (short story)

EXERCISES IN PRECISE IMAGINATION

Take a small incident and in your own writing try to bring it to life. The following could act as opening lines to your narrative. Choose one, or invent your own situation. You may need to write a number of draft copies before your account is ready. Imagine it as being a small part of a novel.

Starting sentences

Disposing of the evidence was more difficult than she had imagined . . .

The intense electric light hurt his eyes. Once again he would have to resist telling the truth . . .

Sitting on the hard chair in the deserted corridor became unbearable. What could she possibly have done? What did the Headmaster want? . . .

Crouched by the open window, the hunted person watched the armed policemen coming cautiously up the drive . . .

There could only be a few seconds of life left. In those seconds she seemed to remember all the events of her life vividly . . .

I knew that something was desperately wrong as soon as she put the phone down and turned to me . . .

It became clear that this was no ordinary country house as soon as the butler opened the door . . .

We have considered single dramatic events, but most stories and novels are made up of a sequence of events. 'Narrative' means 'sequencing of events'. Look at the following group of pictures. They are out of sequence. What order would you put them in to make an interesting narrative?

In small groups, put the pictures into what you think is the best narrative order. You can indicate your ideal sequence by putting it in letter order, e.g. B D C A F, etc.

When you have decided on a sequence, see if you can explain the order you have chosen.

- What story does your sequence tell?

  Now compare your story with those from other groups.

- How many different narratives have been constructed?

- How many different stories come out of the one set of pictures?

- Which are the most interesting?

A

B

C

D

E

F

In making a story, many different sequences can be constructed. The action can start at the beginning, in the middle or at the end. The author can also use flashbacks, memories and dreams. Often authors will plot out the story before starting to write and move the scenes around, as you were moving around the pictures of the character in the pictures.

In later chapters we will look at some of the techniques the writer uses. First, though, in small groups try to construct some plots of your own.

CREATING FICTION FROM NEWSPAPER REPORTS

In small groups, discuss the following newspaper stories.

- How could they be developed into stories?
- Who would be the main characters?
- What would be the best way of narrating the events?
- How would the stories begin, develop, end?
- From whose viewpoint would the stories be told?

Teenage truants save dog

FOUR teenagers were in trouble with their Head Teacher last night in spite of a life-saving good deed.

The four, all from the Newmarsh School in Kingschurch, Lancs., took time off lessons without permission and found themselves in a life and death struggle to save a dog which had become trapped down an old well shaft.

While one of the group went to phone the fire-brigade, the others organised a rope and pulley system and rescued the dog from the 150ft. well-shaft before firemen arrived after a tricky and dangerous operation.

Schoolboy hoax wins day off

A boy fed up with trudging to school in the freezing cold weather, yesterday telephoned the BBC and impersonated his Headmaster. He convinced Radio Rutland to broadcast that his school had been closed because of the conditions.

Mr. James Rudd, the Headmaster, heard the broadcast and managed to get a correction. But he was too late and 500 of the 700 children stayed at home for the day.

Mr. Rudd said today that the boy was being dealt with.

CEMETERY THIEF

A grave was found opened at a cemetery in Southend yesterday. Workmen discovered that someone had dug down to the coffin and stolen a name plate from the lid.

Underground mystery

POLICE were still searching for leads following the discovery of a suitcase containing thousands of pounds in used banknotes at an underground car park in West London. Two men and a woman were seen near the scene of the discovery on Saturday night 'involved in a fierce argument'. Police would like these and any other witnesses to come forward.

Wild man: hunt is on

WORLD famous explorer and wild-life conservationist, Sir Jasper Purcell, yesterday asked for two more volunteers to join him on his journey to the remote Kandari Gorge region of Indigirkiri. Local villagers there have reported siting several species of dinosaur and a 'wild man' who seemed to have survived extinction in some sort of prehistoric time bubble.

The expedition sets off next week to set up camp in the foothills of the Kandari near the torrential river Gush. Sir Jasper agrees that the whole thing could be a hoax, but insists that scientific investigations must be carried out in order to get at the truth.

He still needs two impartial and independent members of the public – 'fit and fearless' – to join the team.

When you have finished your discussion, make a plan of the plots, giving the main sequences of events. Then share the ideas for your plots with other groups.

- How do your ideas compare with theirs?
- How much have you added to the original newspaper reports?
- How much have you changed them?

Here is a story by Maupassant which started from a report in a French newspaper.

At Sea

The following paragraph recently appeared in the press:

Boulogne-sur-Mer, January 22nd: from our correspondent:
'There is consternation among the sea-faring community here, which has been so hard hit during the last two years, at a frightful tragedy a few days ago. The fishing-boat commanded by Captain Javel was driven too far to the west, as it was coming into port, and foundered on the rocks of the breakwater protecting the pier. In spite of the efforts of the lifeboat and the use of the rocket apparatus, four men and the cabin-boy lost their lives. The bad weather continues. Further disasters are feared.'

I wonder who this Captain Javel is. Is he the brother of the one-armed Javel?

If the poor fellow who was washed overboard and now lies dead, perhaps under the wreck of his shattered vessel, is the man I am thinking of, he was involved, eighteen years ago, in another tragedy, terrifying, yet simple, like all the tragedies of the deep.

At that time the elder Javel was skipper of a trawler.

The trawler is the best type of fishing-boat. Strongly built to face any weather, and broad in the beam, she is always tossing about on the waves, like a cork; at sea all the time, continually lashed by the heavy, salt-laden Channel gales, she combs the sea tirelessly, with all sail set, dragging over the side a great net, which scours the ocean-bed, sweeping off and bringing up all the creatures that lurk in the rocks – flat fish clinging to the sand, heavy crabs with crooked claws and lobsters with pointed whiskers.

When the breeze is fresh and the water choppy, fishing starts. The net is attached along the whole length of a pole cased in iron, which is lowered by means of two cables working on two windlasses fore and aft. And the boat drifting to leeward with wind and tide, drags along with her this device for stripping and ransacking the sea-bed.

Javel had his younger brother on board, with a crew of four and a cabin-boy. He had sailed from Boulogne in fine, clear weather to go trawling.

Soon the wind got up and, increasing to gale force, compelled the trawler to run before it. She reached the English coast, but mountainous seas were lashing the cliffs and pounding the beaches, so that it was impossible to make harbour. The little vessel put out again, and made for the French coast. The storm still made it impossible to come alongside the piers, the approaches to the harbours being dangerous with flying foam and roaring waves.

The trawler put about once more, rising to the rollers tossed, battered, drenched with spray, buffeted with deluges of water, but undismayed in spite of everything, for she was accustomed to this sort of heavy weather, which sometimes kept her at sea for five or six days between the two neighbouring countries, unable to make harbour in either.

At last the gale dropped, while she was still some distance out, and, though it was still rough, the skipper ordered the trawl-net to be put down.

So the great net was heaved over the side, and two men forward and two in the stern began to let the cables holding it run out over the windlasses. Suddenly it touched bottom, but, as a huge wave made the boat heel over, the younger Javel, who happened to be forward superintending the paying out of the rope, staggered, and his arm got caught between the cable, momentarily slackened by the heeling of the boat, and the wood of the gunwale over which it passed. He made a desperate effort, trying to raise the rope with his other hand, but the net was already drawing and the tightened cable would not give.

The man cried out in pain. Everyone ran to his help. His brother left the tiller. They tugged at the rope in an attempt to free the limb, which was being crushed. It was useless.

'We must cut it,' said one of the sailors, taking from his pocket a large knife, two slashes of which could have saved the younger Javel's arm.

But cutting the cable meant losing the net, and the net was worth money, a great deal of money – fifteen hundred francs; and it was the property of the elder Javel, with whom having was keeping.

In an agony of anxiety he shouted: 'No! don't cut it; wait a moment; I'll bring her head up into the wind.' And he ran to the tiller and put it hard over.

The boat hardly answered the helm, hampered as she was by the net, which checked her way, and there was also the drag of drift and wind.

The younger Javel had fallen to his knees, with clenched teeth and haggard eyes. He did not say a word.

His brother came back, still afraid that one of the sailors would use his knife. 'Wait, wait, don't cut, we'll cast anchor.'

The anchor was let go, and the whole length of the

chain paid out. Then they began to heave at the capstan to slacken the cables of the net. At last the rope relaxed, and the arm, now useless inside the sleeve of the bloodstained jersey, was freed.

The younger Javel seemed dazed. They took off his jersey, revealing a ghastly sight – a mass of pulped flesh, from which blood was spurting as if under the action of a pump. The man looked at his arm and murmured: 'Buggered!'

As the haemorrhage was making a pool on the deck, one of the crew cried: 'He'll bleed to death; the artery must be tied.'

So they took a piece of coarse, brown, tarred string and putting it round the limb above the wound, they pulled tight with all their force. The flow of blood gradually lessened and finally stopped altogether.

The younger Javel got up, with the arm hanging limp at his side. He took hold of it with the other hand, raised it, turned it round and shook it. Everything was broken, all the bones shattered; it was only joined to the shoulder by the muscles. He examined it sadly and thoughtfully. Then he sat down on a furled sail, and his comrades advised him to bathe the place to prevent gangrene.

They put a bucket near him, and every few minutes he filled a glass with water and bathed the ghastly wound, letting a trickle of fresh water run over it.

'You'd be more comfortable below,' said his brother.

He went below, but came up again an hour later, not liking to be alone. Besides, he preferred the fresh air. He sat down on the sail again and went on bathing his arm.

They were having a good catch. The broad, white-bellied fish were lying about near him, wriggling in their death-throes. He kept his eyes on them, bathing his crushed limb all the time.

As they were just getting back to Boulogne, the wind got up again suddenly; and the little vessel began her mad career once more, pitching and tossing, jarring the poor fellow's injured arm.

Night came on. The weather remained dirty till dawn. When the sun rose, England was in sight, but, as the sea was going down, they set course back for France, beating up against the wind.

Towards evening the younger Javel called his comrades and showed them ugly-looking black marks, where mortification of the mangled portion of the limb was setting in.

The sailors examined it, giving their advice.

'It looks precious like gangrene,' opined one.

'You'd better put salt water on it,' declared another.

So they brought salt water and poured it over the wound. The injured man turned green, ground his teeth and flinched a little; but he did not cry out.

When the smarting ceased, he said to his brother: 'Give me your knife.' His brother handed him the knife. 'Now hold my arm out straight and keep it stretched.'

They did as he asked.

Then he began carving his own flesh. He worked quietly, reflectively, severing the last tendons with the razor-edged blade; and soon there was only the stump left. He uttered a deep sigh and declared: 'It was the only thing to do; I was buggered.'

He seemed relieved, and was breathing heavily, as he resumed his bathing of the stump.

The night was rough again and they could not make land.

When daylight appeared, the younger Javel picked up his severed arm and scrutinized it carefully. Putrefaction was setting in. His comrades also came to examine it; they passed it round from hand to hand, felt it, turned it over and sniffed it.

His brother said: 'You'd better throw it overboard now.'

But the younger Javel fired up at that: 'No, I won't! It's mine, I'd have you know; it's *my* arm, after all.'

He picked it up again and put it between his legs.

'That won't prevent it putrefying,' said the elder brother.

The injured man had an inspiration. When they were long at sea, they used to pack the fish in barrels of salt to preserve them.

He asked: 'I suppose I couldn't put it into brine?'

'That's an idea,' declared the others.

So they emptied one of the barrels which had been filled with the last few days' catch; and they put the arm at the bottom. They heaped salt on the top of it and replaced the fish one by one.

One of the sailors made a joke about it: 'We must take care not to sell it at the auction.'

And everyone laughed except the two Javels.

The wind was still high. They tacked about in sight of Boulogne till ten o'clock the next morning. The injured man went on bathing his arm.

At intervals he got up and walked from one end of the boat to the other. His brother at the tiller watched him, shaking his head.

At last they made the harbour.

The doctor examined the wound and pronounced it quite healthy. He dressed it carefully and ordered rest. But Javel refused to go to bed till he had recovered his arm, and went back as quickly as he could to the harbour to find the barrel, which had been marked with a cross.

They emptied it in his presence, and he picked up his arm, perfectly preserved in the brine, wrinkled, but free from putrefaction. He wrapped it up in a cloth which he had brought for the purpose and went home.

His wife and children carefully examined father's severed arm, feeling the fingers and removing the grains of salt from the nails, then they sent for the joiner to make a miniature coffin.

Next day the whole crew of the trawler followed the funeral of the severed limb. The two brothers, side by side, headed the procession. The parish sexton carried the coffin under one arm.

The younger Javel gave up the sea. He got a small job at the port, and whenever he talked about the accident later, he would add in a confidential whisper: 'If my brother had been willing to cut the trawl rope, of course, I should still have my arm. But with him having's keeping.'

Guy de Maupassant, *At Sea*, translated by
H. N. P. Sloman in *Boule de Suif and Other Stories*

ASSIGNMENTS

MAKING AND PRESENTING

1 Take an everyday routine – your journey to or from school, for example – and make an effort to keep a minute-by-minute account of what happens on this journey. Look around you at the people you pass, at the places you go through, listen to snatches of conversation, the noises, note the smells, perfumes and aromas that waft past your nose. From your collection of sense-impressions, organise a piece of writing based upon the detail of your collected responses to the journey.

2 Outline a **sequence of events** for your own story or novel. Take one small episode and, as in the exercises in precise imagination, bring it to life in words.

3 Make a selection of the class-work on precise imagination and present them as a series of readings (using video or cassette) with an introduction or commentary.

4 Make a radio play of Guy de Maupassant's short story *At Sea*. You might need to improvise it before you come to script it and it might help you to work with a partner or in a small group. If you look at the story closely, you will see that it gives you plenty of opportunity for a range of sound effects.

5 Take one incident from the plots that you developed from the newspaper articles and improvise a short tape-recorded play based upon it. Add any sound effects that you think will help to create the atmosphere.

RESEARCHING AND RESPONDING

1 Do some further research on the fiction of Jack London and Guy de Maupassant. What have they written? What are their chosen themes and settings? When were they writing? What nationality are they? On the basis of your research, you might try to compose a 'mock interview' with one of them for a newspaper article about their life and writing, or you might prefer to write an account for *A Guide to Literature*.

2 Re-read John Braine's account of good and bad writing in fiction (page 30). Then write your own personal account of good and bad writing, giving, where possible, actual examples from stories you know.

3 Write an evaluation of one of your own pieces of imaginative writing, describing both what you felt worked well and what you were displeased with.

4 Write an account of Maupassant's short story *At Sea*, describing both the plot and style of writing and also your personal responses to it.

4 | WORKING WITHIN STORIES

When we pick up a novel the first things we notice are the cover, the title and the author. Look at the following.

- Which covers seem to you most effective?
- What does the title suggest about the nature of the book?
- What does the illustration suggest?
- Do you know the author's work?

A full cover generally includes other important features. Look at the dust-jacket below.

A TYPICAL BOOK-JACKET

The back cover might include notes about the author, extracts from reviews, comments and the publishers 'blurb'. You will sometimes find a photograph of the author here too.

This is the 'spine' of the book. Along the spine you will find the names of the author and the title of the book.

On the front cover of the book you will find the title of the book and the authors name. You will also find a design or picture meant to catch the eye, tell you something about the subject-matter of the book and encourage you to buy it.

¡IMMORTAL SATIRE ON FLEET STREET STOP NOW ON TELEVISION STOP

Lord Copper, newspaper magnate and proprietor of the *Daily Beast*, has always prided himself on his intuitive flair for spotting ace reporters.

There had been the odd blunder, of course. A trick cyclist who had momentarily caught his eye was now on a five-year contract, blithely demolishing the Sports Page. And perhaps Foreign News could be sharpened up a little too? Acting on a dinner-party tip from Mrs Algernon Stitch, he feels convinced that he has hit on just the chap to cover a promising little war in the African Republic of Ishmaelia . . .

Scoop, **turning on a slight case of mistaken identity, is one of Evelyn Waugh's most exuberant comedies, a brilliantly irreverent satire on Fleet Street and its hectic pursuit of hot news.**

WICKED STOP DEADLY STOP BRILLIANTLY FUNNY STOP

Cover illustration by Glen Baxter

A STARTLED BOOT NOTED THE EXOTIC INSCRIPTION WITH SOME DISMAY

 A PENGUIN BOOK
Fiction

ISBN 0-14-010042-3

90000

U.K. £2.99
AUST. $7.99
(recommended)
N.Z. $12.99
(incl. GST)
CAN. $5.95

9 780140 100426

The prices and the international book number is usually found on the back of a paperback book.

At the bottom of the spine you will usually find the name, symbol, trademark or logo of the firm that publishes the book.

Yet a story begins with words and those words must hold the reader's attention. Look at the following openings to various stories and novels.

EMMA WOODHOUSE, handsome, clever, and rich, with a comfortable home and happy disposition, seemed to unite some of the best blessings of existence; and had lived nearly twenty-one years in the world with very little to distress or vex her.

She was the youngest of the two daughters of a most affectionate, indulgent father, and had, in consequence of her sister's marriage, been mistress of his house from a very early period. Her mother had died too long ago for her to have more than an indistinct remembrance of her caresses, and her place had been supplied by an excellent woman as governess, who had fallen little short of a mother in affection.

Jane Austen, *Emma*

October 4th

THIS DIARY is Dr Blanke's idea. I'm seeing him once a week now, travelling up to London by car on early closing days. He is very sympathetic about my little troubles. Cheered me up considerably by saying that my 'condition' wasn't really all that unusual. Though I haven't told him *everything*, must say I feel relieved. He told me that, since I like making notes, to keep a diary might well give me some relief from depressions, headaches, bad dreams and so forth. Added that I might show him my jottings, but only if I felt so inclined. Bought an exercise-book at Wayford's, the thickest one they had. There are a lot of things I'd like to write down, but words don't come to me all that easily; I find it all somewhat embarrassing. Like trying to tell Dr Blanke about my little weakness.

Robert Muller, *The Lost Diaries of Albert Smith*

ON MY NAMING DAY when I come 12 I gone front spear and kilt a wyld boar he parbly ben the las wyld pig on the Bundel Downs any how there hadnt ben none for a long time befor him nor I aint looking to see none agen. He dint make the groun shake nor nothing like that when he come on to my spear he wernt all that big plus he lookit poorly. He done the reqwyrt he ternt and stood and clattert his teef and made his rush and there we wer then. Him on 1 end of the spear kicking his life out and me on the other end watching him dy. I said, 'Your tern now my tern later.' The other spears gone in then and he wer dead and the steam coming up off him in the rain and we all yelt, 'Offert!'

The woal thing felt jus that littl bit stupid. Us running that boar thru that las littl scrump of woodling with the forms all roun. Cows mooing sheap baaing cocks crowing and us foraging our las boar in a thin grey girzel on the day I come a man.

Russell Hoban, *Riddley Walker*

ON MY 23RD BIRTHDAY when I was fed up with London and all the rest of it – boyfriends, marriages (two), jobs (modelling), best friends that are suddenly your best enemies – I had this letter from my girl friend Sophie who was finding peace in an ashram in South India:

'. . . oh Katie you wouldn't know me I'm such a changed person. I get up at 5–*a.m.*!!!! I am an absolute vegetarian let alone no meat no eggs either and am making fabulous progress with my meditation. I have a special mantra of my own that Swamiji gave me at a special ceremony and I say it over and over in my mind. The sky here is blue all day long and I sit by the sea and watch the waves and have good thoughts . . .'

But by the time I got there Sophie had left – under a cloud, it seemed, though when I asked what she had done, they wouldn't tell me but only pursed their lips and looked sorrowful.

Ruth Prawer Jhabvala, *How I Became a Holy Mother*

FUGU is a fish caught off the Pacific shores of Japan. The fish has held a special significance for me ever since my mother died through eating one. The poison resides in the sexual glands of the fish, inside two fragile bags. When preparing the fish, these bags must be removed with caution, for any clumsiness will result in the poison leaking into the veins. Regrettably, it is not easy to tell whether or not this operation has been carried out successfully. The proof is, as it were, in the eating.

Fugu poisoning is hideously painful and almost always fatal. If the fish has been eaten during the evening, the victim is usually overtaken by pain during his sleep. He rolls about in agony for a few hours and is dead by morning. The fish became extremely popular in Japan after the war. Until stricter regulations were imposed, it was all the rage to perform the hazardous gutting operation in one's own kitchen, then to invite neighbours and friends round for the feast.

Kazuo Ishiguro, *A Family Supper*

HEY, I must tell you what happened the other day.

You know how we went up the coast, um, with that young guy. He was like, ah, a self-styled punk. Yeah. Only about fourteen. Well he got involved in London, he was staying there for a while, with these working-class kids; you know, like real punks. They wrecked football trains and he got hooked on cough-mixture and god knows what, dog pills. Well, he came up the coast with us to dry out, and it's just rife with hippies, you know, blonde hair, Balinese gear, god! They went crazy over Richard Clapton, he had a concert there, when he sang 'I've got those Blue Bay blues', you know, about Byron Bay. I mean, that song must have been written ten years ago. Well, o god, he wore a heavy German overcoat, like a military one, and heavy boots, like these great clumping things and he had black pants, and short spiky hair dyed red and he walked onto the sand; I mean this is the middle of summer, the proverbial burning deserts; and I thought: what is this guy going to do? And then I thought: what do punks do in summer? No, really. What do you do in black plastic? It's nonabsorbent right? Surely you have to consider these things. Unless, I don't know punks go in for endurance tests. I mean, it's downright uncomfortable. And black, all that black. It just absorbs the heat. And try to keep looking pasty-faced. They probably raid the chemists for Block-Out. I mean, how are you going to avoid a tan? Well, you just couldn't go out, could you. . . .

Moya Costello, *Brian 'Squizzy' Taylor*

EARLY in 19—, when Srinagar was under the spell of a winter so fierce it could crack men's bones as if they were glass, a young man upon whose cold-pinked skin there lay, like a frost, the unmistakable sheen of wealth was to be seen entering the most wretched and disreputable part of the city, where the houses of wood and corrugated iron seemed perpetually on the verge of losing their balance, and asking in low, grave tones where he might go to engage the services of a dependably professional thief. The young man's name was Atta, and the rogues in that part of town directed him gleefully into ever-darker and less public alleys, until in a yard wet with the blood of a slaughtered chicken he was set upon by two men whose faces he never saw, robbed of the substantial bank-roll which he had insanely brought on his solitary excursion, and beaten within an inch of his life.

Salman Rushdie, *The Prophet's Hair*

The author giveth some account of himself and family, his first inducements to travel. He is shipwrecked, and swims for his life, gets safe on shore in the country of Lilliput, is made a prisoner, and carried up the country.

My father had a small estate in Nottinghamshire; I was the third of five sons. He sent me to Emanuel College in Cambridge, at fourteen years old, where I resided three years, and applied myself close to my studies: but the charge of maintaining me (although I had a very scanty allowance) being too great for a narrow fortune, I was bound apprentice to Mr James Bates, an eminent surgeon in London, with whom I continued four years; and my father now and then sending me small sums of money, I laid them out in learning navigation, and other parts of the mathematics, useful to those who intend to travel, as I always believed it would be some time or other my fortune to do. When I left Mr Bates, I went down to my father; where, by the assistance of him and my uncle John, and some other relations, I got forty pounds, and a promise of thirty pounds a year to maintain me at Leyden: there I studied physic two years and seven months, knowing it would be useful in long voyages.

Jonathan Swift, *Gulliver's Travels*

Look closely at these openings.

- Which ones hold your attention most?
- How much can you tell from them about the kind of story it is going to be?
- How many different kinds of openings can you find?
- Which ones read like autobiography?
- How are the others different?
- When were the stories written? How can you tell?

A good opening is important to any narrative, but it has to continue until the whole story has been told. Here is a complete short story by Stan Barstow.

The Fury

There were times when Mrs Fletcher was sure her husband thought more of his rabbits than anything else in the world: more than tobacco and comfort, more than her – or the other woman. And this was one of those times, this Saturday morning as she looked out from the kitchen where she was preparing the dinner to where she could see Fletcher working absorbedly, and grooming his two favourite Angoras for the afternoon's show in Cressley.

She was a passionate woman who clung singlemindedly to what was hers, and was prepared to defend her rights with vigour. While courting Fletcher she had drawn blood on an erstwhile rival who had threatened to reassert her claims. Since then she had had worse things to contend with. Always, it seemed to her, there was something between her and her rightful possession of Fletcher. At the moment it was the rabbits. The big shed had been full of hutches at one time, but now Fletcher concentrated his attention on a handful of animals in which he had a steady faith. But there were still too many for Mrs Fletcher, who resented sharing him with anything or anybody, and the sight of his absorption now stirred feelings which brought unnecessary force to bear on the sharp knife with which she sliced potatoes for the pan.

'Got a special class for Angoras today,' Fletcher said later at the table. He was in a hurry to be off and he shovelled loaded spoons of jam sponge pudding into his mouth between the short sentences. 'Might do summat for a change. Time I had a bit o' luck.' He was washed and clean now, his square, ruddily handsome face close shaven, the railway porter's uniform discarded for his best grey worsted. The carrying-case with the rabbits in it stood by the door.

Mrs Fletcher gave no sign of interest. She said 'D'you think you'll be back in time for t'pictures?'

Fletcher gulped water. He had a way of drinking which showed his fine teeth. 'Should be,' he answered between swallows. 'Anyway, if you're so keen to go why don't you fix up with Mrs Sykes?'

'I should be able to go out with you, Saturday nights,' Mrs Fletcher said. 'Mrs Sykes has a husband of her own to keep her company.'

'Fat lot o' company he is Saturday night,' Fletcher said dryly. 'Or Sunday for that matter . . . Anyway I'll try me best. Can't say fairer than that, can I?'

'Not as long as you get back in time.'

Fletcher pushed back his chair and stood up. 'I don't

see why not. It shouldn't be a long job today. It isn't a big show. I should be back by half-past seven at latest.'

'Well, just see 'at you are,' she said.

She stood by the window and watched him go down the road in the pale sunshine, carrying case, slung from one shoulder, prevented from jogging by a careful hand. He cut a handsome, well-set-up figure when he was dressed up, she thought. Often too handsome, too well-set-up for her peace of mind.

By half-past seven she was washed, dressed, and lightly made-up ready for the evening out. But Fletcher had not returned. And when the clock on the mantelshelf chimed eight there was still no sign of him. It was after ten when he came. She was sitting by the fire, the wireless blaring unheard, her knitting needles flashing with silent fury.

'What time d'you call this?' she said, giving him no chance to speak. 'Saturday night an' me sittin' here like a doo-lal while you gallivant up an' down as you please.'

He was obviously uneasy, expecting trouble. 'I'm sorry,' he said. 'I meant to get back. I thought I should, but there were more than I expected. It took a long time . . .' He avoided her eyes as he went into the passage to hang up his overcoat. 'Didn't win owt, either,' he muttered, half to himself. 'Not a blinkin' sausage.'

'You knew I specially wanted to see that picture, didn't you?' Mrs Fletcher said, her voice rising. 'I've been telling you all week, but that makes no difference, does it! What does your wife matter once you get off with your blasted rabbits, eh?'

As though he had not heard her Fletcher opened the case and lifted out one of the rabbits and held it to him, stroking the long soft fur. 'You just wasn't good enough, was you, eh?' The rabbit blinked its pink eyes in the bright electric light. 'Nivver mind: you're a beauty all t' same.'

His ignoring of her maddened Mrs Fletcher almost more than she could bear. 'I'm talking to you!' she stormed.

'I heard you; an' I said I'm sorry. What more do you want?'

'Oh, you're sorry, and that's the end of it, I suppose. That's all my Saturday night's worth, is it?'

'I couldn't help it,' Fletcher said. 'I said I couldn't help it.' He put the rabbit back in the case and sat down to unlace his shoes. She watched him, eyes glittering, mouth a thin trap of temper.

'Aye, you said so. You said you'd be home at half-past

seven an' all, and we've seen what that was worth. How do I know what you've been up to while I've been sitting here by myself?'

He looked quickly up at her, his usual full colour deepening and spreading. 'What're you gettin' at now?'

'You know what I'm gettin' at.' Her head nodded grimly.

Fletcher threw down his shoes. 'I told you,' he said with throaty anger, 'an' that's all over. It's been finished with a long time. Why can't you let it rest, 'stead o' keep harping on about it?'

He stood up, and taking the carrying case, walked out in his slippers to the shed, leaving her to talk to the empty room. He always got away from her like that. She grabbed the poker and stabbed savagely at the fire.

On Sunday morning she was shaking a mat in the yard when her neighbour spoke to her over the fence.

'Did you get to the Palace this week, then, Mrs Fletcher?' Mrs Sykes asked her. 'Oh, but you did miss a treat. All about the early Christians and the cloak 'at Jesus wore on the cross. Lovely, it was, and ever so sad.'

'I wanted to see it,' Mrs Fletcher said, 'but Jim didn't get back from Cressley till late. His rabbits y'know.' She felt a strong desire to abuse him in her talk, but pride held her tongue. It was bad enough his being as he was without the shame of everyone's knowing it.

'Oh, aye, they had a show, didn't they?' Mrs Sykes said. 'Aye, I saw him in the bus station afterwards. He was talking to a woman I took to be your sister.'

Mrs Fletcher shot the other woman a look. What was she up to? She knew very well that her sister had lived down south these last twelve months. Her cheeks flamed suddenly and she turned her back on her neighbour and went into the house.

Fletcher was lounging, unshaven and in shirt sleeves, his feet propped up on the fireplace, reading the Sunday papers. She went for him as soon as she had put the thickness of the door between them and Mrs Sykes, who still lingered in the yard.

'You must think I'm stupid!'

'Eh?' Fletcher said, looking up. 'What's up now?'

'What's up? What's up? How can you find the face to sit there with your feet up and ask me that? You must think I'm daft altogether; but it's you 'at's daft, if you did but know it. Did you think you could get away with it? Did you really think so? You might ha' known somebody 'ud see you. And you had to do it in the bus station at that – a public place!'

'I don't even know what you're talking about,' Fletcher said, but his eyes gave him away.

'You'll brazen it out to the very end, won't you?' she said. 'You liar you. "Oh, I've made a mistake," he says. "I'll never see her again," he says. And what do you do but go running back to her the minute you think you can get away with it!'

Fletcher got up, throwing the newspaper to one side.

'I tell you I don't—' Then he stopped, the bluster draining out of him. 'All right,' he said quietly. 'If you'll calm down a minute I'll tell you.'

'You'll tell *me!*' Mrs Fletcher said. 'You'll tell me nothing any more. It's all lies, lies, lies every time you open your mouth. Well I've finished. Bad enough your rabbits, but I draw the line at fancy women. You promised me faithful you wouldn't see her again. You said it sitting in that very chair. And what was it worth, eh? Not a row o' buttons. What d'you think I feel like when me own neighbours tell me they've seen you carryin' on?'

'If you wouldn't listen so much to what t'neighbours say an' take notice o' what I have to tell you—' Fletcher began.

'I've done listening to you,' she said. 'Now I'm having my say.'

'Well, you'll say it to yourself, and rest o' t'street mebbe, but not to me.' He strode across the room and dragged down his coat. 'I'll go somewhere where I can talk to somebody 'at's not next door to a ravin' lunatic.'

'And stop there when you get there,' she told him. 'Go to her. Tell her I've had enough of you. See if she'll sit at home while you traipse about country-side with a boxful o' mucky vermin.'

He was at the door, pulling on his coat.

'And take your things,' she said. 'Might as well make a clean sweep while you're about it.'

'I'm going to our Tom's,' he said. 'I'll send for 'em tomorrow.'

'I'll have 'em ready,' she said.

When the door had closed behind him she stood for a moment, eyes glittering, nostrils dilated, her entire body stiff and quivering with rage. Then suddenly she plucked a vase from the mantelshelf and dashed it to pieces in the hearth. She clenched and unclenched her hands at her sides, her eyes seeking wildly as the fury roared impotently in her.

At half-past ten she was in the kitchen making her supper when she heard the front door open. She went through into the passage and her hands tightened involuntarily about the milk bottle she was holding as she saw Fletcher there.

'Well,' she said. 'Have you come for your things?' Her voice was tight and unnatural and Fletcher took it as a sign of her lingering anger.

He closed the door and stood sheepishly behind it, his eyes avoiding hers. 'I just thought I'd come an' see if you'd calmed down,' he said.

'I thought we'd heard the last of that this morning?' Her eyes were fixed, bright and unmoving, on his face, and Fletcher caught them with his own for an instant and looked away again.

'We were both a bit worked up like,' he said. 'I know how it is when you get mad. You do an' say a lot o' things you don't really mean. That you regret after.'

There was silence for a second before she said, the same tight, strained note in her voice, 'What things?'

'I mean like me walkin' out,' Fletcher said. 'All it needed was a bit o' quiet talkin' an' it wouldn't ha' come to that. It'd ha' been all right if only you'd listened to me.'

'I never expected you to come back,' she said, and moved almost trance-like, across the room to the fire, still watching him intently almost disbelievingly, as though she had expected that with his slamming of the door this morning he would walk off the edge of the world, never to be seen again.

He came over to the hearth to stand beside her. He started to put his hand on her shoulder, but as she moved away slightly he dropped his arm again and looked past her into the fire.

'What I said before, I meant,' he said, speaking quietly, earnestly, with the awkwardness of a man not used to expressing the finer feelings. 'I could ha' told you last night, only I didn't see any point. It was all forgotten as far as I was concerned. Finished. But she was waiting for me when I came out o' show. I told her I didn't want to see her again. There was never owt much between us anyway. But I couldn't get rid of her. She hung on like mad. An' when I looked at her, all painted an' powdered up, I found meself thinkin' what a great fool I'd been ever to risk losing all that mattered for a brazen baggage like her. It took me a couple of hours to get rid of her. She got proper nasty towards the end. Started shoutin' and swearin', right in the street. It was awful.' Fletcher sighed and shook his head and a shudder seemed to run through Mrs Fletcher. 'And I had to jump on a bus in the end and just leave her standing there. There was nowt else I could do bar give her a clout or summat. . . .'

As he finished talking something seemed to snap inside Mrs Fletcher and she began to cry softly. He put his arm round her shoulders, tentatively at first, then, when she offered no resistance, with pressure, drawing her to him.

'Now, lass. Now, then. Cryin' won't do any good. We've had our little bust-up, an' now it's all over an' done with.'

'Oh, why didn't I listen?' she sobbed. 'None of this would have happened then.'

He drew her down into an armchair and held her to him. 'Never mind now, lass. No harm done. Don't cry any more.'

After a time, he said, 'I'll just nip out an' see to the rabbits, then we can get off up to bed.'

She held him to her. 'No leave 'em. Come to bed now.'

He smiled quietly, indulgently. 'Still a bit jealous, eh? Well I reckon they'll manage till morning.'

Later still, in the dark secret warmth of the bed, she clung to him again. 'Did you mean it?' she said. 'When you said you loved nobody but me?'

'I did,' he said.

'Say it, then,' she said, holding him hard.

'I love you, lass,' he said. 'Nobody but you. It'll be better in future. You'll see.'

She could have cried out then. Better in future! Oh, why hadn't she listened? Why, why, why? If only she had listened and heard him in time! For this moment was all she had. There could be no future: nothing past the morning when he would go out and find the rabbits slaughtered in their hutches.

Stan Barstow, from *The Desperadoes*

- What do you think of Stan Barstow's title for the story?
- Why do you think he chose it?
- How well does the first paragraph work?
- How does the first paragraph relate to the very last paragraph of the story?
- Where is this story set?
- What kind of characters are Mr and Mrs Fletcher?
- Why isn't the most dramatic event in the story described?

Now re-read *The Fury* and, keeping close to the actual story, work on one of the following tasks.

- Bring the action forward to the next morning and write an alternative ending to the story.
- Imagine that Mrs Fletcher writes a letter to her husband just after she has broken the vase. What do you think she would put in this letter? How would she reveal her feelings? Write the letter as if you were Mrs Fletcher.

■ Imagine that Mrs Sykes has observed Mrs Fletcher's action. Write a short scene in which she tells either her husband or Mr Fletcher. Try to use the same dialect that they use in the story. Imagine that in the morning, Mr Fletcher visits his girlfriend (look again at his description of her). Give an account of what happened, writing it in the first person, as if you are Mr Fletcher.

A S S I G N M E N T S

MAKING AND PRESENTING

1 Make notes for a story of your own and then write three different openings to it, on one sheet if possible.

2 Here are four poetry superscriptions. Choose two and write an opening paragraph suggested by them:

(a) 'here is the deepest secret nobody knows'
   e e cummings
(b) 'The day dawns over the sea'
   Miroslav Holub
(c) 'If I, like Solomon . . . could have my wish – . . . my wish –'
   Marianne Moore
(d) 'The fire left to itself might smoulder weeks, phone cables melt. Paint peel from off back gates, kitchen windows crack . . .'
   Tony Harrison

3 In a small group, read through Stan Barstow's *The Fury* and turn it into a play for recording on cassette. This will require a very careful reading of the story, as well as considerable discussion of the characters and the sequence of the action.

4 Design a book-jacket for *The Fury*. You will need to find out about the author, and think of what to say about the story itself for the publisher's 'blurb' which describes the story and is usually found either on the back cover or on the inside flap.
You can invent some quotations about the book that might be found in newspaper reviews. Also work out a good idea for a picture for the cover.
If you enjoy this type of work, you could go on to design a book-jacket for one of your own stories, or some of the opening paragraphs that you wrote (questions 1 and 2), filling in details about yourself as the author. It would certainly help if you were to do some research on the different kinds of design work that go into jacket design. Take a look around the school library or the class book shelves.

RESEARCHING AND RESPONDING

1. Do some further research on book-jackets and illustrations (see question 4 above). Find out about illuminated manuscripts. Look at the illustrations of children's books. See if you can find some original illustrations for the novels of Dickens or for Lewis Carroll's *Alice's Adventures in Wonderland*. Prepare an illustrated display to show what you have discovered.

2. Write an account of what you think makes a good opening to a story, illustrating your arguments with a number of examples.

3. Jot down your responses to *The Fury*, or any other short story you have read recently. Look at the plot, the style, the characters. Are there passages that you think particularly well written? Are there parts that seem obscure or confusing? Make a note of the words, sentences or paragraphs that you either like or dislike. Shape your notes either into a presentation for discussion, or into a short essay.

5 | THE VOICES OF STORIES

The vast majority of stories are never recorded. They are told by people at work, in schools, in factories, in offices. They are told in pubs, in cafeterias and coffee bars. They are told, endlessly, inside families.

Each town, each locality, has its own fund of unwritten narratives: love stories, horror stories, ghost stories, comic and tragic stories.

Here, for example, is just one story collected recently from a country woman in England. It was never intended to be written down. It is a ghost story concerning her deceased husband and a certain Annie Luker.

Annie Luker's Ghost

I know what you say about ghosts is quite true. We 'ad one to our cottage. Oh, yes! We come down to cottage arter it were empty, like, and I got Vicar to come and bless cottage. You see, it did belong to old Annie Luker, and she wasn't well liked. Everybody said she 'ad dark dealings; could turn 'erself into a rabbit. Well, arter she died, there weren't no one as 'ud go near. But my 'usband 'e was a clever man, bit too clever, if you ask me, 'e say, 'we'll go to cottage.' So us took it.

Folk in village didn't like it very much, and they come and say to me 'Does 'ee know 'twas Annie Luker's cottage?'

I says, 'Yes, I'll get Vicar to come and bless it.' So we did, and we went there, me and my 'usband, and our daughter Mary. Well, us 'ad been there about three months, when all of a sudden, one night, I 'ears a girt bang. I sits up in bed, and I listens, and someone come in! I could 'ear 'en downstairs. I nudges 'usband, see.

'Bob,' I says, 'wake-up, will 'ee? What be it?' Well, we sat up in bed and then we could 'ear someone coming upstairs – bump, bump, and kerflop, kerflop. 'Usband, 'e got proper cross, and 'e calls out, 'Mary, what be 'ee about? Coming in this time o' night!'

Then us 'eard our Mary, from 'er bedroom next to ours, by the passageway, and she say, 'Dad, oh! Dad, I've been 'ome hours. Whatever is it?' And then 'er goes under blankets like I did.

My 'usband 'e listened, and then we 'eard 'en again, thump, thump, kerflop, kerflop coming along up the stairs toward our door, and all of a sudden, my 'usband – 'oo, nothing much worried 'im – 'e say, 'Oh! 'Tis old Annie Luker!' And 'e come under blankets too.

Well, sometimes she'd come and sometimes she 'ouldn't. Never see 'er, but 'ear 'er, yes. And then, my 'usband, 'e was took ill, and not long ago 'e died. 'Aven't 'eard Annie since. Folks say she knew what she wanted, and she come for 'im.

The habit of telling stories and remembering them and so passing them down through the generations is often called 'the oral tradition'.

In pre-industrial societies the oral tradition and the place of the storyteller are most important. The storyteller has the task of remembering all the great stories of the society and keeping them alive in the imagination of the people. In these societies, storytelling remains a very dramatic affair; using voice and gesture, the storyteller has to engage the interest of the audience and, once engaged, the audience will show their appreciation and join in parts of the story.

Novels, in contrast, are printed, distributed and bought and read quietly by their individual readers. And yet, at the same time, in many ways they depend on the oral tradition, on **telling** and **listening**.

As readers of fiction we have to **hear** the voices of the story. We have to listen to the particular voice of the narrator and also to the various voices of the characters. We must hear them as if they were speaking to us.

The best way to understand the oral element in the story is to read some of the story aloud.

The following stories and excerpts from novels can be read to small groups or to the whole class. Different readings can also be recorded on cassette and presented as radio programmes.

It is suggested that groups start with one of the smaller pieces in section A, then move on to tackle one of the two longer stories in section B.

In your reading, try to bring out the drama of the story by finding the voice or voices which best fit the characters and incidents, and the general mood of the narrative.

SECTION A

This very short story is by the Caribbean writer Robert Henry.

Give and Take

You know Babu, Mass' Bob? Used was to do a little day work for your grandfather, when the yard need clearing and so . . . Him have a little boy, one sweet little boy you see, skin smooth, smooth black, like velvet, and nice wavy hair. Miss Katie tell me them just find him in the shallow water topside the market. . . . Dead. Well sar! The father suffer with fits you know, and like father, like son. Seem like him go for a swim, and the fits take him. But is God in His mercy save him from further sins, for him was goin' dead in jail. Look ya, Mass' Bob, the little boy bad, him bad, him bad so tell! Every day at school him and the boys ketch fight.

Wonder where them tek him? Must be the hospital, for him and the father has was to sleep under the shelf dem in the market. Imagine, a able-body man like Babu, living all these years, and never lif' a finger to build a house. The foxes have holes, and the birds their nests.

Him feel it though. Miss Katie say, when them find the body, you could hear Babu bawl and holler from up the fort; and after him understand proper say the boy dead fe true, him wouldn't go near the body, only bawl and holler and cuss God.

You know is one thing I never do, Mass' Bob? Just the other day up at Jericho, lightning strike a woman what was feeding her baby, kill the woman, and kill the dog under the house, and the blessed infant unscratch!

Babu is a hard man though; him used to charge you grandfather all ten shillings just to chop this little acre. Nobody never see him laugh or anything; only to-day, Babu bawling and cussin' God. The sins of the father . . .

But is God in His mercy save the boy, for him was goin' dead in jail . . . The Lord giveth and the Lord taketh away . . .

Breakfast soon ready you hear sar? You can wash you han' and all that. Breakfast soon ready.

Robert Henry

The following passage is taken from Emily Brontë's 19th-century novel *Wuthering Heights*. Lockwood is speaking, and telling of one of his nightmares after spending the night in the remote farmhouse owned by Heathcliff.

The Nightmare

This time, I remembered I was lying in that oak closet, and I heard distinctly the gusty wind, and the driving of the snow; I heard, also, the fir-bough repeat its teasing sound, and ascribed it to the right cause; but it annoyed me so much that I resolved to silence it, if possible; and, I thought, I rose and endeavoured to unhasp the casement. The hook was soldered into the staple: a circumstance observed by me when awake, but forgotten. 'I must stop it, nevertheless!' I muttered, knocking my knuckles through the glass, and stretching an arm out to seize the importunate branch; instead of which, my fingers closed on the fingers of a little, ice-cold hand! The intense horror of nightmare came over me; I tried to draw back my arm, but the hand clung to it, and a most melancholy voice sobbed, 'Let me in – let me in!' 'Who are you?' I asked, struggling meanwhile, to disengage myself. 'Catherine Linton,' it replied shiveringly . . . ; 'I'm come home: I'd lost my way on the moor!' As it spoke, I discerned, obscurely, a child's face looking through the window. Terror made me cruel; and, finding it useless to attempt shaking the creature off, I pulled its wrist on to the broken pane, and rubbed it to and fro till the blood ran down and soaked the bedclothes; still it wailed, 'Let me in!' and maintained its tenacious gripe, almost maddening me with fear. 'How can I?' I said at length. 'Let *me* go, if you want me to let you in!' The fingers relaxed, I snatched mine through the hole, hurriedly piled the books up in a pyramid against it, and stopped my ears to exclude the lamentable prayer. I seemed to keep them closed above a quarter of an hour; yet the instant I listened again, there was a doleful cry moaning on! 'Begone!' I shouted, 'I'll never let you in, not if you beg for twenty years.' 'It is twenty years,' mourned the voice: 'twenty years. I've been a waif for twenty years!' Thereat began a feeble scratching outside, and the pile of books moved as if thrust forward. I tried to jump up; but could not stir a limb; and so yelled aloud, in a frenzy of fright. To my confusion, I discovered the yell was not ideal. Hasty footsteps approached my chamber door; somebody pushed it open, with a vigorous hand, and a light glimmered through the squares at the top of the bed. I sat shuddering yet, and wiping the perspiration from my forehead: the intruder appeared to hesitate, and muttered to himself. At last he said in a half-whisper, plainly not expecting an answer, 'Is any one here?' I considered it best to confess my presence, for I knew Heathcliff's accents, and feared he might search further if I kept quiet. With this intention, I turned and opened the panels. I shall not soon forget the effect my action produced.

Heathcliff stood near the entrance, in his shirt and trousers, with a candle dripping over his fingers, and his face as white as the wall behind him. The first creak of the oak startled him like an electric shock: the light leaped from his hold to a distance of some feet, and his agitation was so extreme that he could hardly pick it up!

'It is only your guest, sir,' I called out, desirous to spare him the humiliation of exposing his cowardice further. 'I had the misfortune to scream in my sleep, owing to a frightful nightmare. I'm sorry I disturbed you.'

Emily Brontë, *Wuthering Heights*

SECTION B

The Triumph of Jessie Jones

Shortly after Bert had died in the lav, Jessie had had to be carted off to the loony-bin. She just couldn't think what to do next. Bert had always told her what to do. Barbara and Wendy and Eddie had come to see her.

'Mam, you've got to get better quick – brought you a box of "Black Magic" – just to cheer you up!'

They'd talked to her in special voices. Eddie had even shouted and she'd rounded on him. 'Eh, lad, I might be daft but I'm not deaf.'

She'd sat there after they'd driven off in Eddie's 'Avenger' and had gazed at the ladies and gentlemen shuffling about in their carpet slippers or staring vacantly before them.

Suddenly on an afternoon in early March when the sun was shining and she could see snow-drops growing in clusters under the trees in the hospital grounds, it had occurred to her that she was just like the other inmates . . . somehow she hadn't thought of it that way before. They were bloody irritating, she had to say it. A woman called Mildred would keep asking her what time it was. One bloke groaned all the time and there was Rosie who wouldn't stop popping her dentures in and out. Added to all that everything seemed to smell of boiled cabbage and gravy. She'd felt like giving a few sharp blasts on a nice lily of the valley fresh air spray. Basically though it was Rosie's dentures which settled it. She lost them and accused Jessie of pinching them, and they were finally discovered under Jessie's pillow. That was when Jessie decided she was better.

On arrival back at her terrace house she'd looked around with something of a shock. The nets shone whiter than white, the table and sideboard gleamed and there was a gentle aroma of lavender polish. A card saying 'Welcome Home' stood on the mantelpiece.

Every sign of Bert had been removed – no caps, cigarette packets, jackets, shoes had been left. They were saving her.

'Shall you be all right, mam?' Babs had enquired, earnestly. 'Don't want you getting upset again, do we?'

'We've just had a spring-clean, like – the lasses that is,' Eddie had grinned. He was like his Dad, a joker – couldn't stand anything to do with cremis or cancer. He dismissed weepy things by saying they were 'morbid'.

'Yes, love,' she'd said, 'was very nice of you all . . .'

They offered to take her to bingo, for treats at the fish and chip restaurant, and then, as summer was coming on, for day trips to Brid or Scarbro.

'Must get you out, Mam.'

People had been saying that for years. Even Bert had offered occasionally to take her to the club, but she'd always refused – she'd been 'mam', 'our lass', who stayed at home and looked after three kids and then the grand-kids. Mam had nerves, that was a known fact.

Bert in one of his sharp suits would be slapping lavender hair oil on, standing in front of the mirror and humming 'I'll be loving you eternally' or 'When Irish eyes are smiling', and she'd be wondering what he did down there every night and what Irish eyes were smiling at him. He'd been a docker, a bull of a man with a red face, a lined forehead and blue eyes like sapphire chips. He'd not been above laying into her after one of his boozy 'dos' – but that had been early on in the marriage.

One brilliant summer's day she was in the yard pegging out sheets and pillow cases when she saw Edna from next-door leaning on the fence and looking across.

'Eh up,' Edna shouted, 'I've heard there's a nice little job looking after toilets.'

Jessie went on pegging, but she listened.

'Why don't you have a try for it, it 'ud just be up your street?'

Edna had recently been divorced and was working part-time in a newsagent's, selling cigarettes and sweets.

'You need to get out, love – dun't do to stop in so much.'

'Oh I don't suppose I could really.'

But Jessie thought of Rosie's dentures and the smell of boiled cabbage and she screwed up her courage and the following morning, without telling anybody, she put on her best pale blue mac, took her shopping-bag, and set off for the job-centre in town.

She got the job, mainly because she looked too grim to allow customers to slip into the lavs free of charge, also she had the scrupulous cleanliness of the determined cleaner.

'Start on Monday.'

Start on Monday, she was terrified. Her heart fluttered and she wondered whether Bert's heart had done the same when it was giving out. Well, she consoled herself, at least if you were dead, you didn't have to bother about it.

'I've got it,' she announced to Edna when they met later at the fence.

'Geraway!'

'I have . . . but I don't know whether . . .'

'Now, love, what you need is a new look . . . image, you know. You must do something with that hair.'

'Yes,' Jessie said, thinking about Rosie's suet grey face and dusty grey hair through which the dingy white scalp had shone. 'Yes . . . but what?'

At the hands of Debbie at the 'Rhapsody Salon' Jessie underwent a transformation. She emerged as a dizzy, strawberry blonde with a bubble perm. All the way home she kept peeking at herself in shop-windows. This new person amazed her. Her mind began to run on exotic outfits . . . she who for years had worn shapeless 'Courtelle' 'reach-me-downs' and navy-blue or bottle-green polyester skirts. She felt sure an attack of 'nerves' would come on and she waited for the onset of her palpitations and breathlessness . . . but it didn't come. Yes, she promised herself, with her first wage-packet she would buy a new creation.

On Monday morning after a weekend of feeling dizzy and nervous, Jessie started her new job.

'It might be too much for you, Mam,' Babs had said. 'You don't *have* to do it . . .'

They all thought she was a patient . . . she remembered their special voices and that was when she knew, she would be going . . . even if she dropped dead in her lavs, she was going.

Her domain was down by the pier, where the ferries used to chug across to New Holland. She'd once made the trip with Bert and the kids. Bert had spent the voyage drinking bitter in the bar, whilst she'd followed Babs, Wendy and Eddie round, making sure they didn't plop in the water. It had been both exciting and sick-making. What would happen if the ferry sank? She'd read the instructions about life-belts . . . oh, it had been like a journey to the end of the earth!

As she entered the handsome brick building with its heavy oak doors which were fastened back with curly brass hooks, she caught a whiff of that day. Her memories were mostly about averting accidents and placating Bert.

The floor was marble . . . lovely white veined slabs, the lavs had oak doors and their cisterns bore the name 'Dreadnaught'! All the doorknobs and even the hinges on the lavatory seats were brass . . . she would make them shine.

In no time she was mopping that floor, working her mop amongst the white detergent peaks in her bucket and then swirling it across the smooth expanse. The marble came up brilliantly and she paused to admire it.

The customers came in a steady dribble, young girls with bare legs, teetering on spindle-heeled shoes, women with babies, juggling bags and pushchairs. She offered to hold the babies whilst the mothers entered the oak portals. Then there were ladies of her own age murmuring about the heat and their legs and the weight of their shopping bags and the way it cost 5p in old money for a wee-wee . . . and why should women have to pay when men went free?

Somewhere in the middle of the day, she found herself singing – it was a quite extraordinary thing. It began as a dull rumble, not unlike the start of a flushing cistern and then it took off.

'When Irish eyes are smilin' . . .' and 'I'll take you home again Kathleen to where your heart shall feel no pain . . .'

They mingled with the soft leather stroking the coloured glass in the door of the booth which was her little rest-room, the place where the cleaning things were stored and there was an electric kettle for her use.

At 1 p.m. she took a break and sat on a green-painted wooden seat near the lavatory and looked away across the heavy, cold-grey estuary to the horizon where phantom ships dithered in a heat haze. Somewhere in the muddle of her uneasiness a certain comfort was spreading . . . she hardly knew what it was, because it was so unfamiliar to her. She was a woman who had spent a lot of her life being afraid.

At the end of the first week, she bought a black cotton sweater threaded with lurex.

'You should see me Mam,' Jessie heard Wendy muttering to Babs, and got the idea that she disapproved. They thought she was bonkers. Jessie felt a laugh surging up her throat and sneezed.

Daphne Glazer

The Poison Ladies

When you are only four, seven is a hundred and five inches are a mile.

Ben was seven and I was four and there were five inches between us. Ben also had big brown leather patches on the seat of his moley corduroy trousers and dark hairs on his legs and a horn-handled knife with two blades, a corkscrew and a thing he called a stabber.

'Arter we git through the fence,' Ben said, 'We skive round the sloe bushes and under them ash trees and then we're in the lane and arter that there's millions and millions o' poison berries. Don't you eat no poison berries, will you? else you'll die. I swallered a lot o' poison berries once and I was dead all one night afterwards.'

'Real dead?'

'Real dead,' Ben said. 'All one night.'

What does it feel like to be dead?'

'Fust you git terrible belly ache,' Ben said, 'and then your head keeps going jimmity – jimmity – jimmity – bonk – bonk – bonk – clang – bang – jimmity – bonk – clang – bonk all the time.'

'Does it make you sick?'

'Sicking up all the time,' Ben said, 'and seeing old men dancing upside down on the bedroom wall and laughing at you – like my Uncle Perce does when he comes home from *The Unicorn.*'

'I don't want to be dead,' I said, 'I don't want to be dead.'

'Then don't eat no poison berries. You know what poison berries look like, don't you?'

'No.'

'Some are red,' Ben said, 'and some are black. But all on 'em make you sick and give you belly ache and make your head jimmity – jimmity – bonk – clang – bonk – bang – jimmity –'

My blood felt cold. I felt like sobbing and above me where I lay face downwards under the blackberry hedge, giant stalks of cow parsnip stood like frozen white skeleton sentinels against the late summer sky.

'Why don't we start?' I said. I knew we had a long way to go; Ben said so.

Ben got his knife out and opened the stabber.

'I got to see if there's any spies fust,' Ben said. 'You stop here.'

'How long?'

'Till I git back,' Ben said. 'Don't you move and don't you shout and don't you show yourself and don't you eat no poison berries.'

'No,' I said. 'No.'

Ben flashed the knife so that the stabber pierced the blackberry shade.

'You know Ossy Turner?' he said.

'Yes,' I said. 'Yes.'

Ossy had a hare-lip and walked with one drawling foot and a crooked hand. I always felt awfully sorry for Ossy but Ben said:

'Ossy's like that because he come down here and dint look for spies fust – so they got him and done that to him.'

'Who did?'

Ben was crawling away on hairy knees, flashing the stabber in the sunlight, leaving me alone.

'"The Poison Ladies",' Ben said, 'what live down here. In that house I told you about. Them two old wimmin what we're goin' to see if we can see.'

Ben went crawling forward; the brown leather patches on his trousers seat vanished clean from my range of sight. I shut my eyes and lay down alone in dead blackberry leaves and tried to listen for skylarks singing. Whenever I was alone in the fields I listened for the sound of skylarks. The song always seemed to sparkle in the solitude.

But now it was nearly September. It was too late for skylarks and all I could hear was the simmering drone of grasshoppers among yellowing grasses, out in the sun.

It was fifty years before Ben came back. I knew quite well that it was fifty years; I counted every one of them.

'No footmarks,' Ben said.

'I didn't eat any poison berries. I didn't –'

'Let's have a look at your tongue!'

My tongue shot out like a frightened lizard. With big white eyes Ben glared down my throat and said:

'All right. We're going now. Hold your breath.'

'How far is it now?'

'Miles,' Ben said. 'Down the lane and past the shippen and over the brook and then up the lane and across the Akky Duck.'

I didn't know what the Akky Duck was; I thought it must be a bird.

'It's like bridges,' Ben said. 'It's dark underneath 'em where the water goes over.'

'Do the poison ladies live there?'

'They come jist afterwards,' Ben said. 'We hide under the Akky Duck and arter that you can see 'em squinting through the winders.'

The veins about my heart tied themselves in knots as I followed Ben out of the blackberry shade, over the fence, into the lane and past black bushes of sloe powderily bloomed with blue fruit in the sun.

Once I tried to draw level with Ben and walk beside him, just for company, but he turned the stabber on me sharply and said:

'You keep behind me. I'm leader. I know the way, see? I got to git there fust to see if it's all right, see? Else they might do to you what they did to old Ossy, see?'

'Yes, Ben. Yes, Ben. Yes, Ben. Yes, Ben.'

Not long after that we passed a place in the brook where sheep were washed. Ben said I was to look at the water and see how gold it was. That was because it was poison and you'd die if you washed your hands there. Just beyond it great elephant umbrellas of hemlock grew in lush wet shade and Ben said they were poison too.

'Keep in,' he kept saying. 'Keep in. Crouch down. We're coming to the Akky Duck.'

Soon we were crouching under the dark bricks of the bridge. It was suddenly cold and the bricks dripped water. Ferns sprouted green fingers from crevices and Ben said there were snails as big as turnips there, with horns as long as bike-pumps.

'And snakes. And lizards. And rats. And Devil's Coach and Horses.'

'Are they poison too?'

'All on 'em. Everythink's poison down here.'

I wanted to hang on to Ben's coat tails and play horses, but Ben said no, he was going on ahead again to look for spies and that I'd got to wait and stand still and not breathe a word until he whistled a signal back to me.

So I stood under the Akky Duck all alone while Ben went out into the sunlight at the far end to look for spies. I didn't see any snails or lizards or snakes or Devil's Coach and Horses, but water dripped about me in long slow spits, splashing in the shadow.

When Ben whistled at last I jumped clean out of my skin and started running through black pools of water.

'Don't run, you wet ha'puth,' Ben said. 'They'll hear you. They got ears like old sows. They hang down to their shoulders.'

I think I must have shivered as I came out into sunlight, because Ben said:

'You ain't frit are you?'

'No,' I said. 'No, I'm not frit.'

'If you're frit,' Ben said, 'they'll know. Then they'll put both on us in the copper.'

'Why?' I said. 'Why?'

'To boil us up, you wet ha'puth!' Ben said: '*To boil us up.*'

'You said once they poisoned you.'

'So they do,' Ben said. 'Poison you fust, then boil you arterwards.'

Before I could speak again Ben was pointing ahead.

'There it is. That's where they live,' he said. 'That's the house.'

Fifty yards ahead stood a double-bayed house of red brick with a blue slate roof and cowls with foxes' tails on the chimneys. The cowls were black. Half the slates were off the roof and most of the glass was broken in the windows.

When we got a little nearer I could see there were plum trees in the garden, with ripe blue oval fruit shining in the sun. I could see an empty chicken run overgrown with grass and a big red earthenware pot with huge rhubarb leaves growing out of the top like inside-out umbrellas. It was hot now after the tunnel and everywhere the grasshoppers whirred.

I started to say that the house was empty but Ben said:

'Ah! That's what *you* think. That's what the old wimmen *want* you to think.'

'Why do they?'

'They want you to climb the fence and start gittin' the plums and then jist as you're gittin' 'em they spring out an' collar you.'

The veins about my heart tied themselves into tighter, colder knots as we crept along the fence on our hands and knees.

'Crouch down,' Ben kept whispering. 'Crouch down. Don't let 'em see you.'

Then we were in front of the house, in full view of the broken windows, the slateless rafters and the smoky cowls. The sun was on our backs and the light of it sharpened the splintered windows. The plums looked big and luscious now and you could see yellow wasps turning and shimmering madly about the trees.

'The plums are poison anyhow,' Ben said, 'even if they dint collar you. And even if you dint die o' poison the wasps 'd sting you to death.'

All about the house, from the broken window sashes to the stiff black fox tails, there wasn't a single movement in the sun.

Then Ben was clutching my arm and whispering hoarsely and pointing upward.

'There they are. There's one on 'em now. Watching.'

'Where?' I said. 'Where?'

'Up at that window. On the left-hand side.'

Ben didn't know his right hand from his left hand and nor did I. He pointed with the hand he held his knife in and I stared at the right-hand upstairs window but there was nothing there.

'Can't you see her?' Ben said. 'She's got long white pigtails and you can see her big ears.'

I looked at all the windows, one by one, upstairs and down, but there was nothing to be seen except splintered holes in the glass, naked and white-edged in the sunlight.

'She don't have no teeth, this one,' Ben said, 'and her mouth's all green.'

I didn't dare tell Ben I couldn't see anything, but suddenly he grabbed my arm:

'And there's the other one!' he whispered. 'Downstairs. The one with yeller eyes.'

My heart curdled. I started shivering down the whole length of my spine.

'Big yeller eyes she's got,' Ben said. 'Big yeller eyes. Like brimstone.'

All the windows downstairs were empty too and the only yellow I could see was in the clouds of wasps whirling about the laden plum trees.

'Can't you see her?' Ben said. 'Can't you see her?'

'No.'

He turned and looked at me sharply, in derision.

'You'll never see 'em with eyes wide open like that, you wet ha'porth. You gotta squint with 'em. Squint. Like this, see? Like owls do, see?'

Ben had his eyes all screwed up so that they were no more than dark slits.

'Owls can see in the dark,' he said. 'They can see what ain't there when we look. You know that, don't you?'

I knew that; my father had told me so. And suddenly I screwed up my eyes like an owl's too, just like Ben.

And when I looked at the house again it was just as Ben had said. I too could see the two old women at the windows, one upstairs and one down, the two old poison ladies, one with yellow eyes and the other with a green mouth and long white pigtails, both of them with awful ears, like sows.

'I can see them now, Ben,' I said, 'I can see them now.'

'Look out! They're coming!' Ben said. 'They're arter us!'

Then we were running, in terror, faster than wasps, under the Akky Duck, past the hemlock, the gold poison water, the shippen and the blue-black aisles of sloes. My breath was burning my chest and throat but my spine was chilled from the hairs of my neck downward and the knots round my heart coiled more and more tightly, deadly cold.

We didn't stop running until we were out in the big open field at the top of the lane. Then Ben started laughing and I was laughing too.

'We seen 'em!' Ben said. 'Both on 'em! They was there! We seen 'em! They was there!'

'We seen 'em!' I said. 'We seen 'em!'

Ben began turning somersaults in the grass and I tried to turn somersaults too. All the time we were laughing and flinging up our hands and shouting.

'I could see her yeller eyes!'

'And the other one's green mouth!'

'And the white pig-tails!'

'And their big ears!'

Suddenly a rook cackled sharply in the meadows below us, down where the hemlock grew. Ben looked back down the lane, startled, and I was startled too.

'Let's play horses,' Ben said. 'Let's gallop all the way home.'

'I'll be horse,' I said and in a second I was out in front, champing my bit, with Ben holding my coat tails, and a moment later we were away like a cold thin wind.

'We see the poison ladies!' Ben kept shouting. 'We see the ole poison ladies!'

'We see the poison ladies!' Ben kept shouting. 'We see the ole poison ladies!'

'We see the poison ladies!' I echoed. 'We see the old poison ladies!'

'They chased us! They nearly got us!'

'They nearly got us!'

'I bet they don't cut their ole nails fer a million years.'

'I bet they don't cut their old nails for a million years.'

Everything Ben shouted I shouted too. When he laughed I laughed. What he believed I believed. He wasn't afraid and I wasn't afraid. I was only flying home like a wild wind.

When you are only four, seven is a hundred and five inches are a mile.

H. E. Bates

ASSIGNMENTS

MAKING AND PRESENTING

A note on finding stories

(a) Keep a **writer's notebook** – this need only be a simple notepad or scrapbook in which you jot down anything that catches your attention during the day. It could be a joke, a piece of gossip, a snippet of conversation, a newspaper feature or a story that you have read somewhere or heard somewhere. From this kaleidoscope of jottings you are likely to see opportunities for stories of greater length when you look back at the collection.

(b) Ask relatives for **family stories**. There are usually many interesting stories in families. Not all of them will be ready-made for publication straightaway, but many can, with a little thought, be turned into amusing and entertaining short stories.

(c) Listen to **local stories**. There are always local tales, some grim, some amusing, about ghosts or murderous crimes, past tragedies and old heroics. Find out about these – your local library will help you here – and see how you can develop them.

1 Record on cassette some of the stories and memories of your grandparents or other old people in your area. Ask them about the war, about the old days in your area, about their happiest memories, and about some of the sadder ones too.

2 Make a collection of family stories. Choose one and try to develop it into a written short story.

3 Write down a local ghost story in the accent or dialect of the area. Try to capture something of the energy of the 'spoken' word. Have a look at the way the Somerset dialect is used in *Annie Luker's Ghost* on page 50.

4 Re-read the passage on page 53 from *Wuthering Heights*, and design a book cover which expresses the mood of the writing.

RESEARCHING AND RESPONDING

1 Do some research in the library on the life and works of Emily Brontë. Make notes of what you discover and make a list of her written work.

2 Find out what 'oral literature' means, and collect some examples both locally and from other societies.

3 Write a short essay on *The Triumph of Jesse Jones* or *The Poison Ladies*. Try to show how the story has been constructed, what the theme is and how you responded as you read it. At first, jot down brief notes and ideas (which you could discuss in groups), then go on to write up carefully your critical essay.

6 | THE ART OF RE-TELLING

Look at the two pictures below. One was painted in the 18th century and the other in the 20th, but both depend upon earlier stories.

- What myths do they draw on?
- Where have the myths come from?
- Why do you think the artists have been attracted to them?

Stories come out of our lives, our experiences, dreams, conversations, phantasies, but they also come out of other narratives: out of Greek myths, Biblical parables and inherited fairy stories and legends. This chapter is an anthology of such re-tellings.

In small groups, discuss any one set of the following stories. Look closely at the original story.

- What is it about?
- Why do you think it has been chosen by the modern author for re-telling?
- What is the author trying to achieve in its re-telling?
- In your view, is the re-telling successful? Can you say why?
- Why do you think so many authors re-tell the old stories?

NARRATIVE FROM ANCIENT GREECE

Original story: The Punishment of Prometheus

Far, far to the north, amid the freezing mountains of the Caucasus, there stood a tall, cold pillar. Chains of unburstable iron hung from its base and capital. Here the naked Titan was manacled by wrists and ankles, stretched so that he could scarcely twist his body or avert his head.

He waited – then a shadow fell across his face. He rolled his eyes to see what had come between him and the pale, bitter sun.

A vulture with hooked talons and greedy beak hung in the air. Its stony eyes met his. Then it swooped and the Titan writhed and screamed till the mountains cracked. His agony had begun. Again and again the hungry bird flew at him and tore at his undefended liver. When night came with biting frosts and whirling snow, the Titan's wounds healed and he grew whole again. But when the cold sun rose, the self-same shadow fell across his face and the Titan waited for his agony to begin once more. Such was the punishment of Prometheus, maker of men.

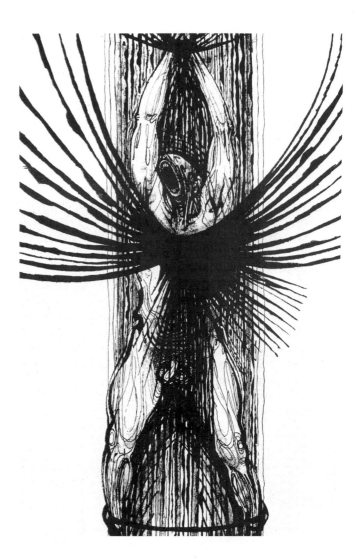

Modern re-tellings

The Vulture

A vulture was hacking at my feet. It had already torn my boots and stockings to shreds, now it was hacking at the feet themselves. Again and again it struck at them, then circled several times restlessly round me, then returned to continue its work. A gentleman passed by, looked on for a while, then asked me why I suffered the vulture. 'I'm helpless,' I said. 'When it came and began to attack me, I of course tried to drive it away, even to strangle it, but these animals are very strong, it was about to spring at my face, but I preferred to sacrifice my feet. Now they are almost torn to bits.'

'Fancy letting yourself be tortured like this!' said the gentleman. 'One shot and that's the end of the vulture.'

'Really?' I said. 'And would you do that?'

'With pleasure,' said the gentleman, 'I've only got to go home and get my gun. Could you wait another half hour?'

'I'm not sure about that,' said I, and stood for a moment rigid with pain. Then I said: 'Do try it in any case, please.'

'Very well,' said the gentleman, 'I'll be as quick as I can.'

During this conversation the vulture had been calmly listening, letting its eye rove between me and the gentleman. Now I realised that it had understood everything; it took wing, leaned far back to gain impetus and then, like a javelin thrower, thrust its beak through my mouth, deep into me. Falling back, I was relieved to feel him drowning irretrievably in my blood, which was filling every depth, flooding every shore.

Franz Kafka

Pincher Martin Shipwrecked on the Bare Rock

He lay with the pains, considering the light and the fact of a new day. He could inspect his wooden left hand if he was careful about the management of the inflamed corner of his eye. He willed the fingers to close and they quivered, then contracted. Immediately he was back in them, he became a man who was thrust deep into a crevice in barren rock. Knowledge and memory flowed back in orderly succession. He became a castaway in broad daylight and the necessity of his position fell on him. He began to heave at his body, dragging himself out of the space between the rocks. As he moved out, the gulls clamoured out of sleep and took off. They came back, sweeping in to examine him with sharp cries then sidling away in the air again. They were not like the man-wary gulls of inhabited beaches and cliffs. Nor had they about them the primal innocence of unvisited nature. They were wartime gulls who, finding a single man with water round him, resented the warmth of his flesh and his slow, unwarranted movements. They

told him, with their close approach, and flapping hover that he was far better dead, floating in the sea like a burst hammock. He staggered and struck out among them with wooden arms.

'Yah! Get away! Bugger off!'

They rose clamorously wheeling, came back till their wings beat his face. He struck out again in panic so that one went drooping off with a wing that made no more than a half-beat. They retired then, circled and watched. Their heads were narrow. They were flying reptiles. An ancient antipathy for things with claws set him shuddering at them and thinking into their smooth outlines all the strangeness of bats and vampires.

'Keep off! Who do you think I am?'

Their circles widened. They flew away to the open sea.

He turned his attention back to his body. His flesh seemed to be a compound of aches and stiffness.

William Golding

NARRATIVE FROM THE BIBLE

Original story: The Prodigal Son

'A certain man had two sons: and the younger of them said to his father, "Father, give me the portion of goods that falleth to me." And he divided unto them his living. And not many days after the younger son gathered all together, and took his journey into a far country, and there wasted his substance with riotous living. And when he had spent all, there arose a mighty famine in that land; and he began to be in want. And he went and joined himself to a citizen of that country; and he sent him into his fields to feed swine. And he would fain have filled his belly with the husks that the swine did eat: and no man gave unto him.

And when he came to himself, he said, 'How many hired servants of my father's have bread enough and

to spare, and I perish with hunger! I will arise and go to my father, and will say unto him, "Father, I have sinned against heaven, and before thee, and am no more worthy to be called thy son: make me as one of thy hired servants."'

And he arose, and came to his father. But when he was yet a great way off, his father saw him, and had compassion, and ran, and fell on his neck, and kissed him. And the son said unto him, 'Father, I have sinned against heaven, and in thy sight, and am no more worthy to be called thy son.' But the father said to his servants, 'Bring forth the best robe, and put it on him; and put a ring on his hand, and shoes on his feet: and bring hither the fatted calf, and kill it; and let us eat, and be merry: for this my son was dead, and is alive again; he was lost, and is found.' And they began to be merry.

Now his elder son was in the field: and as he came and drew nigh to the house, he heard music and dancing. And he called one of the servants, and asked what these things meant. And he said unto him, 'Thy brother is come; and thy father hath killed the fatted calf, because he hath received him safe and sound.' And he was angry, and would not go in: therefore came his father out, and intreated him. And he answering said to his father, 'Lo, these many years do I serve thee, neither transgressed I at any time thy commandment: and yet thou never gavest me a kid, that I might make merry with my friends: but as soon as this thy son was come, which hath devoured thy living with harlots, thou hast killed for him the fatted calf.' And he said unto him, 'Son, thou art ever with me, and all that I have is thine. It was meet that we should make merry, and be glad: for this thy brother was dead, and is alive again; and was lost, and is found.'

A modern version: Home-coming

I have returned, I have passed under the arch and am looking round. It's my father's old yard. The puddle in the middle. Old, useless tools, jumbled together, block the way to the attic stairs. The cat lurks on the banister. A torn piece of cloth, once wound round a stick in a game, flutters in the breeze. I have arrived. Who is going to receive me? Who is waiting behind the kitchen door? Smoke is rising from the chimney, coffee is being made for supper. Do you feel you belong, do you feel at home? I don't know, I feel most uncertain. My father's house it is, but each object stands cold beside the next, as though preoccupied with its own affairs, which I have partly forgotten, partly never known. What use can I be to them, what do I mean to them, even though I am the son of my father, the old farmer? And I don't dare knock at the kitchen door, I only listen from a distance, standing up, in such a way that I cannot be taken by surprise as an eavesdropper. And since I am listening from a distance, I hear nothing but a faint striking of the clock passing over from childhood days, but perhaps I only think I hear it. Whatever else is going on in the kitchen is the secret of those sitting there, a secret they are keeping from me. The longer one hesitates before the door, the more estranged one becomes. What would happen if someone were to open the door now and ask me a question? Would not I myself then behave like one who wants to keep his secret?

Franz Kafka

NARRATIVE FROM FABLES AND FAIRYTALES

Original fable from Aesop: Town Mouse and Country Mouse

A field-mouse invited a friend who lived in a town house to dine with him in the country. The other accepted with alacrity; but when he found that the fare consisted only of barley and other corn, he said to his host: 'Let me tell you, my friend, you live like an ant. But I have an abundance of good things to eat, and if you will come home with me you shall share them all.' So the two of them went off at once; and when his friend showed him peas and beans, bread, dates, cheese, honey, and fruit, the astonished field-mouse congratulated him heartily and cursed his own lot. They were about to begin their meal when the door suddenly opened, and the timid creatures were so scared by the sound that they scuttled into chinks. When they had returned and were just going to take some dried figs, they saw someone else come into the room to fetch something, and once more they jumped to take cover in their holes. At this the field-mouse decided that he did not care if he had to go hungry. 'Good-bye, my friend,' he said with a groan. 'You may eat your fill and enjoy yourself. But your good cheer costs you dear in danger and fear. I would rather gnaw my poor meals of barley and corn without being afraid or having to watch anyone out of the corner of my eye.'

A simple life with peace and quiet is better than faring luxuriously and being tortured by fear.

Modern version:
The Mouse Who Went
to the Country

Once upon a Sunday there was a city mouse who went to visit a country mouse. He hid away on a train the country mouse had told him to take, only to find that on Sundays it did not stop at Beddington. Hence the city mouse could not get off at Beddington and catch a bus for Sibert's Junction, where he was to be met by the country mouse. The city mouse, in fact, was carried on to Middleburg, where he waited three hours for a train to take him back. When he got back to Beddington he found that the last bus for Sibert's Junction had just left, so he ran and he ran and he ran and he finally caught the bus and crept aboard, only to find that it was not the bus for Sibert's Junction at all, but was going in the opposite direction through Pell's Hollow and Grumm to a place called Wimberby. When the bus finally stopped, the city mouse got out into a heavy rain and found that there were no more buses that night going anywhere. 'To the hell with it,' said the city mouse, and he walked back to the city.

Moral: *Stay where you are, you're sitting pretty.*

James Thurber

NARRATIVE FROM FAIRY STORIES

Original story:
Little Red-cap

THERE was once a sweet little maid, much beloved by everybody, but most of all by her grandmother, who never knew how to make enough of her. Once she sent her a little cap of red velvet, and as it was very becoming to her, and she never wore anything else, people called her Little Red-cap. One day her mother said to her, 'Come, Little Red-cap, here are some cakes and a flask of wine for you to take to grandmother; she is weak and ill, and they will do her good. Make haste and start before it grows hot, and walk properly and nicely, and don't run, or you might fall and break the flask of wine, and there would be none left for grandmother. And when you go into her room, don't forget to say, Good morning, instead of staring about you.'

'I will be sure to take care,' said Little Red-cap to her mother, and gave her hand upon it. Now the grandmother lived away in the wood, half-an-hour's walk from the village; and when Little Red-cap had reached the wood, she met the wolf; but as she did not know what a bad sort of animal he was, she did not feel frightened.

'Good day, Little Red-cap,' said he.

'Thank you kindly, Wolf,' answered she.

'Where are you going so early, Little Red-cap?'

'To my grandmother's.'

'What are you carrying under your apron?'

'Cakes and wine; we baked yesterday; and my grandmother is very weak and ill, so they will do her good, and strengthen her.'

'Where does your grandmother live, Little Red-cap?'

'A quarter of an hour's walk from here; her house stands beneath the three oak trees, and you may know it by the hazel bushes,' said Little Red-cap. The wolf thought to himself.

'That tender young thing would be a delicious morsel, and would taste better than the old one; I must manage somehow to get both of them.'

Then he walked by Little Red-cap a little while, and said,

'Little Red-cap, just look at the pretty flowers that are growing all round you, and I don't think you are listening to the song of the birds; you are posting along just as if you were going to school, and it is so delightful out here in the wood.'

Little Red-cap glanced round her, and when she saw the sunbeams darting here and there through the trees, and lovely flowers everywhere, she thought to herself,

'If I were to take a fresh nosegay to my grandmother she would be very pleased, and it is so early in the day that I shall reach her in plenty of time'; and so she ran about in the wood, looking for flowers. And as she picked one she saw a still prettier one a little farther off, and so she went farther and farther into the wood. But the wolf went straight to the grandmother's house and knocked at the door.

'Who is there?' cried the grandmother.

'Little Red-cap,' he answered, 'and I have brought you some cake and wine. Please open the door.'

'Lift the latch,' cried the grandmother; 'I am too feeble to get up.'

So the wolf lifted the latch, and the door flew open, and he fell on the grandmother and ate her up without saying one word. Then he drew on her clothes, put on her cap, lay down in her bed, and drew the curtains.

Little Red-cap was all this time running about among the flowers, and when she had gathered as many as she could hold, she remembered her grandmother, and set off to go to her. She was surprised to find the door standing open, and when she came inside she felt very strange, and thought to herself,

'Oh dear, how uncomfortable I feel, and I was so glad this morning to go to my grandmother!'

And when she said, 'Good morning,' there was no answer. Then she went up to the bed and drew back the curtains; there lay the grandmother with her cap pulled over her eyes, so that she looked very odd.

'O grandmother, what large ears you have got!'

'The better to hear with.'

'O grandmother, what great eyes you have got!'

'The better to see with.'

'O grandmother, what large hands you have got!'

'The better to take hold of you with.'

'But, grandmother, what a terrible large mouth you have got!'

'The better to devour you!' And no sooner had the wolf said it than he made one bound from the bed, and swallowed up poor Little Red-cap.

Then the wolf, having satisfied his hunger, lay down again in the bed, went to sleep, and began to snore loudly. The huntsman heard him as he was passing by the house, and thought,

'How the old woman snores — I had better see if there is anything the matter with her.'

Then he went into the room, and walked up to the bed and saw the wolf lying there.

'At last I find you, you old sinner!' said he; 'I have been looking for you a long time.' And he made up his mind that the wolf had swallowed the grandmother whole, and that she might yet be saved. So he did not fire, but took a pair of shears and began to slit up the wolf's body. When he made a few snips Little Red-cap appeared, and after a few more snips she jumped out and cried, 'Oh dear, how frightened I have been! it is so dark inside the wolf' And then out came the old grandmother, still living and breathing. But Little Red-cap went and quickly fetched some large stones, with which she filled the wolf's body, so that when he waked up, and was going to rush away, the stones were so heavy that he sank down and fell dead.

They were all three very pleased. The huntsman took off the wolf's skin, and carried it home. The grandmother ate the cakes, and drank the wine, and held up her head again, and Little Red-cap said to herself that she would never more stray about in the wood alone, but would mind what her mother told her.

It must also be related how a few days afterwards, when Little Red-cap was again taking cakes to her grandmother, another wolf spoke to her, and wanted to tempt her to leave the path; but she was on her guard, and went straight on her way, and told her grandmother how that the wolf had met her, and wished her good-day, but had looked so wicked about the eyes that she thought if it had not been on the high road he would have devoured her.

'Come,' said the grandmother, 'we will shut the door, so that he may not get in.'

Soon after came the wolf knocking at the door, and calling out, 'Open the door, grandmother, I am Little Red-cap, bringing you cakes.' But they remained still, and did not open the door. After that the wolf slunk by the house, and got at last upon the roof to wait until Little Red-cap should return home in the evening; then he meant to spring down upon her, and devour her in the darkness. But the grandmother discovered his plot. Now there stood before the house a great stone trough, and the grandmother said to the child, 'Little Red-cap, I was boiling sausages yesterday, so take the bucket, and carry away the water they were boiled in, and pour it into the trough.'

And Little Red-cap did so until the great trough was quite full. When the smell of sausages reached the nose of the wolf he snuffed it up, and looked round, and stretched out his neck so far that he lost his balance and began to slip, and he slipped down off the roof straight into the great trough, and was drowned. Then Little Red-cap went cheerfully home, and came to no harm.

A modern version: The Werewolf

It is a northern country; they have cold weather, they have cold hearts.

Cold; tempest; wild beasts in the forest. It is a hard life. Their houses are built of logs, dark and smoky within. There will be a crude icon of the virgin behind a guttering candle, the leg of a pig hung up to cure, a string of dying mushrooms. A bed, a stool, a table. Harsh, brief, poor lives.

To these upland woodsmen, the Devil is as real as you or I. More so; they have not seen us nor even know that we exist, but the Devil they glimpse often in the graveyards, those bleak and touching townships of the dead where the graves are marked with portraits of the deceased in the naïf style and there are no flowers to put in front of them, no flowers grow there, so they put out small, votive offerings, little loaves, sometimes a cake that the bears come lumbering from the margins of the forest to snatch away. At midnight, especially on Walpurgisnacht, the Devil holds picnics in the graveyards and invites the witches; then they dig up fresh corpses, and eat them. Anyone will tell you that.

Wreaths of garlic on the doors keep out the vampires. A blue-eyed child born feet first on the night of St John's Eve will have second sight. When they discover a witch – some old woman whose cheeses ripen when her neighbours' do not, another old woman whose black cat, oh, sinister! *follows her about all the time*, they strip the crone, search for her marks, for the supernumerary nipple her familiar sucks. They soon find it. Then they stone her to death.

Winter and cold weather.

Go and visit grandmother, who has been sick. Take her the oatcakes I've baked for her on the hearthstone and a little pot of butter.

The good child does as her mother bids – five miles' trudge through the forest; do not leave the path because of the bears, the wild boar, the starving wolves. Here, take your father's hunting knife; you know how to use it.

The child had a scabby coat of sheepskin to keep out the cold, she knew the forest too well to fear it but she must always be on her guard. When she heard that freezing howl of a wolf, she dropped her gifts, seized her knife and turned on the beast.

It was a huge one, with red eyes and running, grizzled chops; any but a mountaineer's child would have died of fright at the sight of it. It went for her throat, as wolves do, but she made a great swipe at it with her father's knife and slashed off its right forepaw.

The wolf let out a gulp, almost a sob, when it saw what had happened to it; wolves are less brave than they seem. It went lolloping off disconsolately between the trees as well as it could on three legs, leaving a trail of blood behind it. The child wiped the blade of her knife clean on her apron, wrapped up the wolf's paw in the cloth in which her mother had packed the oatcakes and went on towards her grandmother's house. Soon it came on to snow so thickly that the path and any footsteps, track or spoor that might have been upon it were obscured.

She found her grandmother was so sick she had taken to her bed and fallen into a fretful sleep, moaning and shaking so that the child guessed she had a fever. She felt the forehead, it burned. She shook out the cloth from her basket, to use it to make the old woman a cold compress, and the wolf's paw fell to the floor.

But it was no longer a wolf's paw. It was a hand, chopped off at the wrist, a hand toughened with work and freckled with old age. There was a wedding ring on the third finger and a wart on the index finger. By the wart, she knew it for her grandmother's hand.

She pulled back the sheet but the old woman woke up, at that, and began to struggle, squawking and shrieking like a thing possessed. But the child was strong, and armed with her father's hunting knife; she managed to hold her grandmother down long enough to see the cause of her fever. There was a bloody stump where her right hand should have been, festering already.

The child crossed herself and cried out so loud the neighbours heard her and came rushing in. They knew the wart on the hand at once for a witch's nipple; they drove the old woman, in her shift as she was, out into the snow with sticks, beating her old carcass as far as the edge of the forest, and pelted her with stones until she fell down dead.

Now the child lived in her grandmother's house; she prospered.

Angela Carter

In our own century a number of women writers have taken fairy stories and fables and re-told them from their own point of view. Here is one such tale from the Indian writer, Suniti Namjoshi.

A feminist fable: The Giantess

Thousands of years ago in far away India, which is so far away that anything is possible, before the advent of the inevitable Aryans, a giantess was in charge of a little kingdom. It was small by her standards, but perhaps not by our own. Three oceans converged on its triangular tip, and in the north there were mountains, the tallest in the world, which would perhaps account for this singular kingdom. It was not a kingdom, but the word has been lost and I could find no other. There wasn't any king. The giantess governed and there were no other women. The men were innocent and happy and carefree. If they were hurt, they were quickly consoled. For the giantess was kind, and would set them on her knee and tell them they were brave and strong and noble. And if they were hungry, the giantess would feed them. The milk from her breasts was sweeter than honey and more nutritious than mangoes. If they grew fractious, the giantess would sing, and they would clamber up her leg and onto her lap and sleep unruffled. They were a happy people and things might have gone on in this way forever, were it not for the fact that the giantess grew tired. Her knees felt more bony, her voice rasped, and on one or two occasions she showed irritation. They were greatly distressed. 'We love you,' they said to the tired giantess, 'Why won't you sing? Are you angry with us? What have we done?'

'You are dear little children,' the giantess replied, 'but I have grown very tired and it's time for me to go.'

'Don't you love us anymore? We'll do what you want. We will make you happy. Only please don't go.'

'Do you know what I want?' the giantess asked.

They were silent for a bit, then one of them said, 'We'll make you our queen.'

And another one said, 'We'll write you a poem.'

And the third one shouted (while turning cartwheels), 'We'll bring you many gifts of oysters and pearls and pebbles and stones.'

'No,' said the giantess, 'No.' She turned her back and crossed the mountains.

ASSIGNMENTS

MAKING AND PRESENTING

Throughout history, storytellers and writers have recycled old and familiar stories. This has never been regarded as 'cheating', but as an entirely proper way of bringing stories up to date.

All the great writers and playwrights of the past were happy to use older sources for their material, and you should not hesitate to re-work and re-fashion some of the old stories either, to suit your own needs and values.

Here are some suggestions for you to look at and to try to work into a modern-day interpretation. You may need to go to a library to find the original stories.

1   Look closely at two or three of the following stories (or others which you may have in mind) before you try to work one of them into your own version.

(a) From *The Bible*, for example, the story of David and Goliath, which can be found in the *First Book of Samuel*, chapter 17, verses 49–51, or the story of the Good Samaritan, which can be found in *St Luke's Gospel*, chapter 10, verses 30–37.

(b) Two from **Ancient Greece, the Classical World,** for example the story of Narcissus, or the story of King Oedipus which you can find in the play by Sophocles and in any encyclopaedia.

(c) Any of *Aesop's Fables*, which you will find in any library.

(d) Two from **British literary history,** perhaps the story of Tristan and Iseult, or the legend of Robin Hood.

(e) Something from **Shakespeare,** for example, the story of Romeo and Juliet, or the tragedy of Macbeth.

(f) Or you could **re-work a fairy story** in the same way that Angela Carter has re-told the tale of *Little Red Riding Hood*.

When you have settled upon a story, think what it was that attracted you to it and work out what you want to convey in your modern version. When you have done this, you can begin to construct your own story. You will probably have to think in terms of **revising** and **re-drafting** it before it is ready for a wider audience.

2 In pairs, choose any of the groups of parallel stories in this chapter and make a recording on tape, cutting between the original story and the later version in any way that you think works best. You could go on to add another layer by including parts of your own stories (or even extracts and episodes which fit) by cutting these into your recording. At the end of the recording, explain what effects you were trying to achieve and why you chose the parts that you did.

3 Design an exciting dust-jacket for any of the stories relating to this chapter. Write your own summary of the story for the blurb, and create an image which suggests the nature of the story.

RESEARCHING AND RESPONDING

1 Do some research (in groups or individually) on stories that have been told again and again, but this time extend it to films, television and paintings. What is it about the stories that have made them so popular? Do you notice any important changes in the stories as they are re-told? Make notes and develop them either into a written essay or a display for the classroom.

2 Write an introduction to your own re-telling of an old story. Give an account of the original story. (Where did it first come from? What is the plot? What attracted you to it?) Describe how it changed as you re-told it as a story for our own times.

3 Write a short essay on the re-telling of old stories. Illustrate your argument with quotations from the stories in this chapter and any other re-tellings you have managed to find, including work by yourself and other members of the class.

7 | UNDERSTANDING CHARACTER

Look closely at the following portraits.

- ■ What can you tell about these people from their expression? from their clothes? from any other clues in the picture?
- ■ What kind of background do they come from?
- ■ How do you think they would speak?
- ■ What kind of people do you think they are?
- ■ What might be their weaknesses? their strengths?

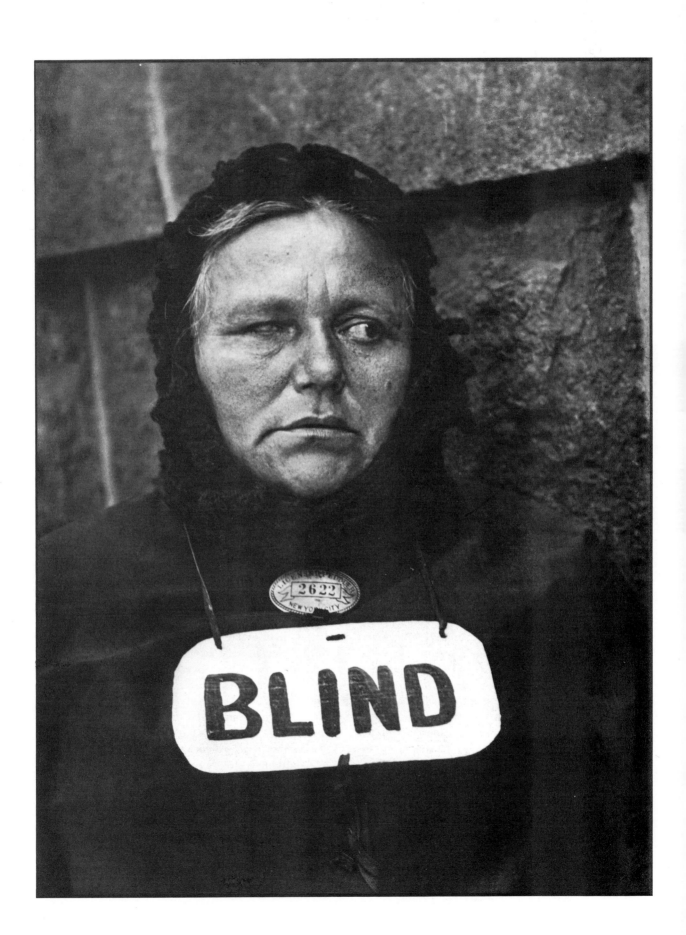

Look at the following titles of some famous novels.

Pamela	*Anna Karenina*
Robinson Crusoe	*Alice's Adventures in Wonderland*
I Am David	*The Wizard of Oz*
Emma	*Kes*
Jane Eyre	*Ulysses*
Oliver Twist	*Doctor Zhivago*
Silas Marner	*Stig of the Dump*
Adam Bede	*Billy Liar*
Pincher Martin	*The Strange Affair of Adelaide Harris*
The Diary of Adrian Mole	*Lord Jim*
The Adventures of Huckleberry Finn	

- What do you notice about all of these titles?
- What do the titles tell us about the novels?
- Do you know who some of the authors are?
- Can you think of other similar titles?

Here is a list of some of the characters created by Charles Dickens.

Mr Tite Barnacle	Miss Podsnap	Mr Venus
Smike	Mrs Clennam	Mr Edmund Sparkler
Wackford Squeers	Mr Boffin	Mr Gradgrind
Mr Snagsby		

- What can you tell about these characters from their names alone?

Reading a novel or story, one of our main interests is with the characters. We want to know what they are like, what happens to them and how they are changed by their experiences.

In their journals and letters, novelists often tell us how they have created their characters, and show how closely they have had to imagine every aspect of their existence. The 19th-century English novelist Anthony Trollope wrote of the author's relationship to his own characters. In the extract below note Trollope's attitudes to women and his assumption that writers are male:

HE MUST LEARN to hate them and to love them. He must argue with them, quarrel with them, forgive them, and even submit to them. He must know of them whether they be cold-blooded or passionate, whether true or false, and how far true, and how far false. The depth and the breadth, and the narrowness and the shallowness of each should be clear to him. And, as here, in our outer world, we know that men and women change – become worse or better as temptation or conscience may guide them – so should these creations of his change, and every change should be noted by him. On the last day of each month recorded, every person in his novel should be a month older than on the first. If the would-be novelist has aptitudes that way, all this will come to him without much struggling – but if it do not come, I think he can only make novels of wood.

It is so that I have lived with my characters, and thence has come whatever success I have obtained. There is a gallery of them, and of all in that gallery I may say that I know the tone of the voice, and the colour of the hair, every flame of the eye, and the very clothes they wear. Of each man I could assert whether he would have said these or the other words; of every woman, whether she would then have smiled or so have frowned. When I shall feel that this intimacy ceases, then I shall know that the old horse should be turned out to grass.

The 19th-century Russian novelist Ivan Turgenev wrote of his own literary characters in a similar way:

IF I WATCH my characters long enough I see them come together, I see them placed; I see them engaged in this or that act and in this or that difficulty, how they look and move and speak and behave always in the setting I have found for them. . . .

Here is an example of a modern novelist, Bruce Chatwin, imagining the Biblical characters, Cain and Abel, in a particular setting. Character, setting and plot come together. From such jottings, stories and novels grow.

Cain and Abel

A possible synopsis for the Murder:

Cain is a painstaking fellow, bent double from constant digging. The day is hot and cloudless. Eagles are floating high above in the blue. The last of the snowmelt still cascades down the valley, but the hillsides are already brown and parched. Flies cluster at the corners of his eyes. He wipes the sweat from his forehead, and resumes his work. His hoe has a wooden handle, with a stone blade hafted on to it.

Somewhere, higher up the slope, Abel is resting in the cool of a rock. He trills at his flute: again and again, the same insistent trills. Cain pauses to listen. Stiffly, he straightens his back. Then, raising his hand against the glare, he peers at his fields along the stream. The sheep have trampled his morning's work. Without having time to think, he breaks into a run . . .

Bruce Chatwin, *The Songlines*

Here are three character sketches taken from different stories.

Lord Jim

He was an inch, perhaps two, under six feet, powerfully built, and he advanced straight at you with a slight stoop of the shoulders, head forward, and a fixed from-under stare which made you think of a charging bull. His voice was deep, loud, and his manner displayed a kind of dogged self-assertion which had nothing aggressive in it. It seemed a necessity, and it was directed apparently as much at himself as at anybody else. He was spotlessly neat, apparelled in immaculate white from shoes to hat, and in the various Eastern ports where he got his living as ship-chandler's water-clerk he was very popular.

Joseph Conrad

Grandma Carter

Our only visitor at Dorinda Gardens was my Grandma Carter. She came in her black bead bonnet, her red nose and the red-rimmed eyes showing like knife-cuts through her black veil, and wearing a black cape of some shiny material, the death-watch beetle of grief. She carried a string bag with her, for wherever she went she seemed always to travel with a few groceries, some sewing, and a bottle of stout. There was the smell of the sharp grocer's about her, something compounded of tea, biscuits, bacon, and pickles, and her tongue was the vinegar. Grief, one thinks, should purge and exalt the soul, but it had made her ugly, bad-tempered and given her also a morbid shuffling humility, a look of guilt and shame. She came every Wednesday to see us, and she would suddenly appear, letting herself in by the back door and saying every time apologetically:

'I came round the back, Gert dear, because I see you done your front.' Then she pushed back her veil to the bridge of her nose, and turning slowly in a circle as a dog does before it lies down to sleep, she would give a sniff and put her string bag down on a chair. Her loneliness, her unhappiness, and her snuffling made us afraid.

V. S. Pritchett

Scrooge

Oh! But he was a tight-fisted hand at the grindstone, Scrooge! a squeezing, wrenching, grasping, scraping, clutching, covetous, old sinner! Hard and sharp as flint, from which no steel had ever struck out generous fire; secret, and self-contained, and solitary as an oyster. The cold within him froze his old features, nipped his pointed nose, shrivelled his cheek, stiffened his gait; made his eyes red, his thin lips blue; and spoke out shrewdly in his grating voice. A frosty rime was on his head, and on his eyebrows, and his wiry chin. He carried his own low temperature always about with him; he iced his office in the dog-days; and didn't thaw it one degree at Christmas.

External heat and cold had little influence on Scrooge. No warmth could warm, no wintry weather chill him. No wind that blew was bitterer than he, no falling snow was more intent upon its purpose, no pelting rain less open to entreaty. Foul weather didn't know where to have him. The heaviest rain, and snow, and hail, and sleet, could boast of the advantage over him in only one respect. They often 'came down' handsomely, and Scrooge never did.

Nobody ever stopped him in the street to say, with gladsome looks, 'My dear Scrooge, how are you? When will you come to see me?' No beggars implored him to bestow a trifle, no children asked him what it was o'clock, no man or woman ever once in all his life inquired the way to such and such a place, of Scrooge. Even the blindmen's dogs appeared to know him; and when they saw him coming on, would tug their owners into doorways and up courts; and then would wag their tails as though they said, 'no eye at all is better than an evil eye, dark master!'

But what did Scrooge care! It was the very thing he liked. To edge his way along the crowded paths of life, warning all human sympathy to keep its distance . . .

Charles Dickens

- How convincing do you find these characters?
- How have the authors built up their descriptions?
- From their descriptions, can you see the characters?
- Could you do an illustration of them?

In some forms of fiction, like detective stories, an author will invent a single hero or heroine and use them again and again. Agatha Christie created Miss Marple. Simenon created Maigret. Dorothy Sayers created Lord Peter Wimsey. Ian Fleming created James Bond.

- Can you think of other examples?
- Can you think of examples from television series?

PROFILES OF TWO ESTABLISHED DETECTIVE CHARACTERS

MARPLE
Miss

A tall thin old lady (not like Margaret Rutherford in the films) with white hair, a pink-and-white face and an expression of great gentleness in china blue eyes, aged 74 when she began in 1928 and used to wear black mittens, more up-to-date at the time of her last case in 1938 or 1939 (though *Sleeping Murder* was published only posthumously in 1976). But shrewd. And with a nose for evil, an intuitive faculty quite different from Hercule Poirot's busy little grey cells. She had a tart appreciation of the importance of gossip, however, 'how often is tittle-tattle, as you call it, true.' In fact, all innocence as she seems, she is a thorough-going cynic, 'it is really very dangerous to believe people. I never have for years.' It is as well that she did not, or the many murderers in the neighbourhood of the quiet village of St Mary Mead, and those encountered in occasional holidays in the Caribbean or at Bertram's Hotel in London, would never have been brought to book, having been compared to their downfall with a delinquent butcher boy or a housemaid who, although she always turned the mattresses every day, 'except Fridays of course', proved to be her master's kept woman.

Creator: Agatha Christie

TIBBS
Virgil

He is a black detective ('despite his dark complexion his features were aquiline') of the Pasadena Police Department in California, though the case that brought him to prominence, *In the Heat of the Night* (1965), took place when he was sent to America's Deep South and encountered race prejudice at its simplest and most hateful, reacting to it with quiet dignity ('They call me *Mister* Tibbs'). His subsequent cases on his home territory have been designed, in his creator's words, 'to help explain the police function to the citizenry at large and to show how modern, enlightened police departments function'. He is modest to a fault about the part he plays in this.

Creator: John Ball

Here is a character sketch of one of the earliest detective heroes,
Sherlock Holmes, written by his inventor Arthur Conan Doyle.

Sherlock Holmes

His very person and appearance were such as to strike
the attention of the most casual observer. In height he
was rather over six feet, and so excessively lean that
he seemed to be considerably taller. His eyes were
sharp and piercing . . . and his thin hawk-like nose
gave his whole expression an air of alertness and
decision. His chin, too, had the prominence and
squareness which mark the man of determination. His
hands were invariably blotted with ink and stained
with chemicals, yet he was possessed of extraordinary
delicacy of touch, as I frequently had occasion to
observe when I watched him manipulating his fragile
philosophical instruments.

His limits:

1. Knowledge of Literature. – Nil.
2.   ,,   ,, Philosophy. – Nil.
3.   ,,   ,, Astronomy. – Nil.
4.   ,,   ,, Politics.   – Feeble.
5.   ,,   ,, Botany.   – Variable. Well up
     in belladonna, opium, and
     poisons generally. Knows
     nothing of practical gar-
     dening.
6.   ,,   ,, Geology. – Practical, but
     limited. Tells at a glance dif-
     ferent soils from each other.
     After walks has shown me
     splashes upon his trousers,
     and told me by their colour
     and consistence in what part
     of London he had received
     them.
7.   ,,   ,, Chemistry. – Profound.
8.   ,,   ,, Anatomy. – Accurate, but
     unsystematic.
9.   ,,   ,, Sensational   Literature. –
     Immense. He appears to know
     every detail of every horror
     perpetrated in the century.
10. Plays the violin well.
11. Is an expert singlestick player, boxer and
     swordsman.
12. Has a good practical knowledge of British law.

Special Characteristics – kept cigars in the coal-
scuttle, his tobacco in the toe end of a Persian slipper
and his unanswered correspondence transfixed by a
jack-knife into the very centre of his wooden
mantelpiece. Deerstalker cap and Inverness cape,
test-tubes, magnifying glass and Stradivarius violin.
Not only possessed far greater mental brilliance than
his predecessors, but also good social and cultural
background, perfect integrity, status of a scientist; a
master of disguise, an accomplished actor and great
physical strength. He is unemotional, reasons with
ice-cold logic, vast technical knowledge. Heavy
smoker, takes long walks through city streets at night,
holds poor opinion of police, bachelor with no interest
in opposite sex.

Sir Arthur Conan Doyle, *A Study in Scarlet*

■ How does Holmes compare with his modern counterparts?

■ How, would you say, have detective heroes and heroines changed?

■ How lifelike are the modern heroes?

■ How lifelike do you think a hero or heroine should be?

Not all characters in fiction are heroes or heroines. Some authors set out deliberately to create **anti-heroes** or **anti-heroines.** More often, though, authors want to create characters who are not ideal but are closer to the muddle and mix of human life.

Here are two stories that are firmly based on character. The first is by an American writer and is a single character sketch. The second is by an Italian, and is a more dramatic recreation of two characters in action.

Cameron (44:40)

When I knew Cameron he was a very old man and wore carpet slippers all the time and didn't talk any more. He smoked cigars and occasionally listened to Burl Ives' records. He lived with one of his sons who was now a middle-aged man himself and starting to complain about growing old.

'God-damn it, there's no getting around the fact that I'm not as young as I used to be.'

Cameron had his own easy chair in the front room. It was covered with a wool blanket. Nobody else ever sat in that chair, but it was always as if he were sitting there, anyway. His spirit had taken command of that chair. Old people have a way of doing that with the furniture they end their lives sitting in.

He didn't go outside any more during the winter, but he would sit out on the front porch sometimes in the summer and stare past the rose bushes in the front yard to the street beyond where life calendared its days without him as if he had never existed out there at all.

That wasn't true, though. He used to be a great dancer and would dance all night long in the 1890s. He was famous for his dancing. He sent many a fiddler to an early grave and when the girls danced with him, they always danced better and they loved him for it and just the mention of his name in that county made the girls feel good and would get them blushing and giggling. Even the 'serious' girls would get excited by his name or the sight of him.

There were a lot of broken hearts when he married the youngest of the Singleton girls in 1900.

'She's not that pretty,' refrained the sore losers and they all cried at the wedding.

He was also a hell of a good poker player in a county where people played very serious poker for high stakes. Once a man sitting next to him was caught cheating during a game.

There was a lot of money on the table and a piece of paper that represented twelve head of cattle, two horses and a wagon. That was part of a bet.

The man's cheating was made public by one of the other men at the table reaching swiftly across without saying a word and cutting the man's throat.

Cameron automatically reached over and put his thumb on the man's jugular vein to keep the blood from getting all over the table and held him upright, though he was dying until the hand was finished and the ownership of the twelve head of cattle, two horses and a wagon was settled.

Though Cameron didn't talk any more, you could see events like that in his eyes. His hands had been made vegetable-like by rheumatism but there was an enormous dignity to their repose. The way he lit a cigar was like an act of history.

Once he had spent a winter as a sheepherder in 1889. He was a young man, not yet out of his teens. It was a long lonely winter job in God-forsaken country, but he needed the money to pay off a debt that he owed his father. It was one of those complicated family debts that it's best not to go into detail about.

There was very little exciting to do that winter except look at sheep but Cameron found something to keep his spirits up.

Ducks and geese flew up and down the river all winter and the man who owned the sheep had given him and the other sheepherders a lot, an almost surrealistic amount, of 44:40 Winchester ammunition to keep the wolves away, though there weren't any wolves in that country.

The owner of the sheep had a tremendous fear of wolves getting to his flock. It bordered on the ridiculous if you were to go by all the 44:40 ammunition he supplied his sheepherders.

Cameron heavily favoured this ammunition with his rifle that winter by shooting at the ducks and geese from a hillside about two hundred yards from the river. A 44:40 isn't exactly the greatest bird gun in the world. It lets go with a huge slow-moving bullet like a fat man opening a door. Cameron wanted those kind of odds.

The long months of that family-debted exile winter passed slowly day after day, shot after shot until it was finally spring and he had maybe fired a few thousand shots at those ducks and geese without hitting a single one of them.

Cameron loved to tell that story and thought it was very funny and always laughed during the telling. Cameron told that story about as many times as he had fired at those birds years in front of and across the bridge of 1900 and up the decades of this century until he stopped talking.

Richard Brautigan

Seen in the Canteen

I knew at once that something would happen. The two were looking at each other across the table with expressionless eyes, like fish in an aquarium. But one could see that they were strangers and quite incomprehensible to each other, two unknown animals, each watching and distrusting the other.

She had arrived first; a huge woman in black, obviously a widow – a widow from the country up in town on business was how I placed her as soon as I saw her. Her kind of people also came to the popular 60-lire canteen where I ate: black marketeers, big and small operators alike, with a taste for economy remaining with them from their days of poverty, but with sporadic outbursts of extravagance every now and again when they remembered that their pockets were full of 1,000-lire notes – outbursts that made them order spaghetti and beefsteak, while we others, thin bachelors eating on meal tickets, eyed them enviously and gulped down spoonfuls of vegetable soup. The woman must have been quite a rich marketeer; she sat down, occupying a whole side of the table, and began pulling out of her bag pieces of white bread, fruit, carelessly wrapped cheese, and spreading them all over the cloth. Then, with her black-rimmed fingers, she began mechanically picking at grapes and bits of bread, and shovelling them into her mouth where they vanished in a slow chewing motion.

It was at this moment that he approached and saw the empty chair at a still uncluttered corner of the table. He bowed. 'May I?' The woman glanced up and went on chewing. He tried again. 'Excuse me – may I?' The woman shrugged her shoulders and let out a grunt from a mouth full of chewed bread. The man raised his hat slightly and sat down. He was an old man, neat but rather shabby, with a starched collar, wearing an overcoat although it was not winter; a flex from a deaf-aid instrument hung from his ear. I felt sorry for him at once, sorry for the air of good breeding emanating from his every gesture. He was obviously a gentleman who had come down in the world, fallen suddenly from a world of compliments and bows to one of shoves and digs in the ribs, without ever understanding how it had all happened but continuing to bow among the crowd in the canteen as if he were at a court reception.

Now they were face to face, the newly-rich woman and the ex-rich man, animals unknown one to the other; the woman broad and short with her large hands resting on the table like the claws of a crab, and breathing as if she had a crab in her throat too; the old man sitting on the edge of his chair with his arms pressed against his sides, his gloved hands paralysed with arthritis, and little blue veins protruding from his face, like lichen on a red stone.

'Excuse my hat,' he said. The woman looked at him out of the yellows of her eyes. She understood nothing about him at all.

'Excuse me,' repeated the man, 'for keeping my hat on. There's rather a draught.'

The large widow smiled then, at the corners of her mouth, covered with soft down like an insect's; a stiffened smile, almost without moving a muscle of her face, like a ventriloquist's.

'Wine,' she said to a passing waitress.

At that word the eyes of the old man with the gloves flickered; he obviously liked his wine, the veins at the top of his nose bore witness to the long careful drinking of a gourmet. But he must have given up drinking for some time. The widow was now dropping pieces of white bread into her glass of wine and still chewing steadily.

Perhaps the old man with the gloves suddenly felt a pang of shame, as if he were courting a woman and was afraid of appearing mean. 'Wine for me too!' he called.

Then at once he seemed to have repented of saying this; perhaps he thought that if he finished his pension before the end of the month he would have to starve for days, muffled in his overcoat in his cold attic. He did not pour the wine into his glass. 'Perhaps,' he thought, 'if I don't touch it I can give it back, say I no longer want it, then I won't have to pay for it.'

And, indeed, the desire for wine had already passed, as had also the desire to eat; he rattled his spoon in the tasteless soup, chewing with his few remaining teeth, while the large widow swallowed forkfuls of macaroni dripping in butter.

'Let's hope they'll be quiet now,' I thought. 'That one or the other will finish soon and go.' I don't know what I was afraid of. Each of them were monstrous beings in their way, and under their slow crustacean-like appearances both were charged with a reciprocal terrible hatred. I imagined a battle between them like a slow tearing to pieces of monsters at the bottom of the sea.

The old man was already surrounded, almost besieged, by the wrappings from the widow's food scattered over the table; confined to a corner with his tasteless soup and his two poor coupon rolls, he tried to pull them nearer as if afraid they would get lost in the enemy camp, but with an involuntary move of his gloved and paralysed hand he pushed a piece of cheese off the table, and it fell to the ground.

The widow seemed to loom up in front of him more enormous than ever; she was grinning. 'Excuse me . . . excuse me,' said the old man with the gloves. She looked at him as one looks at a new kind of animal, but did not reply.

'Now,' I thought. 'Now he'll shout out "Enough of this" – and tear off the tablecloth!'

Instead he bent down, and with clumsy movements searched for the cheese under the table. The big widow stopped, looked at him for a moment, then almost without moving dropped one of her enormous paws to the floor, picked up the piece of cheese, brushed it, popped it into her insect's mouth, and had swallowed it before the old man with the gloves re-emerged.

Finally he straightened up, aching with the effort, red with confusion, his hat crooked and the flex of his hearing aid awry.

'Now,' I thought. 'Now he'll take up a knife and kill her!'

Instead, however, he seemed unable to console himself for the unfavourable impression he felt he had created. Obviously he longed to talk, to say anything at all to dispel the uncomfortable atmosphere. But he could not think of a single phrase that did not refer to the incident, did not sound like an excuse.

'That cheese,' he said. 'Such a pity, really – I'm so sorry . . .'

The large widow did not just want to humiliate him by her silence, she wanted to squash him completely.

'Oh, it doesn't matter at all,' she said. 'At Castel Brandone I've got cheeses this size,' and she moved her hands apart. But it was not the space between her hands that impressed the old man.

'Castel Brandone?' he said, and his eyes lit up. 'I was at Castel Brandone as a second lieutenant! In '95; for the shooting. If you come from there, you must know the Counts of Brandone d'Asprez!'

The widow was not just grinning now, she was laughing. Laughing and turning round to see if any others had noticed this ridiculous old man.

'You wouldn't remember,' went on the old man. 'You certainly wouldn't remember – but that year at Castel Brandone, for the shooting, the King came! There was a reception at the d'Asprez' castle. And it was there that what I am about to tell you happened.'

The large widow looked at her watch, ordered a plate of liver and began hurriedly eating, without listening to him. The old man with the gloves knew that he was talking to himself, but he did not stop; it would have made a bad impression to stop, he must finish the story he had begun.

'His Majesty entered the brilliantly lit drawing-room,' he continued with tears in his eyes, 'and on one side were the ladies in evening dress curtseying, and on the other us officers standing at attention. And the King kissed the countess's hand and greeted first one and then another. Then he came up to me . . .'

The two quarter-litre bottles of wine were side by side on the table; that of the widow almost finished, that of the old man still full. Without thinking the widow poured some wine out of the full bottle and drank it. The old man noticed this, even in the heat of his story-telling; now there was no more hope, he would have to pay for it. And perhaps the widow would drink it all. But it would be impolite to point out her mistake, and besides it might hurt her feelings. No, it would be too indelicate.

'And His Majesty asked me: "And you, Lieutenant?" Just like that he asked. And I, standing at attention: "Second Lieutenant Clermont de Fronges, Your Majesty." And the King said: "Clermont! I knew your father; a fine soldier!" And he shook my hand . . . Just like that he said it: "A fine soldier!"'

The large widow had finished eating and got up. Now she was rummaging in her bag which was propped on the other chair. She bent over the chair and all that could be seen above the table was her behind, an enormous fat woman's behind, covered in black. Old Clermont de Fronges was facing this big waggling behind. He went on telling his story, his face transfigured: 'The whole room brilliant with chandeliers and mirrors. And the King shaking me by the hand. "Bravo, Clermont de Fronges," he said to me . . . and the ladies all standing round in evening dress . . .'

Italo Calvino

ASSIGNMENTS

MAKING AND PRESENTING

1 One way of inventing a character is to produce a confidential file on a particular character, and then to see that person as a whole person.

The confidential file   Confidential files are kept by a great many organisations. You can probably think of some of them, but here are a few suggestions:

schools	police	RSPCA
fraud squad	drugs squad	HM Customs and Excise
secret services	private detectives	businesses
Army, Navy, RAF	Interpol	

You can decide which organisation is going to keep 'your' file, and then you need to work out who the file is going to be about. Make a confidential file on a piece of A4 card.

NAME _____

In this section you write down details about your character:	In this section you can fill in details of the reasons why your character is on anyone's confidential file.	Attach or 'draw' a photograph of your character here
■ name ■ aliases ■ known friends ■ places frequented ■ physical description Include anything that will help to create an identity for your character.	■ Has a crime been committed? ■ Is your character a suspect or a victim? You can list any evidence or objects related to the case: letters, newspaper cuttings, diary pages, photographs, sketch maps. These will tell something more about your character and help to build up a full picture. If you have invented a lot of material, it might be better to present it on separate sheets.	You could add fingerprints here.

The whole person   The confidential file only tells a small part of your character's story: the part discovered so far by those keeping the file. You can now go on to give your character's version of events. This will give you a chance to show other sides to your character.

2 Tell the story of *Seen in the Canteen* on page 78 from the viewpoint of **either** the old man **or** the old woman, but keep your account close to the details given by Calvino.

3 Conduct an imaginary interview with one of your favourite characters from a book. When you have written it out, record it on tape (ask a partner to help). In the interview, your character must display those qualities that he or she are known for in the book.

4 Write a character sketch **either** of someone in your group **or** of a member of your family **or** of yourself. See if, in one short paragraph, you can bring out the qualities that are really distinctive about the person you have chosen. It would be worth while looking back at the examples given at the start of this chapter.

5 Prepare a short talk on the following proposition:
'Bad characters in books or on television can have a bad effect on their readers or viewers. Therefore censorship of bad characters would be in the interests of us all.'

RESEARCHING AND RESPONDING

1 Think back over some of the stories that you have read (you can even include comics or magazine stories) and try to remember some of the characters from fiction that have left a strong impression or memory with you. Jot down the names of **five** characters and then quickly write down what it is that makes you remember them so strongly. Look back to the pen-pictures of Miss Marple and Virgil Tibbs on page 75. Write a similar brief pen-picture of one of the characters that you have remembered.

2 Take any well-known detective hero or heroine (Miss Marple or Sherlock Holmes, for example, or one from a television series) and write down some aspects of the character that have made him or her so popular.

3 The novelist, E. M. Forster wrote about 'flat' characters and 'round' characters. The **flat** characters he described as types whom one could recognise instantly. The **round** characters, he said, could change and were unpredictable. How does this view fit in with your own understanding of characters in fiction? Can you think of any characters whom you could classify as 'flat' or 'round'?
You might extend this idea to film and television. Are there any characters in the programmes that you watch who slot easily into 'flat' and 'round' categories? Write about some such characters either from books or film and discuss whether E. M. Forster's ideas about the subject are helpful to you when thinking about the nature of 'character'.

4 Look up the work of E. M. Forster in the library and see how he sets about the process of character construction. Among his most famous books are *Where Angels Fear to Tread*, *A Passage to India* and *Howards End*.

5 Find out about one of the title characters listed on page 72. Write an account for classroom presentation.

8 | UNDERSTANDING DIALOGUE

Characters, as we have seen, reveal themselves through their physical appearance and their actions, but generally they show their nature through what they say and how they say it. Characters reveal themselves through their speech, through their dialogue.

In Raymond Brigg's cartoon story *When the Wind Blows* we are presented with two central characters. As we read the dialogue between them, we quickly become aware of the kind of characters they are and how they view what's happening in the world around them.

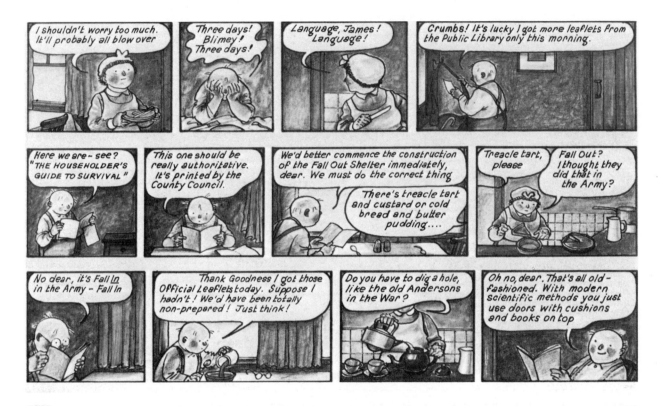

In this cartoon, **the characters reveal themselves through their dialogue,** that is, through the words that they say to each other. Now that you have read through this piece of the cartoon, try to imagine James and Hilda as characters and jot down four different aspects of their individual characters.

- What does their language tell us about their understanding of nuclear warfare?

- Why do you think Raymond Briggs, the author, has chosen these two characters to write a story about the nuclear holocaust?

- This is just the start of the story. What effect has the story so far had on you? Do you think the characters as they have been introduced to us so far have caught your interest?

- What particular effect do you think the author is aiming at in this cartoon? Do you think that he has achieved what he wanted?

Look at the picture of two men fighting. Think about how the argument might have started and how it developed to this pitch of anger. It might help you if you think about where it is all taking place and about why there is a group of people there. Think back to the start of the argument and try to re-create the dialogue that took place and led up to the fight.

Read the following passages of dialogue from two novels. Study them carefully and see how they are written. Read them out loud to see if you catch the tone in which the dialogue is spoken. Discuss what kind of characters the speech reveals.

Pip and the Convict

'Hold your noise!' cried a terrible voice, as a man started up from among the graves at the side of the church porch. 'Keep still, you little devil, or I'll cut your throat!'

A fearful man, all in coarse grey, with a great iron on his leg. A man with no hat, and with broken shoes, and with an old rag tied round his head. A man who had been soaked in water, and smothered in mud, and lamed by stones, and cut by flints, and stung by nettles, and torn by briars; who limped, and shivered, and glared and growled; and whose teeth chattered in his head as he seized me by the chin.

'O! Don't cut my throat, sir,' I pleaded in terror. 'Pray don't do it, sir.'

'Tell us your name!' said the man. 'Quick!'

'Pip, sir.'

'Once more,' said the man, staring at me. 'Give it mouth!'

'Pip. Pip, sir.'

'Show us where you live,' said the man. 'Point out the place!'

I pointed to where our village lay, on the flat in-shore among the alder-trees and pollards, a mile or more from the church.

The man, after looking at me for a moment, turned me upside down, and emptied my pockets. There was nothing in them but a piece of bread. When the church came to itself — for he was so sudden and strong that he made it go head over heels before me, and I saw the steeple under my feet — when the church came to itself, I say, I was seated on a high tombstone, trembling, while he ate the bread ravenously.

'You young dog,' said the man, licking his lips, 'what fat cheeks you ha' got.'

I believe they were fat, though I was at that time undersized for my years, and not strong.

'Darn me if I couldn't eat 'em,' said the man, with a threatening shake of his head, 'and if I han't half a mind to't!'

I earnestly expressed my hope that he wouldn't, and held tighter to the tombstone on which he had put me; partly, to keep myself upon it; partly, to keep myself from crying.

'Now lookee here!' said the man. 'Where's your mother?'

'There, sir!' said I.

He started, made a short run, and stopped and looked over his shoulder.

'There, sir!' I timidly explained. 'Also Georgiana. That's my mother.'

'Oh!' said he, coming back. 'And is that your father alonger your mother?'

'Yes, sir,' said I; 'him, too; late of this parish.'

'Ha!' he muttered then, considering. 'Who d'ye live with — supposin' you're kindly let to live, which I han't made up my mind about?'

'My sister, sir — Mrs Joe Gargery — wife of Joe Gargery, the blacksmith, sir.'

'Blacksmith, eh?' said he. And looked down at his leg.

After darkly looking at his leg and me several times, he came closer to my tombstone, took me by both arms, and tilted me back as far as he could hold me; so that his eyes looked most powerfully down into mine, and mine looked most helplessly up into his.

'Now lookee here,' he said, 'the question being whether you're to be let to live. You know what a file is?'

'Yes, sir.'

'And you know what wittles is?'

'Yes, sir.'

After each question he tilted me over a little more, so as to give me a greater sense of helplessness and danger.

'You get me a file.' He tilted me again. 'And you get me wittles.' He tilted me again. 'You bring 'em both to me.' He tilted me again. 'Or I'll have your heart and liver out.'

Charles Dickens, *Great Expectations*

Ben's Return

Benjamin Braddock graduated from a small Eastern college on a day in June. Then he flew home. The following evening a party was given for him by his parents. By eight o'clock most of the guests had arrived but Benjamin had not yet come down from his room. His father called up from the foot of the stairs but there was no answer. Finally he hurried up the stairs and to the end of the hall.

'Ben?' he said, opening his son's door.

'I'll be down later,' Benjamin said.

'Ben, the guests are all here,' his father said. 'They're all waiting.'

'I said I'll be down later.'

Mr Braddock closed the door behind him. 'What is it,' he said.

Benjamin shook his head and walked to the window.

'What is it, Ben.'

'Nothing.'

'Then why don't you come on down and see your guests.'

Benjamin didn't answer.

'Ben?'

'Dad,' he said, turning around, 'I have some things on my mind right now.'

'What things?'

'Just some things.'

'Well can't you tell me what they are?'

'No.'

Mr Braddock continued frowning at his son a few more moments, glanced at his watch, then looked back at Benjamin. 'Ben, these are our friends down there,' he said. 'My friends. Your mother's friends. You owe them a little courtesy.'

'Tell them I have to be alone right now.'

Charles Webb, *The Graduate*

Writing dialogue well requires considerable skill and practice. Here are some valuable guiding points by the novelist Dianne Doubtfire.

YOU CANNOT, of course, put down everything your characters would really say in the given circumstances. You have only to listen to five minutes of true-life dialogue to realise that normal conversation would be unbearably tedious in a novel. You must prune and edit your speeches, directing them towards what is essential for the forward movement of your story and the delineation of character.

Every line of dialogue must be precisely tailored for the person concerned. In a good novel you can usually tell who is speaking even from isolated sentences; everyone has his individual choice of words, and manner of framing remarks. Here for instance, are twenty different ways of saying Yes. Imagine that a man has been asked to close a door which he has just left ajar: Yes; Yeah; O.K.; Oky-doke; Right; Certainly; Of course; Indeed; Indeedy; Will do; Sure thing; All right; If you say so; Why not?; Delighted; Yep; *So* sorry; Huh; Righty-ho. Or just a silence to denote the absence of a negative response. You should know which of these replies any of your characters would use, depending, of course, on the person who made the request. The same man might easily say 'Delighted' to one woman and 'Huh' to another!

Always read your speeches aloud; this helps to reveal the faults. Avoid the stilted 'he did not' and 'she would not' when 'he didn't' and 'she wouldn't' would be normal speech. Be careful not to make your characters speak as if they were reading an essay or addressing a meeting. This is a special danger if you are making somebody voice one of your own pet theories; it is a temptation to climb on to the soap box with him and enjoy the sound of your own voice.

It is, of course, perfectly in order to use ungrammatical speech for a character who would normally speak that way. It is not only in order, it is essential. The same applies to strong language. You must suit the language to the character. You are showing people as they *are* not as you might like them to be, and no matter how much you may disapprove of swearing, you wouldn't make your builder's mate say 'Damn' when he drops a brick on his toe! A novelist must allow his creations to use their own authentic vocabulary, but he is naturally free to exercise his personal discrimination in the choice of theme and characters in the first place.

Don't be afraid of the simple 'he said' and 'she said'. It is the sign of the amateur to search for alternatives when they are not really necessary: 'he expostulated'; 'she gushed'; 'he averred', etc. 'Said' can be used a great deal more than one would expect, without disturbing the reader. In my Penguin copy of *England Made Me* by Graham Greene, I found no less than sixteen 'saids' on one page, but you would never notice them unless you were on the look-out. It is only necessary to use alternatives if you want to express a particular manner of speech, such as 'whispered' or 'shouted'.

If it is clear who is speaking, just set down the speech on its own. Beware, however, of going on for too long in this way; we all know how annoying it is to have to count back to see who started!

The Craft of Novel Writing

Read through the passage on the previous page. Try to pick out at least six points made by the writer.

■ Which are the most important?

■ Can you add any further points of your own about writing dialogue?

■ Could there be stories where Dianne Doubtfire's advice would not apply? What kind of stories would these be? How would their dialogue be constructed?

Here are the main rules for the layout of dialogue in fiction.

CHECKLIST FOR DIALOGUE LAYOUT

1 Only the words actually spoken go inside the inverted commas: '. . . .' Compare this with the comic-strip method of placing the words actually spoken inside the voice bubble.

2 Each new speaker is given a new line. This means that the speeches work down the page and it allows us to follow more easily who it is that is speaking. It also adds a sense of space and room to the page layout. This even happens for very short words, for example:
   'Well can't you tell me what they are?'
   'No.'

3 Each speech begins with a capital letter and ends with a full-stop.

4 Punctuation marks which are a part of a sentence in the speech are placed inside the inverted commas:
   'Ben?' he said, opening his son's door.

5 We separate the speech from the narrative part by using a comma:
   'I'll be down later,' Benjamin said.
   even when the narrative part is placed in the middle of a sentence:
   'Can I be told,' he said, 'or will the knowledge kill me?'
   Notice here that in the second part of the sentence, beginning
   , 'or will the knowledge . . .'
   the word 'or' does not need a capital letter because it is counted as part of the whole spoken sentence, which is:
   'Can I be told, or will the knowledge kill me?'

6 It is common in print for the speeches to be indented (that is, for a space to be left between the margin and the start of the speech) and although it is not usual for this to be done when you are handwriting, you might find that it is a way of getting space into your work and of making the page look more attractive to the reader. What you want to avoid is to have all the speeches of different characters following on, one after another, across the page.

The following short story is built up through dialogue, through a phone conversation. As we follow the discussion, so we are drawn into the characters and events of the story.

Yellow Trains

'I am unhappy,' said the girl to her friend. She looked out of the window through the shimmering folds of the net curtains to the parked cars in the street; their windscreens snapped in the sunshine and a small dog rummaged in the gutter. 'I am so unhappy,' she repeated, and across the city the friend sighed and murmured.

'Yesterday,' she said, 'I was so happy I could have cried. Listen, I rode in a train with blue seats, bright bright blue, and there was this factory chimney smoking white against the sky and the sky was grey like velvet. Do you know what I mean? And clouds like carvings. I tell you, I sat there looking and I could have cried.'

'He isn't,' asked the friend delicately, 'coming?'

'He isn't coming. There is this business with the office and his mother that he must go to on Saturday come what may and something about someone for whom he has to hold keys to a flat. He isn't coming.'

'People,' said the friend, after a pause, 'get so involved.'

The girl watched the small dog nose an empty tin. She looked at the sky above the rooftops and at the thread of vapour from an aeroplane. 'I sat in that train and I wasn't thinking of anything in particular. I wasn't thinking: tomorrow, tomorrow, tomorrow. It was just a state of mind. And today . . . Listen, I'm looking at the sky now, and it's nothing. Nothing at all. And yesterday there were these clouds like sculptures. I don't understand how what you see is a question of what you feel.'

The friend, across streets and parks and rooftops, sighed again. 'Did he phone, or what?'

'He phoned.'

'Excuse me a minute,' said the friend, 'I've got something on the stove.'

The girl saw a pigeon with pink twiggy legs walk round and round, round and round. She saw a child go past chanting incantations. She saw an old woman put down a carrier bag and stand for a moment, hunched up.

The friend came back. 'Sorry. I expect he just couldn't get out of it.'

'Possibly. Probably. I made pizza. And got that beer he likes. He phoned very late last night. I feel as though I've put on pounds and pounds.'

'Sorry?' said the friend.

'Weight. Yesterday I felt as though I was floating slightly. Walking along the platform at Clapham Junction. Like bubbles going up through you. And these yellow trains dashing all over the place, yellow like daffodils. I thought, I'm always going to remember feeling like this.'

'Mmn.'

'And the funny thing is I do now. Remember. I'm miserable, I'm pissed off, I feel as heavy as a rock. But it's all there still, underneath. The floating feeling, and the clouds, and the yellow trains. Only I can't get at it any more.'

'Is he going to call again?' asked the friend.

The girl twitched the curtain; the cars shimmered and flashed. 'Actually, yesterday I wanted things just to stop there. Until I said go on. I wanted to keep it – feeling like that. I wanted to learn what it was like.'

'Looking forward to something,' the friend began, 'is . . .'

'I wasn't really looking forward. Don't you see? It was just being like that. Happy. Now I'm unhappy and it's nothing, it's a no-feeling. It doesn't exist.'

The friend said, 'Mmn – I'm not so sure about that.' After a moment she added, 'I'm sure he'll call again.'

'I expect he's calling now,' said the girl. 'I expect he's desperately trying to get through, dialling and hanging up again and asking the operator if the line's engaged talking or out of order. Dialling and dialling.'

The friend coughed. 'Excuse me. Where does his mother live?'

'In Surrey. Reigate. His sister lives with her. She has red hair and works in the library. What I can't get over is how things push on like they do and take you with them whether you want it or not. Days. They drag you on. One day you're with the yellow trains like daffodils and the next you're sitting here with a knot in your insides. Sometimes I'm not sure if I can go through with life if this is the way it's going to be.'

'Oh, come on now . . .' said the friend. After a moment she went on, 'Hello? Are you still there?'

'I'm here. There's this dog outside that's got its paw muddled up in a bit of plastic. Do you think I should go out and help it?'

The friend said, 'I don't know. Of course he wouldn't have known about you making the pizza.'

'It's all right – the dog's got its paw out of the plastic. I couldn't get the big olives so I had to use the other kind. I had them in my bag when I was walking along the platform at Clapham Junction and now there they are in the fridge. Same bloody olives. Funny, when you come to think about it.'

The friend said sadly, 'I suppose you're in love with him.'

'Is that my trouble? God, how unoriginal. And here was I going on about clouds and yellow trains. Oh, and there was Battersea Power Station. I didn't tell you about Battersea Power Station. It looked like a temple. Egyptian, I think. Do you imagine he's going to see someone else instead?'

'Look, don't think about that kind of thing.'

'I'm not. It's not a question of thinking. I'm not thinking about anything. I just get attacked from time to time.'

'I know,' said the friend, after a moment.

The girl said. 'Do you remember the way when you were a child you always wanted it to be next week? Today was so boring. Next week was always Christmas and birthdays and going to the cinema.'

'He'll ring up,' said the friend. 'You see. Next week. Tomorrow.'

'Ah. Will he? Since when were birthdays always last week? And yellow trains.'

'These trains . . .'

'Sorry about the trains.' The girl saw sparrows float down from a tree and hop among crisp packets and paper bags. 'He said it was a pity and we'd have to fix something another time. He ran out of coins and had to go.'

Miles away, across roads and buses and taxis, the friend said, 'Then that's how it is. Another time. There's always other times.'

'I don't want other times,' said the girl. 'I want yesterday. I want to be so happy like I was yesterday. I want to go back into yesterday and settle down there and live there for ever. I want to spend the rest of my life riding out of Clapham Junction on yellow trains, looking at the smoke against those clouds. I don't want to be here; I want to be there. I want to be sitting on those bright blue seats, watching the houses go by. I don't like now, I want to be then.'

The friend sighed. 'Go and eat that pizza. It won't keep.'

Penelope Lively, *Corruption*

ASSIGNMENTS

MAKING AND PRESENTING

A note on writing dialogue

It takes care, skill and inner concentration to write dialogue successfully. This is because you do not only have the job of getting the **form** of it written down properly – the inverted commas, capital letters, full-stops, question-marks and other features of written dialogue – but also because you are at the same time trying to build up a picture of the type of people your characters are. One of the most effective ways of doing this is through the things that they say. Before starting your own writing, re-read Dianne Doubtfire's comments.

I   Choose two of the following situations and construct short passages of dialogue to develop the scenes.
   (a) Angry and complaining customers in a restaurant . . .
   (b) A completely unqualified candidate being interviewed for a highly skilled job . . .
   (c) A teacher wrongly accusing a pupil of causing trouble . . .
   (d) A daughter or a son arrives home well after midnight to face angry and anxious parents . . .
   (e) A couple on a first date . . .
   When you have built up a short dialogue, you might begin to consider how you can develop the narrative further.

2　Write a story which uses dialogue with one of the following titles:
The Interrogation
A Family Misunderstanding
A Conflict with Authority
Caught Red-handed!

3　Continue as your own cartoon story the narrative of *When the Wind Blows*. Notice that the conventions for writing dialogue in comics are different from those for stories.

RESEARCHING AND RESPONDING

1　Do some research on the life and writings of Ernest Hemingway in order to produce a talk either on tape or to the class. Among his most famous books are *A Farewell to Arms, For Whom the Bell Tolls,* and *The Old Man and the Sea.* He led a dramatically active life, was awarded the Nobel Prize for Literature in 1954 and committed suicide in 1961. He would make an ideal subject for a literature research project.

2　Make a similar study of the work of Ursula Le Guin, author of *The Wizard of Earthsea* and many other science fiction stories.

3　Read *Yellow Trains* and write a critical review of this story concentrating your remarks (a) on the use of dialogue and (b) on the way in which this helps to build up character.

9 | SETTING THE STORY

All narratives have some kind of setting. Look at the following pictures.
Imagine they are settings for your own stories.

■ What kind of stories do they suggest?

Many novels are named after the places where the events take place:

Wuthering Heights
The House of Seven Gables
Northanger Abbey
Mansfield Park
North and South
A Passage to India
A Room with a View
Wide Sargasso Sea
Vermilion Sands

Stig of the Dump
Brighton Rock
Animal Farm
The Secret Garden
Hotel du Lac
Watership Down
Miguel Street
On the Black Hill

Can you think of any other novels where the titles derive from the setting?

So important is place in the composition and structure of novels that some novels have begun in their author's mind with no more than a sense of the setting where the action will take place.

The novel *Room at the Top* began with a picture in the author's mind of a lonely place on Bingley Moor. The novelist John Braine described the first idea of the novel in a newspaper article:

> But after a pork pie and rather a lot of bitter at a nearby pub I went to bed cheerful. And the ideas – or rather the pictures – did come. Before I fell asleep I noted them all down. One in particular I knew was important: a lonely place on Bingley Moor by a disused brickworks and a car parked there with a young man sitting alone in it. It was dusk and the lights were going up in the valley. Looking back I know now that this is when the deepest part of me began to ponder over 'Room at the Top'.

The novelist P.D. James has given a similar account of the importance of place in her work:

> **WHAT PEOPLE** usually ask is 'How do you get your ideas?' And here the writer is as much at a loss as the questioner. Something sparks off the creative imagination; a character, a place, an original idea for the murder itself. With me it is often the setting; a desolate stretch of coast, an old and sinister house, an atmospheric part of London, a closed community such as a Nurses Home, a village, a forensic science laboratory. The central idea germinates over weeks, sometimes months and becomes clothed with the flesh of characters; literally the plot thickens. It is almost as if the whole book and the people already exist in some limbo outside myself and it is my business, by a long process of thought and effort, to get in touch with them and put them down on paper.
>
> This is a lonely, disciplined and often frustrating process, and to the question 'Do you enjoy writing?' I can only reply that I may not always be happy when writing but I would be miserable if I didn't write. And that is probably what it means to be an author.

In the following passage, on the Docklands development in London, the contemporary writer Penelope Lively sees the location with the sharp eye of the novelist.

Lost in the unreality of Docklands

I AM CURIOUS about Docklands, partly for fictional purposes, partly because the violence and speed of such change in a landscape cannot but fascinate, and to some degree horrify.

I wangled a visit to one of the mammoth commercial developments now in full swing of construction: £60 million worth of steel, reinforced concrete, and glass curtain walling shooting thirty stories into the skies within a year. Fast track, the system is called, as well it might be. Glass dominates Docklands: smoke grey, black, turquoise; reflective surfaces in which sail clouds, the Meccano outlines of cranes, and the diminished, doomed rooftops of the last streets of old terraced housing.

Why, I asked the site architect who showed me around. 'It's quickest,' he said. 'You can slap it on just like that. The snag is, bits pop out.' Construction sites are dangerous places; wearing a hard helmet, I picked my way gingerly over concrete floors in which huge holes yawned, across heaps of girders, along airy catwalks, and was too chicken to brave the 'scenic' lift.

The building's innards spew out on every side: great hanks of coloured wiring, networks of gleaming pipes. The ground floor is half-finished; up in the sky they are still pouring concrete; the curtain walling is a patchwork of blue mirrors. Work goes on twenty-four hours a day; five hundred on shift-work.

'We've got half Ireland here,' said my guide. Later I went over to the Business Efficiency Centre: racks of glossy brochures and nobody much about except a receptionist who inquired keenly if I was interested in space (office, she meant, not infinite). When I said apologetically no, just information, there were no hard feelings.

I came away with an armful of elegantly produced material in which enthusiastic prose vies with futuristic illustration to present a self-contained utopia in which retail and business amenities coexist in a pleasant marine atmosphere, with the outer world kept at bay by entrance barriers and security patrols; ducting links will be provided to the Docklands fibre-optic network facility; there will be street furniture within the common areas of the infrastructure; the urinals will be controlled by miser valves.

Alongside all of this, the fragmented surviving streets and the carcasses of half-submerged barges still visible at Canary Wharf, seem of archaeological rather than historical significance. And as for people. . . On the platform of that jolly blue and red toytown railway, I got talking to an elderly couple, Docklands residents all their lives.

For how much longer? I wondered. They were resigned about the future of their council flat: 'I'll tell you what they'll do, they'll let the building run down till it's not worth propping up, and then they'll say, 'Right, we'll have to develop this, won't we?' Nothing else we can do with it, is there?' Cynical laughter.

- What kind of novel could be set in the Docklands?
- What kind of characters might it use?
- What kind of plot?
- What might be its main themes?

Why do you think place is so important in the novel?   John Braine gave
the following answer:

PEOPLE are places and places are people. This isn't intended to dazzle you with its originality; it's simply another working-rule. Whenever you write about places you also write about people. It isn't always that you mention the people when you write about the place. Sometimes it's necessary, sometimes it isn't. On the whole the best way is to concentrate on making the reader see the place.

The most revealing place of all is the home. Imagine yourself suddenly in the home of a complete stranger. Within five minutes you'll have an accurate general picture of what sort of person he is. There are obvious guides like the kind of books or, for that matter, the absence of books, and the pictures and ornaments and the quality of the furniture. There are different kinds of tidiness from the house-proud to the clinically obsessive; different kinds of untidiness from profusion to squalor. There is over and above all the atmosphere of a home. Some people have the gift of creating comfort, some have not. But be careful about this. If you describe a home properly, if you see it accurately, there's no need to say anything about the atmosphere. Your description says it for you. Or, to be more precise, your reader instantly makes the inference, just as his eye in the cinema will make the inference of falling between a shot of a man swaying on a window sill ten storeys up and the same man hitting the ground.

This isn't to say that we are exclusively the creatures of our economic environment. We aren't, for instance, made what we are by our homes (using the word in its narrowest sense). We make our homes. We were there first, so to speak. We even make impersonal places like offices and factories bear the imprint of our personality – pin-ups on the wall behind the workbench, trendy executive toys, gold pens, silver mounted portraits on the executive's desk (or, equally revealing, nothing at all).

- Imagine a room without its owner. By describing the objects in the room and its atmosphere, suggest the character of its owner.

- Imagine any workplace. By a close description of its appearance, bring out the characters of those who work there.

In the following passages Charles Dickens reveals how he begins his novels by closely imagining the settings in which the action takes place.

Twenty-second December 1840

Dear George,

The child lying dead in the little sleeping-room, which is behind the open screen. It is winter-time, so there are no flowers; but upon her breast and pillow, and about her bed, there may be strips of holly and berries, and such free green things. Window overgrown with ivy. The little boy who had that talk with her about angels may be by the bedside, if you like it so; but I think it will be quieter and more peaceful if she is quite alone. I want it to express the most beautiful repose and tranquillity, and to have something of a happy look, if death can.

The child has been buried inside the church, and the old man, who cannot be made to understand that she is dead, repairs to the grave and sits there all day long, waiting for her arrival, to begin another journey. His staff and knapsack, her little bonnet and basket, etc., lie beside him. 'She'll come to-morrow,' he says when it gets dark, and goes sorrowfully home. I think an hour-glass running out would help the notion; perhaps her little things upon his knee, or in his hand.

I am breaking my heart over this story, and cannot bear to finish it.

Ever and always heartily,
Charles Dickens to George Cattermole, *Letters*

Further ideas for a novel: jottings by Charles Dickens

. . . Beginning with the breaking up of a large party of guests at a country house; house left lonely with the shrunken family in it; guests spoken of, and introduced to the reader that way. – OR, beginning with a house abandoned by a family fallen into reduced circumstances. Their old furniture there, and numberless tokens of their own comforts. Inscriptions under the bells downstairs – 'Mr. John's Room,' 'Miss Caroline's Room.' Great gardens trimly kept to attract a tenant: but no one in them. A landscape without figures. Billiard room: table covered up, like a body. Great stables without horses, and great coach-houses without carriages. Grass growing in the chinks of the stone-paving, this bright cold winter day.

Some authors create vast imaginary worlds where the narrative action takes place.

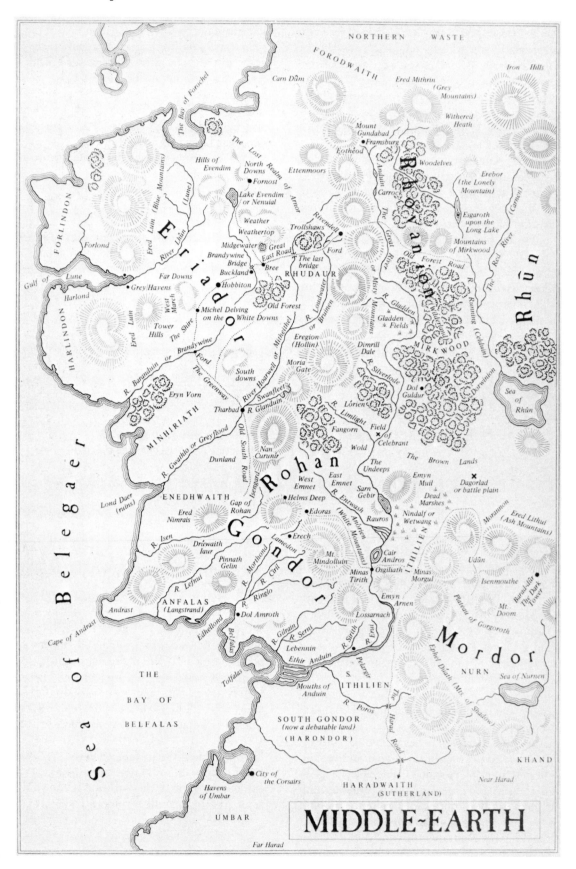

Others work to imagine the exact spot where the major events are to happen.

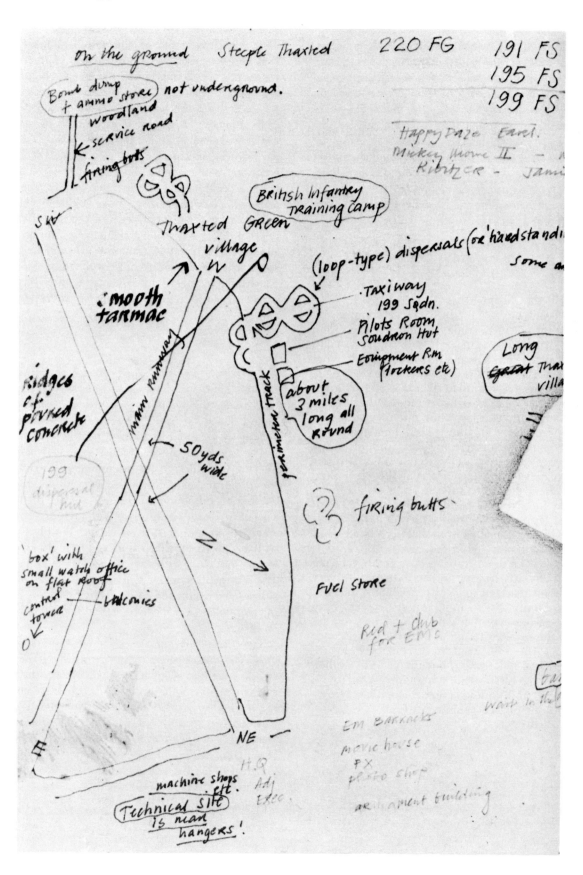

Consider the following openings of stories. They all describe the place where the events are to take place.

THE VERANDAH, which was lifted on stone pillars, jutted forward over the garden like a box in the théatre. Below were luxuriant masses of flowering shrubs, and creepers whose shiny leaves, like sequins, reflected light from a sky stained scarlet and purple and apple-green. This splendiferous sunset filled one half of the sky, fading gently through shades of mauve to a calm expanse of ruffling grey, blown over by tinted cloudlets; and in this still evening sky, just above a clump of darkening conifers, hung a small crystal moon.

There sat Major Gale and his wife, as they did every evening at this hour . . .

Doris Lessing, *The De Wets Come to Kloof Grange*

EXCEPT for the Marabar Caves – and they are twenty miles off – the city of Chandrapore presents nothing extraordinary. Edged rather than washed by the river Ganges, it trails for a couple of miles along the bank, scarcely distinguishable from the rubbish it deposits so freely. There are no bathing-steps on the river front, as the Ganges happens not to be holy here; indeed there is no river front, and bazaars shut out the wide and shifting panorama of the stream. The streets are mean, the temples ineffective, and though a few fine houses exist they are hidden away in gardens or down alleys whose filth deters all but the invited guest. Chandrapore was never large or beautiful, but two hundred years ago it lay on the road between Upper India, then imperial, and the sea, and the fine houses date from that period. The zest for decoration stopped in the eighteenth century, nor was it ever democratic. There is no painting and scarcely any carving in the bazaars. The very wood seems made of mud, the inhabitants of mud moving. So abased, so monotonous is everything that meets the eye, that when the Ganges comes down it might be expected to wash the excrescence back into the soil. Houses do fall, people are drowned and left rotting, but the general outline of the town persists, swelling here, shrinking there, like some low but indestructible form of life.

Inland, the prospect alters.

E.M. Forster, *A Passage to India*

THE HOUSE is full of voices, full of movements, Whichever room one is in, one can hear in other rooms the sounds of talk and coming and going. The windows are open to the sea, to the murmuring wash of the waves, and the salt tangy air. The front door stands wide, admitting a quadrilateral of sunlight onto the carpet, and small Beth, her fair head blazing white with day, runs in, and out again, seeing and not seeing the meticulously-illuminated Turkey pattern, the grandfather clock counting its way towards four, and Gran making her way downstairs for tea, holding the banister rail all the way, patient at her own slowness. Reaching the foot of the stairs she straightens her cardigan, and advances with careful steadiness towards the living-room door, hand outstretched for the brass doorknob. The hand has crooked finger-joints and three rings, and a fretwork of blue veins beneath the brown freckles.

Jill Paton Walsh, *Unloading*

The *Nellie*, a cruising yawl, swung to her anchor without a flutter of the sails, and was at rest. The flood had made, the wind was nearly calm, and being bound down the river, the only thing for it was to come to and wait for the turn of the tide.

The sea-reach of the Thames stretched before us like the beginning of an interminable waterway. In the offing the sea and the sky were welded together without a joint, and in the luminous space the tanned sails of the barges drifting up with the tide seemed to stand still in red clusters of canvas sharply peaked, with gleams of varnished spirits. A haze rested on the low shores that ran out to sea in vanishing flatness. The air was dark above Gravesend, and farther back still seemed condensed into a mournful gloom, brooding motionless over the biggest, and the greatest, town on earth.

The Director of Companies was our captain and our host. We four affectionately watched his back as he stood in the bows looking to seaward. On the whole river there was nothing that looked half so nautical. He resembled a pilot, which to a seaman is trustworthiness personified. It was difficult to realize his work was not out there in the luminous estuary, but behind him, within the brooding gloom.

Between us there was, as I have already said somewhere, the bond of the sea.

Joseph Conrad, *Heart of Darkness*

This is the first chapter of *Waterland* by Graham Swift. As the title suggests, the narrative is set in a particularly powerful location, the Fens in East Anglia.

About the Stars and the Sluice

'And don't forget,' my father would say, as if he expected me at any moment to up and leave to seek my fortune in the wide world, 'whatever you learn about people, however bad they turn out, each one of them has a heart, and each one of them was once a tiny baby sucking his mother's milk . . .'

Fairy-tale words; fairy-tale advice. But we lived in a fairy-tale place. In a lock-keeper's cottage, by a river, in the middle of the Fens. Far away from the wide world. And my father, who was a superstitious man, liked to do things in such a way as would make them seem magical and occult. So he would always set his eel traps at night. Not because eel traps cannot be set by day, but because the mystery of darkness appealed to him. And one night, in midsummer, in 1937, we went with him, Dick and I, to set traps near Stott's Bridge. It was hot and windless. When the traps had been set we lay back on the river-bank. Dick was fourteen and I was ten. The pumps were tump-tumping, as they do, incessantly, so that you scarcely notice them, all over the Fens, and frogs were croaking in the ditches. Up above, the sky swarmed with stars which seemed to multiply as we looked at them. And as we lay, Dad said: 'Do you know what the stars are? They are the silver dust of God's blessing. They are little broken-off bits of heaven. God cast them down to fall on us. But when he saw how wicked we were he changed his mind and ordered the stars to stop. Which is why they hang in the sky but seem as though at any time they might drop . . .'

For my father, as well as being a superstitious man, had a knack for telling stories. Made-up stories, true stories; soothing stories, warning stories; stories with a moral or with no point at all; believable stories and unbelievable stories; stories which were neither one thing nor the other. It was a knack which ran in his family. But it was a knack which my mother had too – and perhaps he really acquired it from her. Because when I was very small it was my mother who first told me stories, which, unlike my father, she got from books as well as out of her head, to make me sleep at night.

And since my mother's death, which was six months before we lay by the eel traps under the stars, my father's yen for the dark, his nocturnal restlessness, had grown more besetting. As if he were constantly brooding on some story yet to be told. So I would see him sometimes, inspecting his vegetable patch by the moonlight, or talking to his roosting chickens, or pacing up and down by the lock-gates or the sluice, his movements marked by the wandering ember of his cigarette.

We lived in a lock-keeper's cottage by the River Leem, which flows out of Norfolk into the Great Ouse. And no one needs telling that the land in that part of the world is flat. Flat, with an unrelieved and monotonous flatness, enough of itself, some might say, to drive a man to unquiet and sleep-defeating thoughts. From the raised banks of the Leem, it stretched away to the horizon, its uniform colour, peat-black, varied only by the crops that grew upon it – grey-green potato leaves, blue-green beet leaves, yellow-green wheat; its uniform levelness broken only by the furrowed and dead-straight lines of ditches and drains, which, depending on the state of the sky and the angle of the sun, ran like silver, copper or golden wires across the fields and which, when you stood and looked at them, made you shut one eye and fall prey to fruitless meditations on the laws of perspective.

And yet this land, so regular, so prostrate, so tamed and cultivated, would transform itself, in my five- or six-year-old mind, into an empty wilderness. On those nights when my mother would be forced to tell me stories, it would seem that in our lock-keeper's cottage we were in the middle of nowhere; and the noise of the trains passing on the lines to King's Lynn, Gildsey and Ely was like the baying of a monster closing in on us in our isolation.

A fairy-tale land, after all.

My father kept the lock on the River Leem, two miles from where it empties into the Ouse. But because a lock-keeper's duties are irregular and his pay, set against the rent-free cottage in which he lives, is scant, and because, in any case, by the nineteen-thirties, the river-traffic on the Leem had dwindled, my father also grew vegetables, kept chickens and trapped eels. It was only in times of heavy rain or thaw that these secondary occupations were abandoned. Then he would have to watch and anticipate the water-level. Then he would have to raise the sluice which cut across the far side of the stream like a giant guillotine.

For the river in front of our cottage divided into two channels, the nearer containing the navigation lock, the farther the sluice, with, in between, a solidly built brick-faced pier, a tiny island, on which stood the cabin housing the sluice engine. And even before the river had visibly risen, even before its colour had changed and it began to show the milky brown of the Norfolk chalk hills from which it flowed, Dad would know when to cross the lock-gates to the cabin and begin – with a groaning of metal and throbbing of released water – to crank up the sluice.

But under normal conditions the sluice remained lowered, almost to the river bottom, its firm blade holding back the slow-flowing Leem, making it fit for the passage of boats. Then the water in the enclosure above it, like the water in the lockpen, would be smooth and placid and it would give off that smell which is characteristic of places where fresh water and human ingenuity meet, and which is smelt over and over again in the Fens. A cool, slimy but strangely poignant and nostalgic smell. A smell which is half man and half fish. And at such times Dad would have plenty of leisure for his eel traps and vegetables, and little to do with the sluice, save to combat rust, grease the cog-wheels and clear away from the water the accumulations of flotsam.

For, flood or no flood, the Leem brought down its unceasing booty of debris. Willow branches; alder branches; sedge; fencing; crates; old clothes; dead sheep; bottles; potato sacks; straw bales; fruit boxes; fertiliser bags. All floated down on the westerly current, lodged against the sluice-gate and had to be cleared away with boat-hooks and weed-rakes.

And thus it was that one night, in midsummer, when God's withheld benedictions were shining in the sky, though this was several years after Dad told us about the stars, but only two or three since he began to speak of hearts and mother's milk, and the tump-tumping of the pumps was drowned now, in the evening, by the roar of ascending bombers – it was, to be precise, July, 1943 – that something floated down the Leem, struck the iron-work of the sluice and, tugged by the eddies, continued to knock and scrape against it till morning. Something extraordinary and unprecedented, and not to be disposed of like a branch or potato sack or even a dead sheep. For this something was a body. And the body belonged to Freddie Parr, who lived less than a mile away and was my age, give or take a month.

Look carefully at the following piece of writing. Although it comes from a much longer book, it is complete in itself. It depends not only on its action and dialogue but also on its sense of place.

The Arrival of the Grasshopper

The same year the grasshoppers came on the land. It was said that they came from Abyssinia; after two years of drought up there, they travelled South and ate up all vegetation on their way. Before we ever saw them, there were strange tales circulating in the country of the devastation that they had left behind them – up North, maize and wheat and fruit-farms were all one vast desert where they had passed. The settlers sent runners to their neighbours to the South to announce the coming of the grasshoppers. Still you could not do much against them even if you were warned. On all the farms people had tall piles of firewood and maize-stalks ready and set fire to them when the grasshoppers came, and they sent out all the farm-labourers with empty tins and cans, and told them to shout and yell and beat the tins to frighten them from landing. But it was a short respite only, for however much the farmers would frighten them the grasshoppers could not keep up in the air for ever, the only thing that each farmer could hope for was to drive them off to the next farm to the South, and the more farms they were scared away from, the hungrier and more desperate were they, when in the end they settled. I myself had the great plains of the Masai Reserve to the South, so that I might hope to keep the grasshoppers on the wing and send them over the river to the Masai.

I had had three or four runners announcing the arrival of the grasshoppers, from neighbourly settlers of the district, already, but nothing more had happened, and I began to believe that it was all a false alarm. One afternoon I rode over to our dhuka, a farm-shop of all goods, kept for the farm-labourers and the squatters by Farah's small brother Abdullai. It was on the high-road, and an Indian in a mule-trap outside the dhuka rose in his trap and beckoned to me as I passed, since he could not drive up to me on the plain.

'The grasshoppers are coming, Madam, please, on to your land,' said he when I rode up to him.

'I have been told that many times,' I said, 'but I have seen nothing of them. Perhaps it is not so bad as people tell.'

'Turn round kindly, Madam,' said the Indian.

I turned round and saw, along the Northern horizon, a shadow on the sky, like a long stretch of smoke, a town burning, 'a million-peopled city vomiting smoke in the bright air,' I thought, or like a thin cloud rising.

'What is that?' I asked.

'Grasshoppers,' said the Indian.

I saw a few grasshoppers, perhaps twenty in all, on the path across the plain as I rode back. I passed my manager's house and instructed him to have everything ready for receiving the grasshoppers. As together we looked North the black smoke on the sky had grown up a little higher. From time to time while we were watching it, a grasshopper swished past us in the air, or dropped on the ground and crawled on.

The next morning as I opened my door and looked out, the whole landscape outside was the colour of pale dull terracotta. The trees, the lawn, the drive, all that I could see, was covered with the dye, as if in the night a thick layer of terracotta-coloured snow had fallen on the land. The grasshoppers were sitting there. While I stood and looked at it, all the scenery began to quiver and break, the grasshoppers moved and lifted, after a few minutes the atmosphere fluttered with wings, they were going off.

That time they did not do much damage to the farm, they had been staying with us over the night only. We had seen what they were like, about an inch and a half long, brownish grey and pink, sticky to touch. They had broken a couple of big trees in my drive simply by sitting on them, and when you looked at the trees and remembered that each of the grasshoppers could only weigh a tenth of an ounce, you began to conceive the number of them.

The grasshoppers came again; for two or three months we had continued attacks of them on the farm. We soon gave up trying to frighten them off, it was a hopeless and tragi-comical undertaking. At times a small swarm would come along, a free-corps which had detached itself from the main force, and would just pass in a rush. But at other times the grasshoppers came in big flights, which took days to pass over the farm, twelve hours incessant hurling advance in the air. When the flight was at its highest it was like a blizzard at home, whistling and shrieking like a strong wind, little hard furious wings to all sides of you and over your head, shining like thin blades of steel in the sun, but themselves darkening the sun. The grasshoppers keep in a belt, from the ground up to the top of the trees, beyond that the air is clear. They whir against your face, they get into your collar and your sleeves and shoes. The rush round you makes you giddy and fills you with a particular sickening rage and despair, the horror of the mass. The individual among it does not count, kill them and it makes no difference to anybody. After the grasshoppers have passed and have gone towards the horizon like a long streak of thinning smoke, the feeling of disgust at your own face and hands, which have been crawled upon by grasshoppers, stays with you for a long time.

A great flight of birds followed the advance of the grasshoppers, circled above them and came down and walked in the fields when they settled, living high on the horde: storks and cranes – pompous profiteers.

At times the grasshoppers settled on the farm. They did not do much harm to the coffee-plantation, the leaves of the coffee-trees, similar to laurel-leaves, are too hard for them to chew. They could only break a tree here and there in the field.

But the maize-fields were a sad sight when they had been on them and had left, there was nothing there now but a few laps of dry leaves hanging from the broken stalks. My garden by the river, that had been irrigated and kept green, was now like a dust-heap – flowers, vegetables and herbs had all gone. The shambas of the squatters were like stretches of cleared and burnt land, rolled even by the crawling insects, with a dead grasshopper in the dust here and there as the sole fruit of the soil. The squatters stood and looked at them. The old women who had dug and planted the shambas, standing on their heads, shook their fists at the last faint black disappearing shadow in the sky.

A lot of dead grasshoppers were left behind the army everywhere. On the high-road, where they had sat, and where the wagons and carts had passed, and had driven over them, now, after the swarm had gone, the wheel-tracks were marked, like rails of a railway, as long as you could see them, with little bodies of dead grasshoppers.

The grasshoppers had laid their eggs in the soil. Next year, after the long rains, the little black-brown hoppers appeared – grasshoppers in the first stage of life, that cannot fly, but which crawl along and eat up everything upon their march.

Karen Blixen, *Out of Africa*

A S S I G N M E N T S

MAKING AND PRESENTING

1. Read Charles Dickens's letter to George Cattermole on page 95 and his further jottings on ideas for stories. Take **one** of these and work on it in order to develop your own outline of a short story, then go on to write out the story in full.

2. Find a picture or photograph of a place which captures your imagination (or use one of the photographs at the beginning of this chapter), and write a short passage which captures the atmosphere of the place.
There are various ways of approaching this. You could describe it from the **outside**, writing in detail about how you see it; you could imagine yourself **inside** the scene shown by the picture and describe what you see around you; or you might try to describe it **through the eyes of another person** – an old man or woman, a visitor from another world.

3 Write a short story placing it directly in the setting provided by Karen Blixen in her story *The Arrival of the Grasshopper*.

4 Think of a place that you know well, a place that has perhaps a special meaning or power for you. Think of the ways that place has changed across the years or through the centuries, and will go on changing in the years to come.

Now develop ideas for a series of linked short stories, all of which take place in this same setting, although they could happen hundreds of years apart, both in the past and in some future time of your own invention. You could perhaps try to write four short stories, one of which takes place at the present time.

Remember, the stories must all be set in the **same place**. You could, if you wanted, provide some running link; something could keep turning up in each story or something could be lost in one story and turn up in the next. You might want to produce a series of drawings or maps to show how the place changes across the years.

5 Take some of the locations in the following list and **describe in detail** a number of places, real or imaginary that spring to your mind.

(a) a place of great mystery
(b) a place of horror
(c) a place of secrecy
(d) a place of quiet and harmony
(e) a place of imprisonment
(f) a place of great magic and unknown power
(g) a place of happiness and celebration
(h) a place of great loneliness
(i) a place of great destruction
(j) a place of decay and desolation

You might find that some of these settings come easily to you or even that you know of such places in your own experience. Other settings will require the power of imagination.

6 Look at the map and plan reproduced in this chapter. Design your own map or plan which could be used as the basis of a story. It might be best at the start if you were to work on an area that you know well and develop other features which suit your story as they arise.

7 Make a cassette recording on 'The power of place in literature'. You might wish to include some of the passages from this chapter and also some of the writing by the class. Music could also be used to add further atmosphere.

8 Prepare a display with illustrations, photographs and texts, on 'The Settings of Fiction'.

RESEARCHING AND RESPONDING

1 Look again at the list of novel titles on page 93 and see if you can make your own list of titles based on **place**. Make a note of the authors and of the dates of publication.

2 See if you can find in your library the novel that Dickens is describing in the notes which he gives in the letter. What is its title? When was it first published? Who are the main characters? What happens in the narrative?

3 Using the library, see what you can discover about the following writers (all referred to in this chapter): Doris Lessing, J.R.R. Tolkien, Karen Blixen, P.D. James. Make notes on one of them for a short introduction to the class.

4 Take one of the stories or novels that you have read recently. Imagine you are its author. Write a letter to a friend outlining the way the story first developed and, in particular, how you decided on the setting for the story.

5 Drawing on a number of examples (from your own reading as well as from this chapter), write an essay on the importance of setting in fiction.

10 | PLOT

> **PLOT** the plan, design, scheme or pattern of events in a play, poem or work of fiction; the organisation of incident or character in such a way as to induce curiosity and suspense in the reader.

Look carefully at the picture below.

What happens in fiction is called **the plot**. The plot is the whole structure of the incidents as presented by the work.

- If you were to base a story or novel on the picture above, what would be the plot of the story?
- What would happen to your main characters?
- Where would this scene be located in your plot? Would it be at the beginning, in the middle, or at the end?

Plots can be very complex or very simple. The following story has a very simple plot.

Svayamvara

Once upon a time there was a little princess who was good at whistling.

'Don't whistle,' said her mother.

'Don't whistle,' said her father, but the child was good at it and went on whistling.

Years went by and she became a woman. By this time she whistled beautifully. Her parents grieved. 'What man will marry a whistling woman?' said her mother dolefully.

'Well,' said her father, 'we will have to make the best of it. I will offer half my kingdom and the princess in marriage to any man who can beat her at whistling.'

The king's offer was duly proclaimed, and soon the palace was jammed with suitors whistling. It was very noisy. Most were terrible and a few were good, but the princess was better and beat them easily. The king was displeased, but the princess said, 'Never mind, father. Now let me set a test and perhaps some good will come of it.' The she turned to the suitors, 'Do you acknowledge that you were beaten fairly?'

'No,' they all roared, all except one, 'we think it was magic or some sort of trick.'

But one said, 'Yes.' 'Yes,' he said, 'I was beaten fairly.' The princess smiled and turning to her father she pointed to this man. 'If he will have me,' she said, 'I will marry him.'

Svayamvara – the choosing of a husband by the bride herself (Sanskrit Dictionary).

Suniti Namjoshi

The plot of *Svayamvara* could be sketched out as follows:

- There is a princess who is good at whistling.
- Her parents are anxious that she should find a husband.
- They arrange a whistling contest.
- The princess beats all the men, but chooses the one who admits that he was beaten fairly.

There is a conflict – (1) and (2) – which leads to the main event of the story (3) and is resolved, with a twist (4).

- What is the story about?
- How does this story compare with other fairy stories you know?
- What does the author make us consider by developing the plot in this way?

The next short story is by the Caribbean author Undine Giuseppi.

Journey by Night

He stood alone, leaning against a post, and shifting his weight from one foot to the other. It was late, and the taxi-stand was empty. The street was silent. He looked up and down, hoping that some vehicle would come in sight, for he wanted to get home. But none came.

The silence began to pall. He started to whistle, but there was no mirth in it, and he soon stopped. Midnight, ten miles away from home! What was he to do? To begin to walk that distance was out of the question.

A dark cloud passed across the sky, hiding the few pale stars that had been there. The noise of a falling dust-bin reached his ear. Some dog must have been scattering its contents.

Instinctively his hand felt for his wallet. Yes, it was still there. If only he had a stick! But he had nothing with which he might protect himself. He began to walk up and down, up and down.

What was that in the distance? At last two headlights were drawing near. He stepped into the middle of the street and held up his hand, and the car stopped.

'Taxi?' he asked. 'Valencia?'

'Get in,' said the driver, opening the door.

He sat beside the driver, glad to be on his way home at last. He had felt so lonely while he had been waiting. If only someone would say something! In the semi-darkness of the car he turned to look at the other passengers, but no one else was there.

The driver said nothing to him as the car sped along. Suppose . . .

No, he mustn't allow himself to think of that. He glanced at the driver, and again his hand went to his wallet. He had heard of passengers being attacked at night and robbed. But surely . . . No, that couldn't happen to him.

If only he could see the other man's face clearly! But he had no idea who the driver was. He kept his eye intently on him during the seemingly interminable journey.

Now they were approaching a spot where the road branched off in another direction. There were tall, dark bushes around. The car slowed down, and the driver was looking at him. Then the driver took something short and black from the side-pocket of the car. It looked like an iron tool. Would the driver attack him with that?

'Stop!' he heard himself screaming, and his heart beat so fast with fear that he could hardly breathe.

But the car did not stop. Faster and faster instead it went. Now they were nearing his destination. Did the driver intend to take him past and then . . .

'Put me down here,' he cried out.

Still with his eyes on the driver, he quickly stepped from the car as it came to a standstill. He fumbled in his wallet for his fare, but the taxi was no longer there.

'No night passengers for me again,' exclaimed the driver, as with a sigh of relief he hurriedly moved off. And his hand tenderly caressed the heavy spanner with which he had meant to defend himself had that queer passenger attacked him.

Read the story closely then try to analyse the whole piece by looking at the following questions:

- What is the setting of the story?
- How important are the characters?
- How much use is made of dialogue?
- How is the suspense built up?
- When does the story reach a climax?
- How does the story close?
- What kind of story is *Journey by Night*?
- Is it, in your view, a successful piece of story-writing?

In the traditional short story the plot often begins, moves up a slope of increasing excitement or suspense, reaches a point of climax and then quickly descends and ends. If you were to plot it as a graph, it would look like this:

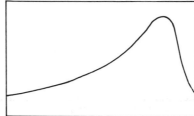

- Looking at the story *Journey by Night,* where would you say the moment of climax is?
- How well does the plot of the story fit the graph?

The plot of a story often goes through four stages:

1 Exposition   The part of the story that sets the scene and introduces characters.

2 Complication   The part of the story where the lives of the characters are complicated in some way.

3 Climax   The point where suspense is highest and matters are most threatening.

4 Resolution   A solution for the complication is introduced – it may not be a happy one!

The best way of understanding these stages is to see them at work in a story. In *Journey by Night,* the **exposition** is where the story begins, with the man waiting for the taxi:

> He stood alone, leaning against a post, and shifting his weight from one foot to the other. It was late, and the taxi-stand was empty. The street was silent. He looked up and down, hoping that some vehicle would come in sight, for he wanted to get home. But none came.

The **complication** comes when the man thinks that the driver is a thief:

> Suppose . . .
> No, he mustn't allow himself to think of that. He glanced at the driver, and again his hand went to his wallet. He had heard of passengers being attacked at night and robbed. But surely . . . No, that couldn't happen to him.

The **climax** of the narrative comes when the man screams 'Stop!' but the taxi drives on:

> 'Stop!' he heard himself screaming, and his heart beat so fast with fear that he could hardly breathe.

And the **resolution** of the story works as a kind of twist in the tail when we are led to see that the taxi-man acted as he did because he was more terrified than his passenger:

> 'No night passengers for me again,' exclaimed the driver, as with a sigh of relief he hurriedly moved off. And his hand tenderly caressed the heavy spanner with which he had meant to defend himself had that queer passenger attacked him.

You can now try to analyse the next short story, *The Visitor*, and work out the four stages:

exposition ● complication ● climax ● resolution

It is interesting to ask yourself with this story whether it has a resolution and whether it fits into the pattern illustrated by the graph of story narrative.

The Visitor

It was the beginning of a new day. A thin white sun rose over the bleak hills; black silhouettes of trees looked brittle against the pale skies. The ground was hard and dry, and around a small, whitewashed cottage the frosted grass seemed to be bristling, as if anticipating the approach of an intruder. This cottage was the only sign of civilization for miles around.

Inside the cottage, McGill was lying on an old coat he had found the previous day. He lay there a long time, staring up at the thatch sticking through the beams of the roof, and thinking. A narrow shaft of sunlight caught his eye. It was coming through a hole in the door. It seemed as if its very brightness had pierced through the door. It made a little spot of light appear on the smooth, earthen floor. It flickered, as if winking at him. McGill watched it for a while, and then it occurred to him that someone might be outside. He got up and pushed his long, black hair out of his eyes, and went to the door. He paused, fingering his rough, black beard, and then lifted the latch. The door swung open.

Outside stood a child, about eight or perhaps twelve years old: it was hard to say. Her large green eyes gazed up at him. 'May I come in?' she said. She almost whispered it. McGill thought for a moment, and then drew back to let her in.

She stepped lightly inside, and sat down on a little wooden stool by the fire. McGill stared at her. Her frame was so small and frail, and he was almost afraid that she would melt before the fire. He could see her more clearly now, for the fire lit up her quaint features. She had red, wispy hair, and a pale skin, which looked as cold as marble. She wore a light cotton dress, and on her feet no shoes, so that her toes twitched with the warmth of the fire, which was very meagre, and McGill felt ashamed.

McGill asked her if she would like something warm to drink. She answered, yes, a little milk. He gave it to her in a wooden bowl, and when she took it, her tiny hands curled round it like tendrils round a smooth tree-trunk. She sipped at it, and said that it was good. This pleased McGill, and he smiled secretly to himself.

When she had finished, she stood up and said that she had to go. McGill did not argue, but unlatched the door and pulled it open for her. On the doorstep she paused and looked up at him. She reached up, and curled her tiny hands around his neck, and kissed his rough hairy cheek with ice-cold lips. Then she was gone.

Every day she came, and every day she sat by the fire and drank a little milk with McGill. And he grew to love her, and called her his fairy-child, and when she left, he only lived to see her come again.

But one day she did not come. And many times that day McGill opened his door and called for her, but still she did not come. The next day she also did not visit him, and McGill spent his time searching for her in the hills, but there was no sign of her.

After three days, McGill decided to go down into the village in the valley and look for her.

When he arrived there, he was laughed at and scorned, and he could not breathe, for the air was choked with mocking voices and cruel thoughts. But he had to find her.

Then he saw her. She was holding the hand of a burly, well-dressed woman who was scolding her for something. The child was crying. McGill saw that she had shoes on her feet, and her hair was combed and tied back with a green ribbon. She turned and caught sight of him – her eyes were unchanged. She held out her slender white arms to him, and McGill ran to gather her into his arms. The woman screamed something incomprehensible to McGill, and tried to pull her away from him. McGill was angry for the first time in his life. He did not like the feeling; but all he knew was that he wanted to stop this woman screaming and pulling the child away from him. He wanted to get up into the clean, pure air of the hills, and take the child with him. He closed his hands around the woman's neck, and in a few minutes she lay quietly on the cobbled road, motionless. McGill turned to pick up the child, but in a moment iron arms seized him, and he was dragged away, frustrated and bewildered.

Patricia Cresswell

■ What is the plot of this story?
■ Can you divide it into the four elements
exposition ● complication ● climax ● resolution?

- Does the story have a resolution?
- How well does this story fit the graph of story narrative?
- What would you say was the theme of the story?

People have found various ways of picturing the plot of a story. Some have seen it as a series of bookmarks placed at different heights.

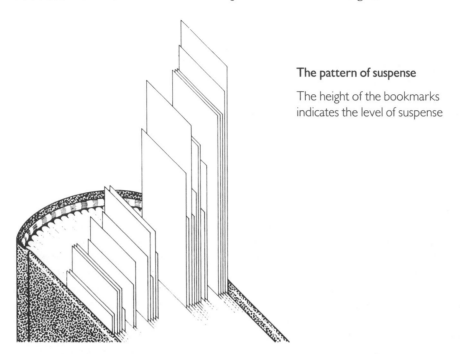

The pattern of suspense

The height of the bookmarks indicates the level of suspense

Others have shown the plot of a detective story in terms of the reader walking down a corridor.

Detection and suspense novels compared

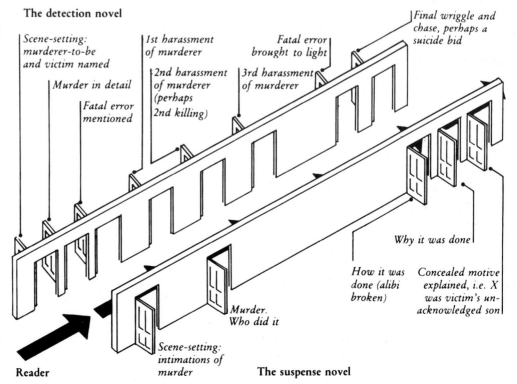

The detection novel

Scene-setting: murderer-to-be and victim named

Murder in detail

Fatal error mentioned

1st harassment of murderer

2nd harassment of murderer (perhaps 2nd killing)

3rd harassment of murderer

Fatal error brought to light

Final wriggle and chase, perhaps a suicide bid

Why it was done

How it was done (alibi broken)

Concealed motive explained, i.e. X was victim's un-acknowledged son

Murder. Who did it

Scene-setting: intimations of murder

Reader

The suspense novel

WHERE DO PLOTS COME FROM?

Writers come by their plots in many different ways. They gather them from conversations, from newspapers and from their own experience. In the following account, the author Patricia Highsmith describes how the plot for her story *The Barbarians* came directly from her own personal experience, living by herself in a flat in New York.

I LIVED in a cold-water flat on East 56th Street in Manhattan, on the first floor, and my back window had a fire escape with a ladder that led to the ground ten feet below. One day shortly after I had moved in, I entered the apartment and saw five or six boys, aged about fifteen and younger, hunched over my books and paint boxes which I had not yet put away. They rushed past me in a fast stream down the hall and out the door. I had left the window slightly open, and they had come in from the fire escape. I erased with turpentine the daubs they made on one of my suitcases. It was a disturbing experience. On another day, I was at my desk working when I heard yelling and shouting, and a great clanging of shoes on iron, and the boys started a free-for-all on the fire escape only two yards from where I sat. Absent-mindedly, I retreated, and a few seconds later was amused to find myself standing in the far corner of the room like a scared rat, still frowning with concentration as I tried to compose the last half of the sentence that was in the typewriter across the room.

I do not understand people who like to make noise; consequently I fear them, and since I fear them, I hate them. It is a vicious emotional cycle. On this occasion, my heart was beating absurdly fast, and I waited until the boys had decided to leave, as I was much too cowardly to speak to them. I might certainly call this an 'emotional experience'.

Several months later, I was inspired as a result of this to write a short story called 'The Barbarians'. A young architect with overtime work is tortured by the noise of soccer players in a vacant lot below his window every Saturday and Sunday afternoon. The players reply to his requests for less noise with taunts and insults, and the architect reaches such a pitch of nerves that he drops an eight-pound stone on the head of one of the players in the lot. The architect ducks back. The injured man is carried away but returns the next day to play with a bandaged head. But the police do not arrive. The architect is only heckled after that: his windows are broken when he comes home from work; there is chewing gum in his doorlock; and he is mildly beaten up when he encounters a couple of the players at night. The architect is afraid to ask for police help, because what he did was more serious than their heckling. The story ended with the situation unresolved.

from *Plotting and Writing Suspense Fiction*

Georges Simenon, the Belgian-French writer of detective stories, works in a similar way. He begins only with a few notes on his main characters written on an envelope, and a vague sense of a setting, and then he starts the hard labour of composition.

Here is the envelope of jottings which led to his novel *The Brothers Rico*.
And this is what Simenon says about the period of writing.

SIMENON: As soon as I have the beginning I can't bear it very long; so the next day I take my envelope, take my telephone book for names, and take my town map – you know, to see exactly where things happen. And two days later I begin writing. And the beginning will always be the same, it is almost a geometrical problem: I have such a man, such a woman, in such surroundings. What can happen to them to oblige them to go to their limit? That's the question. It will be sometimes a very simple incident, anything which will change their lives. Then I write my novel chapter by chapter.

INTERVIEWER: What has gone on the planning envelope? Not an outline of the action?

SIMENON: No, no. I know nothing about the events when I begin the novel. On the envelope I put only the names of the characters, their ages, their families. I know nothing whatever about the events that will occur later. Otherwise it would not be interesting to me.

INTERVIEWER: When do the incidents begin to form?

SIMENON: On the eve of the first day I know what will happen in the first chapter. Then, day after day, chapter after chapter, I find what comes later. After I have started a novel I write a chapter each day, without ever missing a day. Because it is a strain, I have to keep pace with the novel. If, for example, I am ill for forty-eight hours, I have to throw away the previous chapters. And I never return to that novel.

from Writers at Work

Suggested rules for the construction of detective stories

I	THE CRIMINAL must be someone mentioned in the early part of the story, but must not be anyone whose thoughts the reader has been allowed to follow.
II	ALL SUPERNATURAL or preternatural agencies are ruled out as a matter of course.
III	NOT MORE THAN ONE secret room or passage is allowable.
IV	NO HITHERTO UNDISCOVERED poisons may be used, nor any appliance which will need a long scientific explanation at the end.
V	NO CHINAMAN must figure in the story.
VI	NO ACCIDENT must ever help the detective, nor must he ever have an unaccountable intuition which proves to be right.
VII	THE DETECTIVE must not himself commit the crime.
VIII	THE DETECTIVE must not light on any clues which are not instantly produced for the inspection of the reader.
IX	THE STUPID FRIEND of the detective, the Watson, must not conceal any thoughts which pass through his mind; his intelligence must be slightly, but very slightly below that of the average reader.
X	TWIN BROTHERS and doubles generally, must not appear unless we have been duly prepared for them.

In small groups, discuss these rules.

- When do you think they were constructed?
- How seriously are they intended?
- Which rules would you accept as a writer of detective stories?
- Which would you want to break?
- Have the rules changed since this was written?
- Do you think there is a system of rules for writing such stories? for writing all stories?

In this chapter we have looked at **plot** and **theme**. We have looked at the development of some stories through the gradient of **exposition**, **composition**, **climax** and **resolution**. We have looked at the principle of **suspense** and the place of **rules** in some fiction. In the light of these terms, discuss the following story.

Witches' Loaves

MISS MARTHA MEACHAM kept the little bakery on the corner (the one where you go up three steps, and the bell tinkles when you open the door).

Miss Martha was forty, her bank-book showed a credit of two thousand dollars, and she possessed two false teeth and a sympathetic heart. Many people have married whose chances to do so were much inferior to Miss Martha's.

Two or three times a week a customer came in in whom she began to take an interest. He was a middle-aged man, wearing spectacles and a brown beard trimmed to a careful point.

He spoke English with a strong German accent. His clothes were worn and darned in places, and wrinkled and baggy in others. But he looked neat, and had very good manners.

He always bought two loaves of stale bread. Fresh bread was five cents a loaf. Stale ones were two for five. Never did he call for anything but stale bread.

Once Miss Martha saw a red and brown stain on his fingers. She was sure then that he was an artist and very poor. No doubt he lived in a garret, where he painted pictures and ate stale bread and thought of the good things to eat in Miss Martha's bakery.

Often when Miss Martha sat down to her chops and light rolls and jam and tea she would sigh, and wish that the gentle-mannered artist might share her tasty meal instead of eating his dry crust in that draughty attic. Miss Martha's heart, as you have been told, was a sympathetic one.

In order to test her theory as to his occupation, she brought from her room one day a painting that she had bought at a sale, and set it against the shelves behind the bread counter.

It was a Venetian scene. A splendid marble palazzo (so it said on the picture) stood in the foreground – or rather forewater. For the rest there were gondolas (with the lady trailing her hand in the water), clouds, sky, and chiaroscuro in plenty. No artist could fail to notice it.

Two days afterward the customer came in.

'Two loafs of stale bread, if you bleese.'

'You haf here a fine bicture, madame,' he said while she was wrapping up the bread.

'Yes?' says Miss Martha, revelling in her own cunning. 'I do admire art and' (no, it would not do to say 'artists' thus early) 'and paintings,' she substituted. 'You think it is a good picture?'

'Der balace,' said the customer, 'is not in good drawing. Der bair spective of it is not true. Goot morning, madame.'

He took his bread, bowed, and hurried out.

Yes, he must be an artist. Miss Martha took the picture back to her room.

How gentle and kindly his eyes shone behind his spectacles! What a broad brow he had! To be able to judge perspective at a glance and to live on stale bread! But genius often has to struggle before it is recognized.

What a thing it would be for art and perspective if genius were backed by two thousand dollars in bank, a bakery, and a sympathetic heart to – But these were day-dreams, Miss Martha.

Often now when he came he would chat for a while across the showcase. He seemed to crave Miss Martha's cheerful words.

He kept on buying stale bread. Never a cake, never a pie, never one of her delicious Sally Lunns.

She thought he began to look thinner and discouraged. Her heart ached to add something good to eat to his meagre purchase, but her courage failed at the act. She did not dare affront him. She knew the pride of artists.

Miss Martha took to wearing her blue-dotted silk waist behind the counter. In the back room she cooked a mysterious compound of quince seeds and borax. Ever so many people use it for the complexion.

One day the customer came in as usual, laid his nickel on the showcase, and called for his stale loaves. While Miss Martha was reaching for them there was a great tooting and clanging, and a fire-engine came lumbering past.

The customer hurried to the door to look, as any one will. Suddenly inspired, Miss Martha seized the opportunity.

On the bottom shelf behind the counter was a pound of fresh butter that the dairyman had left ten minutes before. With bread knife Miss Martha made a deep slash in each of the stale loaves, inserted a generous quantity of butter, and pressed the loaves tight again.

When the customer turned once more she was tying the paper around them.

When he had gone, after an unusually pleasant little chat, Miss Martha smiled to herself, but not without a slight fluttering of the heart.

Had she been too bold? Would he take offence? But surely not. There was no language of edibles. Butter was no emblem of unmaidenly forwardness.

For a long time that day her mind dwelt on the subject. She imagined the scene when he should discover her little deception.

He would lay down his brushes and palette. There would stand his easel with the picture he was painting in which the perspective was beyond criticism.

He would prepare for his luncheon of dry bread and water. He would slice into a loaf – ah!

Miss Martha blushed. Would he think of the hand that placed it there as he ate? Would he –

The front door bell jangled viciously. Somebody was coming in, making a great deal of noise.

Miss Martha hurried to the front. Two men were there. One was a young man smoking a pipe – a man she had never seen before. The other was her artist.

His face was very red, his hat was on the back of his head, his hair was wildly rumpled. He clinched his two fists, and shook them ferociously at Miss Martha. At *Miss Martha*.

'*Dummkopf!*' he shouted with extreme loudness; and then '*Tausenmier!*' or something like it in German.

The young man tried to draw him away.

'I vill not go,' he said angrily, 'else I shall told her.'

He made a bass drum of Miss Martha's counter.

'You haf shpoilt me,' he cried, his blue eyes blazing behind his spectacles. 'I vill tell you. You vas von *meddlingsome old cat!*'

Miss Martha leaned weakly against the shelves and laid one hand on her blue-dotted silk waist. The young man took the other by the collar.

'Come on,' he said, 'you've said enough.' He dragged the angry one out at the door to the sidewalk, and then came back.

'Guess you ought to be told, ma'am,' he said, 'what the row is about. That's Blumberger. He's an architectural draftsman. I work in the same office with him.

'He's been working hard for three months drawing a plan for a new city hall. It was a prize competition. He finished inking the lines yesterday. You know, a draftsman always makes his drawing in pencil first. When it's done he rubs out the pencil lines with handfuls of stale bread crumbs. That's better than India rubber.

'Blumberger's been buying the bread here. Well, to-day – well, you know, ma'am, that butter isn't – well, Blumberger's plan isn't good for anything now except to cut up into railroad sandwiches.'

Miss Martha went into the back room. She took off the blue-dotted silk waist and put on the old brown serge she used to wear. Then she poured the quince seed and borax mixture out of the window into the ash can.

O. Henry

MAKING AND PRESENTING

1 **Plot structure** In the table below, one part of each plot structure has been given. Fill in the other three sections and try to build up a complete story outline. Use **one** of these as a basis for a story of your own creation.

EXPOSITION	COMPLICATION	CLIMAX	RESOLUTION
Plot 1 *A survival story* In attempting a round-the-world, single-handed yacht race, you hit a reef and are stranded on a mid-ocean island where there seems to be no sign of life . . .			
Plot 2 *A love story*	'She could not believe her eyes. In spite of everything that he had promised her, there he was, with another girl, laughing and joking . . . all those things her friends had told her seemed to be coming true . . . She turned away.'		
Plot 3 *A spy story*		'Despite all those years of training, she had allowed herself to become trapped. The night patrol was coming ever closer and would soon search this room. The only window looked out upon a 40-foot drop . . .'	
Plot 4 *Death of a hero*			Imagine that the picture on page 104, at the start of this chapter, illustrates the resolution and the final scene of a story. Write an outline of the four preceding stages.

2 Imagine that the picture on page 104 illustrates the climax and resolution of a novel in which the hero dies. Write the last few paragraphs of the novel.

3 Using no more words than Undine Giuseppi in her story *Journey by Night*, write your own suspense story.

RESEARCHING AND RESPONDING

1 Look back at the patterns of suspense as they are shown on pages 107–9 and either on your own or with a partner, try to think up other ways of illustrating the pattern of the build-up of suspense in any book that you are familiar with or are working on at the moment.
The 'bookmark' and 'corridor' diagrams on page 109 are meant to simplify and clarify the extremely complex structure of a book. Try to invent your own representation of suspense. Could it be shown as a map, as a journey, as a board-game, or in some other graphic way? Make a drawing or diagram for display.

2 Most film stories follow the same plot structure as that outlined on page 107. Watch a TV drama or film and try to write notes as the plot develops. Can you see any pattern to it? Does it reflect the outline given in this chapter? Did you notice any variations on the pattern?
You might find that such stories are made more complex by the introduction of a **sub-plot** which runs parallel to, or intertwines with, the **main plot**. Such sub-plots are common in crime stories or TV soap operas.
Make a note of your observations for classroom discussion or for your own study of plot in narrative.

3 Discuss in groups the rules for writing detective stories which appear on page 111.
- Which ones are intended seriously?
- Which ones are light-hearted or frivolous?
- Which rules do you agree with? Why?
- Which ones do you disagree with? Why?

Now make a list of your own rules for writing various types of stories: spy stories, science fiction stories, love stories, war stories, murder mysteries, horror stories, etc.

4 Write your personal response to any novel or story (including those in this chapter) and deal separately with
- character
- dialogue
- setting
- plot.

5 Outline the plots of any three short stories not used in this chapter. To what extent do they fit the pattern:
exposition ● complication ● climax ● resolution?

11 | SYMBOLS IN NARRATIVE

This is the cover of a recent book of stories by the writer Alice Walker.

The image of the black hand holding the flowers is an illustration for one of the stories in the collection.

B

IN LOVE & TROUBLE
ALICE WALKER

STORIES OF BLACK WOMEN

$2.95   A Harvest/HBJ Book

The Flowers

It seemed to Myop as she skipped lightly from hen house to pigpen to smokehouse that the days had never been as beautiful as these. The air held a keenness that made her nose twitch. The harvesting of the corn and cotton, peanuts and squash, made each day a golden surprise that caused excited little tremors to run up her jaws.

Myop carried a short, knobby stick. She struck out at random at chickens she liked, and worked out the beat of a song on the fence around the pigpen. She felt light and good in the warm sun. She was ten, and nothing existed for her but her song, the stick clutched in her dark brown hand, and the tat-de-ta-ta-ta of accompaniment.

Turning her back on the rusty boards of her family's sharecropper cabin, Myop walked along the fence till it ran into the stream made by the spring. Around the spring, where the family got drinking water, silver ferns and wild flowers grew. Along the shallow banks pigs rooted. Myop watched the tiny white bubbles disrupt the thin black scale of soil and the water that silently rose and slid away down the stream.

She had explored the woods behind the house many times. Often, in late autumn, her mother took her to gather nuts among the fallen leaves. Today she made her own path, bouncing this way and that way, vaguely keeping an eye out for snakes. She found, in addition to various common but pretty ferns and leaves, an armful of strange blue flowers with velvety ridges and a sweetsuds bush full of the brown, fragrant buds.

By twelve o'clock, her arms laden with sprigs of her findings, she was a mile or more from home. She had often been as far before, but the strangeness of the land made it not as pleasant as her usual haunts. It seemed gloomy in the little cove in which she found herself. The air was damp, the silence close and deep.

Myop began to circle back to the house, back to the peacefulness of the morning. It was then she stepped smack into his eyes. Her heel became lodged in the broken ridge between brow and nose, and she reached down quickly, unafraid, to free herself. It was only when she saw his naked grin that she gave a little yelp of surprise.

He had been a tall man. From feet to neck covered a long space. His head lay beside him. When she pushed back the leaves and layers of earth and debris Myop saw that he'd had large white teeth, all of them cracked or broken, long fingers, and very big bones. All his clothes had rotted away except some threads of blue denim from his overalls. The buckles of the overalls had turned green.

Myop gazed around the spot with interest. Very near where she'd stepped into the head was a wild pink rose. As she picked it to add to her bundle she noticed a raised mound, a ring, around the rose's root. It was the rotted remains of a noose, a bit of shredding plowline, now blending benignly into the soil. Around an overhanging limb of a great spreading oak clung another piece. Frayed, rotted, bleached, and frazzled – barely there – but spinning restlessly in the breeze. Myop laid down her flowers.

And the summer *was* over.

■ 'Myop laid down her flowers.
And the summer was over.'
How do these last two lines resolve the story?

Novelists and storytellers often use symbols
in their narratives. The symbol stands not
only for itself but also for a number of other
things. In the cartoon *House and Woman*,
Thurber shows his attitude towards his
mother by using the house to symbolise the
power of the woman.

House and Woman

Me and my shadow.

Is industry appealing enough to students?

Pluck sixthform boys and girls from the classroom, let them shadow industrial managers at work for a week and the answer is 'yes'.

At Esso, we've proved the value of workshadowing so conclusively that it's now a permanent part of <u>our</u> curriculum.

In Industry Year 1986, we put forward the highest number of managers to be shadowed. In 1987, we increased this number. This year, it goes up again.

The sixthformers come from all kinds of schools. And whether they shadow the company secretary or a plant manager, they attend every meeting.

Nobody holds back just because a shadow is present. The shadow has to see industry as it really is. Otherwise it's a waste of time.

For teachers, we have made a film and video on workshadowing.

If your school would like a copy on free loan, please write to us (stating 16mm, VHS or BETA format) at Viscom Limited, Park Hall Road Trading Estate, London SE21 8EL.

We hope it sheds more light.

Esso

Quality at work for Britain for 100 years.
A MEMBER OF THE EXXON GROUP.

■ How is Esso being
symbolised?

In the next story – *The Captain's Hat* – which is by a young writer, the hat is the actual hat of the captain but it also comes to represent the relationship between the captain and the young boy who admires him. The hat takes on a symbolic meaning which unifies the story.

The Captain's Hat

And when it became dark his uncle would reach up, unhook the treasured captain's hat from the polished hat stand and hand it to him. He yearned for the day when he could reach the hat himself, when he was as tall as his uncle. They would enter the oak panelled kitchen, where the crackling flames warmed his ears, poking beneath the unwieldy hat. Perched on a stool, next to the old ship wheel, his eyes would stream as he gallantly sipped uncle's broth. 'Only real sailors can drink this, lad.' For uncle's approval he would tip back his head to swallow the last dregs only to hear that deep familiar chuckle as the hat bounced on the hard tiles. While uncle rapped his pipe on the arm of his chair the boy would rock eagerly, waiting. 'You'll make a fine sailor,' he would say, the big strong hand lifting the hat out of the boy's eyes. As uncle lit the pipe, the boy, too, would breathe in, excitedly, knowing the aroma signalled an adventure from under the thick moustache. 'When I was in the Straits of Malaga', he would begin, easing back into his creaky chair. He may have heard the story before but for the boy these evenings were always a time of wonder and admiration.

But it would be even better tomorrow because uncle had already lent him the captain's hat.

Shrilly nagging, the phone woke him. Upstairs in bed, the boy heard his father step into the hall and answer in his usual fashion. There was a long silence, his father only whispering, 'Thank you very much for calling', before clattering the receiver down. His mother called out, questioning. The boy, oblivious, heard his uncle's name mentioned, put the captain's hat on and crept onto the landing to listen. The voices were muted, the boy had to strain his ears. 'What do we tell him? He's only young, he won't understand suicide. He worships him.' He crept to the top of the stairs to hear better. 'It's so terrible. What made him do it?'

He wished he knew what was happening rather than being jumbled up. Rubbing the sleep from his eyes he wanted to warn his parents but daren't for fear of being seen. The glare of the landing light dazed him. The silence was claustrophobic. Confused by his parents' words, he wished he was older so he could understand. If he was uncle, he would understand. His mother sobbed. Wondering, he crept further down the stairs. A cold dawning gradually came to him. It was a question he didn't want to ask. 'It's too much of a shock, I can't believe it. Why did he try to kill himself?' The boy screamed. He hated his uncle. A sense of betrayal overwhelmed him. The loss of the uncle he believed in was more than he could bear. An image shattered now revealed a weak man. He could, would, never show his uncle that the captain's hat fitted properly now. With repulsion he tore it from his head and hurled it down the stairs using all his strength. The boy protected himself from the reality with his arms and rocked to and fro.

The hat was trampled upon as his parents rushed to him.

Emma Gray

Now look closely at the following passage taken from Penelope Mortimer's *The Pumpkin Eater*. In the novel, Mrs Jake is married, for the fourth time, to a script-writer. She discovers that he is having an affair with an actress. In the last chapter of the book Mrs Armitage makes her way to a tower she is having built on the wing of her country cottage. The building of the tower is the one thing in her life that *she* has chosen.

In the Tower

I went to the tower. There, in a cell of brick and glass, I sat and watched the wall of sky that rose ten feet away from my lookout window. Nothing else existed. Nobody else lived. A thick mist packed the surrounding valleys and rain, very fine rain, fell incessantly to obscure the world further. The birds clattered, invisible: or sometimes drifted like burnt paper across the window, were carried up and away again, lying on their wings as though half asleep.

I seemed to be alone in the world. My past, at last, was over. I had given it up; set it free; sent it back where it belonged, to fit into other people's lives. For one's past grows to a point where it is longer than one's future, and then it can become too great a burden. I had found, or had created, a neutrality between the past that I had lost and the future that I feared: an interminable hour which passed under my feet like the shadow of moving stairs, each stair recurring again and again, flattening to meet the next, a perfect circle of isolation captive between yesterday and tomorrow, between two illusions. Yesterday had never been. Tomorrow would never come. Darkness and light succeeded each other. The thick log in the grate became a heap of ash. Did this mean time continuing? I didn't believe it. The high tower, rising like a lighthouse in a sea of mist, was inaccessible to reality. Even the birds flung themselves about as though there were no trees, no earth to settle on.

I had been married for twenty-four years, more than half my life. The children who were born during my first wedding night now walked heavily about, frowning, groping in worn handbags for small change; their clothes were beginning to grow old and many of them must have stopped falling in love. I found it hard to understand this, as I found it hard to grasp the idea of distance, or as I always found it hard to believe in the actuality of other people's lives. For further proof, there were my own children, who until recently I had loved and cared for. Some were still growing up. Some merely grew thinner or fatter, but the size of their feet, the length of their arms, the circumference of their wrists and ankles would never change, except from disease. In them, in their memories and dreams, I existed firmly enough, however unrecognizable to myself. I stood over stoves, stirring food in a saucepan; I bent and picked things up from the floor; I stepped from side to side in the ritual of bed-making; I ran to the garden calling 'Rain!' and stretched up for the clothespegs, cramming them into one fist and hurrying in, bedouined with washing. I shook thermometers, spooned out medicine; my face hung pinkly over the bath, suspended in steam, while I scrubbed at the free, tough flesh over a kneecap, removing stains. I glowered, frightening, and then again sagged, sank, collapsed with the unendurable labours of a Monday. All this, and more, I saw myself perform in my children's memories, but although I knew that at one time it was so, I could not recognize myself. My children could remember stories of my own childhood, although they found them boring; but I was severed even from those old, clear images which determine, as I had previously thought, everything. The images of my childhood had disappeared.

But on the hill, in the tower, there were no children to identify me or to regulate the chaos of time. It was very light, the glare of the mist more accurate than sunshine. I had taken the telephone receiver off its rest: it lay like an unformed foetus on the table, its cord twisted in thick knots. No postman, milkman, baker or grocer walked on the gravel. The sound of their footsteps, of their low gears grinding up the track, would in any case have been muffled, and I would not have known they were there until they rang the bell. But I was safe. I had ordered no milk or bread, no cornflakes, flour, butter, cocoa, cat food, assorted jellies, biscuits, bacon, honey, cake, salad cream, sugar, tea, currants, chutney, tomato ketchup, gelatine, cream of tartar, soap, detergents, salt, shoe polish, cheese, sausages, rice, baking powder, margarine, orange squash, black-currant syrup, tins of soup or beans or salmon, disinfectant or instant coffee. The women who came to clean, in their fitted coats and Wellington boots, with wedding rings embedded in fingers glazed and pudgy as crystallized fruit, sat home by their fires and cared for their families. Only the wild cats knew I was there. They lay upstairs, spread out on separate beds, with their stomachs heaving and their feet crossed, sleeping as though they were tired.

From time to time I put another log on the fire. I was very aware of comfort. The heat in the tower made irregular, small noises: a sudden thud through the pipes, a creaking, the slow hiss as a log blistered. I sat down again by the window. A man serving a life sentence will never again have children. Capable, strong, alert to love, he stares from his tower and cannot prevent his body growing older. His body is an uninhabited house and the outside walls are the last to crumble. I was alone with myself, and we watched each other with steady, cold, inward eyes: the past and its consequence, the reality and its insubordinate dream. . . . I bolted the doors and went up to the highest room in the tower. It is all glass, this room, but it was surrounded by cloud, and I couldn't even see the ground. I opened one of the windows and looked down, but I could only see a bed of mist. To be dead would be a perfect solution for me, I thought. But I couldn't bear the idea of pain, the possibility that I would be a broken mess on the gravel, bleating for help. I used to be physically very brave, but now if I pricked my finger I couldn't look at it. I shut the window and went downstairs again.

- What do you think the tower stands for in this passage?
- What does the highest room represent?
- Why does Mrs Armitage shut the windows and go downstairs?

In art and literature a mountain may often represent a struggle, a goal towards which human beings may strive. The story may be of a journey towards the highest point, a dangerous journey, an uphill journey, an adventure into the unknown.

Look at the painting 'The Human Mountain'. It represents all human life as a movement up the mountain. It is a deeply symbolic painting.

Study for *The Human Mountain*, c. 1910.

Novelists have often used the mountain in the same way as the painter, using it as a symbol of human endeavour.

In one of the earliest English novels, *The Pilgrim's Progress* by John Bunyan, first published in 1678, the main character, Christian, has to climb the Hill of Difficulty.

I BEHELD THEN that they all went on till they came to the foot of the Hill Difficulty, at the bottom of which was a spring. There were also in the same place two other ways, besides that which came straight from the gate: one turned to the left hand, and the other to the right, at the bottom of the hill; but the narrow way lay right up the hill, and the name of that going up the side of the hill is called Difficulty. Christian now went to the spring (Isa. xlix. 10), and drank thereof to refresh himself, and then began to go up the hill, saying,

'The hill, though high, I covet to ascend;
The difficulty will not me offend,
For I perceive the way to life lies here.
Come, pluck up, heart, let's neither faint nor fear.
Better, though *difficult*, the right way to go,
Than wrong, though *easy*, where the end is woe.'

The other two also came to the foot of the hill. But when they saw that the hill was steep and high, and that there were two other ways to go; and supposing also that these two ways might meet again with that up which Christian went, on the other side of the hill; therefore they were resolved to go in those ways. Now the name of one of those ways was Danger, and the name of the other Destruction. So the one took the way which is called Danger, which led him into a great wood; and the other took directly up the way to Destruction, which led him into a wide field, full of dark mountains, where he stumbled and fell, and rose no more.

I looked then after Christian, to see him go up the hill, where I perceived he fell from running to going, and from going to clambering upon his hands and his knees, because of the steepness of the place. Now, about the midway to the top of the hill was a pleasant arbour, made by the Lord of the hill for the refreshment of weary travellers. Thither, therefore, Christian got, where also he sat down to rest him.

Thus pleasing himself a while, he at last fell into a slumber, and thence into a fast sleep, which detained him in that place until it was almost night. Now, as he was sleeping, there came one to him, and awakened him, saying, 'Go to the ant, thou sluggard; consider her ways, and be wise.' (Prov. vi. 6.) And, with that, Christian suddenly started up, and sped on his way, and went apace till he came to the top of the hill.

The following map shows Christian's symbolic journey.

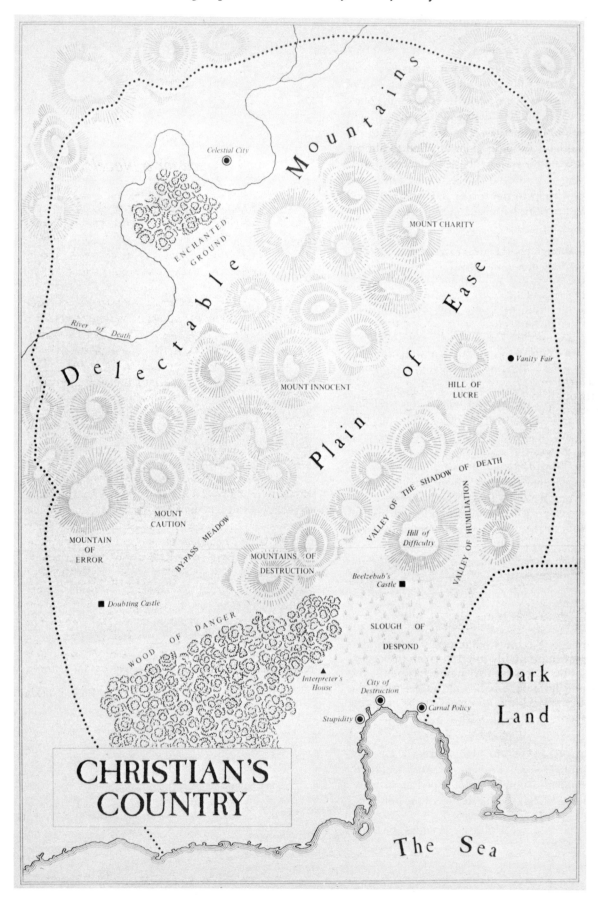

TWO SHORT SYMBOLIC STORIES

A Message from the Emperor

The emperor – so the story goes – has sent you, his wretched subject, a shadow that has fled to almost vanishing-point remoteness from the imperial sun, the emperor has from his deathbed sent you, personally, a message. He made the messenger kneel at his bedside, and he whispered the message in his ear; so concerned was he about it that he had the man whisper it back to him. With a nod he confirmed that the recitation had been correct. And in the presence of the entire company assembled to witness his death – all walls that were in the way have been knocked down and on the broad, soaring sweep of the staircase the notables of the empire are forgathered in a circle – in the presence of all these people he has dispatched the messenger. The messenger is already on his way; a powerful, indefatigable man; stretching now this arm, now that arm before him, he forces a path for himself through the throng; whenever he encounters resistance he points to his breast, where the sun sign is; and he is making good progress, better than anyone else would. But the throng is so vast, their dwellings endless. Were he suddenly in open country, how he would fly, and it would doubtless not be long before you heard the majestic pounding of his fists on your door. Instead of that, how unavailing are his efforts; he is still pushing his way through the apartments of the innermost palace; he will never get beyond them; and if he did, nothing would be gained; he would have to fight his way down the stairs; and if he succeeded in doing that, nothing would be gained; he would still have the courtyards to cross; and beyond the courtyards the other, outer palace to penetrate; and more staircases and courtyards; and yet a third palace; and so on for millennium after millennium; and were he finally to burst from the outermost gate – but it can never, never happen – the capital would lie before him, the mid-point of the world, its lees piled high. No one gets through this far and certainly not with a message from a dead man. But you, you sit at your window and dream about it as evening comes.

Franz Kafka

A Sketch for a Novel?

A very short History of the Skyscraper:

Everyone knows that the Tower of Babel was conceived as an attack on Heaven. The officials in charge of the construction were few. The work-force was innumerable: and in order that commands might not be misconstrued, every worker was required to speak the same language.

Little by little, as the courses of masonry succeeded one another, the Highest Authority became anxious that the concept of a war against Heaven might be meaningless: worse, that God in His Heaven might not exist. At an emergency session of the Central Committee, it was decided to launch a probe into the sky. Salvoes of missiles were fired off, vertically; and when these returned to Earth, bloodstained, here was proof that God, after all, was mortal; and that work on the Tower should proceed.

He, for His Part, resented being pricked in the backside. One morning, with a disdainful puff, he unsteadied the arm of a mason on one of the uppermost terraces, causing him to drop a brick on to the head of a fellow mason below. It was an accident. Everyone knew it was an accident, but the mason below began shouting threats and insults. His comrades tried to calm him, in vain. Everyone took sides in the quarrel without knowing what the quarrel was about. Everyone, in his righteous anger, refused to listen to what his neighbour was saying, and used language intended to confuse. The Central Committee was helpless: and the work gangs, each of whom now spoke a different language, took refuge from each other in remotest regions of the Earth.

Bruce Chatwin

ASSIGNMENTS

MAKING AND PRESENTING

1 Write your own story or opening to a story based on Munch's picture 'The Human Mountain' on page 120.

2 Write a short story where, as in *The Captain's Hat,* a simple object comes to take on symbolic meaning.

3 **The status symbol** These days, many people put their money towards buying status symbols; that is, symbols with which they hope to display their wealth and position in life. Such status symbols could be large cars, expensive gold jewellery or luxury yachts.
Write a story in which a person becomes totally obsessed with a status symbol.

4 Make a collage using symbols that you have cut out of newspapers or magazines. Think up a title for the completed collage and use it for a classroom display on symbolism.

RESEARCHING AND RESPONDING

1 Advertisers often use symbols in their attempts to sell their goods. Make a collection of advertisements from newspapers and magazines, from posters and television, and try to identify those adverts which have deliberately used symbols in this way.

2 Look at the following list of words and write down the first things that come into your mind as you read each word:

fire	a river
snakes	sunset
falling leaves	a swan flying
a rose	a tower
gold	moon

As an experiment, select five of these words and separately ask ten people (friends, parents, teachers) the first things they think of when you mention each word. Write down each response and consider whether, on the basis of the answers, you think there could be any special symbolic significance in the words in the list.
Analyse the responses you receive and consider whether they give you material for a story involving symbolism or one in which a symbol could become the central focus.

3   Re-read the extract from *The Pilgrim's Progress* and look at the map of Christian's Country on page 122.
John Bunyan's book was first published in 1678. Try to construct a map of the modern world on the same lines as Bunyan's symbolic vision. How have things changed? Is the world any different in symbolic terms from the world that Bunyan described? Are there new or different horrors, vices, temptations or pleasures that you would need to include?

4   Do some further research on the life and writings of John Bunyan, looking particularly at his novel *The Pilgrim's Progress*. Make notes on John Bunyan either for your own study or to report back to the class.

5   Using the library, make a study of the life and work of any one of the authors looked at in this chapter: John Bunyan, James Thurber, Alice Walker, Penelope Mortimer, Franz Kafka, Bruce Chatwin.

6   Re-read the story *The Flowers* by Alice Walker.
   • Where and when is the story set?
   • Who is its central character?
   • What is its theme?
   • Does it remind you of another story where people are exiled from a garden?
   • Why is the last sentence so important?
   • In what way is the story symbolic?
   • In response to these questions write an account of the story.

12 | FIRST-PERSON NARRATIVE

Stories can be narrated in a number of different ways. It all depends on the viewpoint that the author wishes to adopt.

Look at the following story. It is a re-telling of the myth of Icarus by a young writer.

Icarus

We stood on the edge of the cliff, staring down at the blue green water and watching the white waves crashing wildly against the cliffs.

In our hearts, we hesitated. Would our wings work? Would we really be able to fly like one of those gulls now calling overhead?

We knew the risks we were taking – Daedalus had warned me, 'Fly not near the water, my son, nor near the sun, or the wax on your wings will melt'.

As I remembered this, I heard Daedalus say in his gentle voice, 'My son, it is time to go'.

Together we stepped over the cliff. I felt myself falling, down, down, down.

Panic took a hold on me. I flapped my wings swiftly, firmly. My speed of flight downwards lessened, then suddenly I was rising and flying over to my father who was circling around, waiting.

Together, we flew out over the sea.

Then I saw the sun.

Like a red ball of fire, it hung in the sky. I wondered how it stayed there, why it was so red and angry-looking. I flew nearer. I heard Daedalus cry out, 'Icarus, remember my warning!'

I paid no heed. I was still inside the safety margin but the sun fascinated me.

I flew nearer. I wondered if I could get close enough to touch it. I think I went mad then. I flew towards it, ever nearer it.

Then suddenly I realized that my wings were not pushing me through the air as fast as they had been.

The wax was beginning to melt.

I tried to make my wings work again, by beating harder, but it was no use.

Then they gave such a little amount of power that I began to lose height.

I fell slowly at first, then faster and faster.

Daedalus watched as his son fell into the sea. It was too far away for him to be of any help.

Sadly he flew towards the place. He saw some feathers floating on the water, but nothing more.

- How has the author decided to tell her story?
- Who is the main narrator of the passage?
- Why has the author chosen to tell most of her story from Icarus's viewpoint?
- Why do you think she shifts her narrative at the end to Daedalus's position?
- How does the form of narration change when it shifts to Daedalus?
- What effect does the shift have?
- Do you see any problems with the way in which the story has been structured?
- How successful do you find this re-telling of the Icarus myth?

As you will have discovered, most of the Icarus story is told through first-person narration. This is one of the main ways of telling a story. In it the storyteller adopts the voice of autobiography and the listener or, reader, imagines that he is listening to an intimate first-hand account of experience. Indeed, some of the first novels written were presented so cunningly as autobiography (in the Preface to *Robinson Crusoe*, for example, Daniel Defoe wrote: 'the Editor believes the thing to be a just History of Fact') that many readers seriously believed they were reading true accounts.

By using first-person narration, authors can thus draw their readers into believing the imaginative world of their creation.

Look at three following examples of fiction. The first by a young writer. The second is taken from a work of fiction by the novelist Susan Hill. They use the device of first-person narration to draw the reader into their imaginative worlds. They read like direct autobiography.

On the Run

No, I haven't been to jail, not yet anyway, I'm just being hunted, hunted for what I've done. I'll get this straight between you and me now, I'm not ashamed of anything, I'm not ashamed of killing that girl . . .

I went up to the Youth Club a few weeks ago. There was a party on, quite a big thing. Anyhow, I was introduced to this girl about the same age as me. From the moment I met her, I don't know why, I hated her. She was a common little slut and everything she did got on my nerves. Later on that evening, I found out that she had pinched my guy. That night, I went round to her house, after the party, and asked her if, the next day, she would come over the fields with me for a walk – you know, I told her the boys would probably be there. She thought I was her friend. No, I was her worst enemy. I suppose you have guessed what happened. It was as easy as winking. When she turned round I knifed her. I didn't think I had killed her as it needed so little effort on my part . . .

I didn't dare go back home. I was prepared not to. Everyone knew that I was going out with her alone and if I came back all by myself they would start wondering what had happened. At the moment I'm just wondering what to do. Every movement or sound makes me jump. I have no food, just a five-pound note. I can't go into the city as someone might recognize me but I can't go on without food.

Just lately I have found out that one crime leads to another. Last night I slept out in the open and I was terrified. An owl flew through one of the trees nearby. I wanted to scream but I couldn't. I was too scared to scream, besides I couldn't afford to be heard. I was so terrified I had to run, run to get rid of some of my fears. I came to a farmhouse. The dog started barking so I became very still and tried to be quiet but I nearly started crying. The dog stopped barking and I crept up to the farm kitchen (the dog was round the other side of the farm). I knew how to break in quietly. You have to keep pressing all the way round the window-frame and the glass will become loose. The windows were quite old and they were easy to take out.

I climbed into the kitchen. It was very dark. I could see a lot of weird shapes. From one corner of the room I heard a big clock ticking very slowly. I was cold, tired and hungry and very much afraid. I suppose you will think me silly, but for one second I imagined I heard Susan's voice. She's the girl I murdered. I can tell you, I nearly fainted with fright. I told myself not to be so daft and then I felt that horrible feeling that comes over you when you know you have no one to turn to, nowhere to go and nothing to live for. I felt I was just being hunted, like an animal, but that's what I treated Susan like.

I stole all the food I could find. I was glad to get out of the place. All I could find, though, was one tin of biscuits. The next morning I went near the village, hoping no one would recognize me. I felt very near to suicide but I just couldn't bring myself to it. Strange isn't it that I can just kill someone straight off and yet be too scared to kill myself?

I went past a shop which sold newspapers. Splashed all over the front page I read 'Police Seek Killer of Teenage Girl' and underneath there was a photograph of me. I knew the police would be after me soon, but I hadn't realized how soon! I went back over the fields wondering what to do. I doubt if my parents would have helped me. I doubt if they will help me now, so I think I'm going to give myself up. I must escape from this feeling of being hunted, no peace, no rest until I know I am forgiven. No one will forgive me though, not even this 'God' they talk of. No, my life is not worth living any more. It is worse than being in jail; in jail you know you deserve all you get. You are being punished. On the run you are in your own prison, only you know you deserve a much harder punishment, a much harder jail.

Gillian Tritton

I Began to Remember

Last night, the snow fell. And then I began to remember. And today is Christmas Eve, and still it snows, and still I go on remembering, and the memories will keep me company.

I sit here, beside the window, and watch the snow, and the blackbird who comes and sits under the flowering bush, and after a while hops out further, to find the food that I have thrown. The yellow flowers of the bush are dusted with snow, and the bare branches of the tall tree are outlined delicately in white. And I sit here, beside the window, and my lamp throws its light in a pool onto the ground below, but there is no snow so close to the building, the overhang of the roof above deflects it.

And all last night, and all today, I have sat here quietly and remembered. Remembered joy and sorrow, nights and days, summer and winter, in that perfect place.

I remember my room at the very top of the tall old house, and the view out over the churchyard, and the gravestone of my two dead brothers. Remember the stone church and the fields beyond, remember the wood and the lanes and Ladyman Barrow.

And Nancy in the Rectory kitchen, and Sam Hay who whistled through the gap in his teeth. And m'lord at the Hall, and my lady. Old Betsy Barlow with one leg, Pether the church-warden. And Mr Vale, the verger, Father's right hand. And his curate with the bobbing Adam's-apple and the new, new wife.

Father, and Mother, and brother Will.

Last night, the snow fell, and I began to remember. Today it is Christmas Eve. And I remember that Christmas best of all, when I was nine years old, and the snow lay like a goose-down quilt over the earth, and I walked across the churchyard, through the deep, soft drifts, to listen to Father say Evensong, by the light of the candles.

I remember the carol singers coming with their lanterns across the snow, and their voices, and the sound of the flute and the fiddle. Remember sitting on the stairs with brother Will, and our mother handing around the plate of mince pies in the hall below, and not looking up at us or noticing.

And in the kitchen the sweet rich smells and the dark, dark fruit in the china bowl, and a cat on a cushion and a lemon rolling onto the stone-flagged floor.

Remember sleeping and waking in the thin blue light of Christmas morning. And the great stoves blazing in the icy church, and the brown savoury skin of the roasted fowl, and the death of Seth Locke and the birth of Thomas Tumney's baby; and on St Stephen's Day the stiff dead body of the tiny frozen shrew, the feel of Seth Locke's hand to my warm touch, and the new, new baby in the crook of my arm.

And the skating with torches, and the great, great beauty of that snow-covered world.

I remember. For that was the last country Christmas. The next spring, Father was made a canon of the Cathedral and we went away, away from the Rectory and the little stone church, and the grave of our two dead brothers; away from the fields and the wood, the lanes and the stream and the ditches, and the great wide barrow. Away from the country to the city, where we were happy enough in another tall house, joined to a row of others and set in the Close, but where our life ever after was so very, very different.

And after that, it seemed, I left behind my childhood, that magic time, set within a circle and lit from within, so that the memory of it, coming to me down all the years, is golden as the light of a lantern falling across the snow.

Susan Hill

- Consider the characters in these photographs.
- Consider the setting.
- Consider when the photographs were taken.
- Take one of the two characters and using the technique of first-person narration, tell his or her story.
- Try to make the way you tell the story fit the character you have imagined.

The Lesson

Back in the days when everyone was old and stupid or young and foolish and me and Sugar were the only ones just right, this lady moved on our block with nappy hair and proper speech and no makeup. And quite naturally we laughed at her, laughed the way we did at the junk man who went about his business like he was some big-time president and his sorry-ass horse his secretary. And we kinda hated her too, hated the way we did the winos who cluttered up our parks, and pissed on our handball walls and stank up our hallways and stairs so you couldn't halfway play hide-and-seek without a goddamn gas mask. Miss Moore was her name. The only woman on the block with no first name. And she was black as hell, cept for her feet, which were fish-white and spooky. And she was always planning these boring-ass things for us to do, us being my cousin, mostly, who lived on the block cause we all moved North the same time and to the same apartment then spread out gradual to breathe. And our parents would yank our heads into some kinda shape and crisp up our clothes so we'd be presentable for travel with Miss Moore, who always looked like she was going to church, though she never did. Which is just one of the things the grown-ups talked about when they talked behind her back like a dog. But when she came calling with some sachet she'd sewed up or some gingerbread she'd made or some book, why then they'd all be too embarrassed to turn her down and we'd get handed over all spruced up. She'd been to college and said it was only right that she should take responsibility for the young ones' education, and she not even related by marriage or blood. So they'd go for it. Specially Aunt Gretchen. She was the main gofer in the family. You got some ole dumb shit foolishness you want somebody to go for, you send for Aunt Gretchen. She been screwed into the go-along for so long, it's a blood-deep natural thing with her. Which is how she got saddled with me and Sugar and Junior in the first place while our mothers were in a la-de-da apartment up the block having a good ole time.

Toni Cade Bambara

Miles City, Montana

My father came across the field carrying the body of the boy who had been drowned. There were several men together, returning from the search, but he was the one carrying the body. The men were muddy and exhausted, and walked with their heads down, as if they were ashamed. Even the dogs were dispirited, dripping from the cold river. When they all set out, hours before, the dogs were nervy and yelping, the men tense and determined, and there was a constrained, unspeakable excitement about the whole scene. It was understood that they might find something horrible.

The boy's name was Steve Gauley. He was eight years old. His hair and clothes were mud-colored now and carried some bits of dead leaves, twigs, and grass. He was like a heap of refuse that had been left out all winter. His face was turned in to my father's chest, but I could see a nostril, an ear, plugged up with greenish mud.

I don't think so. I don't think I really saw all this. Perhaps I saw my father carrying him, and the other men following along, and the dogs, but I would not have been allowed to get close enough to see something like mud in his nostril. I must have heard someone talking about that and imagined that I saw it.

Alice Munro

I was born in 1927, the only child of middle-class parents, both English, and themselves born in the grotesquely elongated shadows, which they never rose sufficiently above history to leave, of that monstrous dwarf Queen Victoria. I was sent to a public school, I wasted two years doing my national service, I went to Oxford; and there I began to discover I was not the person I wanted to be.

John Fowles

I speak as the boy's mother which is what I've been asked to do. If you say it will help him somehow, then I'll have a go. It is a strange thing to be asked – my Kevin being so different from myself in every way imaginable – but I'm going to try and be clear about the whole business because I do care about him, even though I could never get close to the person I still call my son. That boy was just a bolt out of the blue and there isn't much you can do about those.

David Pownall

- What kind of novels have these openings been taken from?
- When do you think they were written?
- How are they like the openings of autobiography?
- How successful, in your view, are they as first paragraphs?

The use of first-person narrative by storytellers divides into two main groups. In the first group the character telling the story is the central character, the central protagonist. This is so, for example, in Mark Twain's novel *Huckleberry Finn* in which the hero (Huck) tells the whole story in his own immediate speech:

YOU don't know about me, without you have read a book by the name of *The Adventures of Tom Sawyer*, but that ain't no matter. That book was made by Mr Mark Twain, and he told the truth, mainly. There was things which he stretched, but mainly he told the truth. That is nothing. I never seen anybody but lied, one time or another, without it was Aunt Polly, or the widow, or maybe Mary. Aunt Polly — Tom's Aunt Polly, she is — and Mary, and the Widow Douglas, is all told about in that book — which is mostly a true book; with some stretchers, as I said before.

Now the way that the book winds up, is this: Tom and me found the money that the robbers hid in the cave, and it made us rich. We got six thousand dollars apiece — all gold. It was an awful sight of money when it was piled up. Well, Judge Thatcher, he took it and put it out at interest, and it fetched us a dollar a day apiece, all the year round — more than a body could tell what to do with. The Widow Douglas, she took me for her son, and allowed she would sivilize me; but it was rough living in the house all the time, considering how dismal regular and decent the widow aa in all her ways; and so when I couldn't stand it no longer, I lit out. I got into my old rags and my sugar-hogshead again, and was free and satisfied. But Tom Sawyer he hunted me up and said he was going to start a band of robbers, and I might join if I would go back to the widow and be respectable. So I went back.

The widow she cried over me, and called me a poor lost lamb, and she called me a lot of other names, too, but she never meant no harm by it. She put me in them new clothes again, and I couldn't do nothing but sweat and sweat, and feel all cramped up. Well, then, the old thing commenced again. The widow rung a bell for supper, and you had to come to time. When you got to the table you couldn't go right to eating, but you had a wait for the widow to tuck down her head and grumble a little over the victuals, though there warn't really anything the matter with them.

In the second group the character telling the story is not the central protagonist but a spectator, an observer who has watched the drama unfold. In some cases the observer merely narrates to us a story that he or she has heard from another. Look, for example, at the way the following two stories begin.

Fear

After dinner we gathered on deck. The Mediterranean lay without a ripple, its surface shot with the silver radiance of the full moon. The great ship glided along, sending up to the star-strewn sky a snaky column of black smoke. In our wake foamed and whirled a white streak of water, ploughed up by the swift passage of the vessel, churned by the screw, and emitting such brilliant flashes of brightness that it seemed like liquid moonlight, all bubbling and boiling.

Six or seven of us stood there in silent admiration, our eyes turned towards the distant shores of Africa, whither we were bound. The captain, who had joined us and was smoking a cigar, resumed a conversation begun at the dinner-table.

'Yes, I knew what fear was that day. My ship lay for six hours spiked on a rock with the seas breaking over her.'

Guy de Maupassant

The Blank Page

By the ancient city gate sat an old coffee-brown, black-veiled woman who made her living by telling stories.

She said:

'You want a tale, sweet lady and gentleman? Indeed I have told many tales, one more than a thousand, since that time when I first let young men tell me, myself, tales of a red rose, two smooth lily buds, and four silky, supple, deadly entwining snakes.'

The old beldame for a while says nothing, only giggles a little and munches with her toothless mouth.

'We,' she says at last, 'the old women who tell stories, we know the story of the blank page. But we are somewhat averse to telling it, for it might well, among the uninitiated, weaken our own credit. All the same, I am going to make an exception with you, my sweet and pretty lady and gentleman of the generous hearts. I shall tell it to you.'

Karen Blixen

- ■ What do you think are the advantages of the first method?
- ■ What are the advantages of the second method?
- ■ What do you think might be some of their disadvantages in telling a story?

The following short stories illustrate in full the two first-person narrative devices. In the first story, *The Use of Force*, the narrator is the central protagonist who tells his own story directly.

The Use of Force

They were new patients to me, all I had was the name, Olson. Please come down as soon as you can, my daughter is very sick.

When I arrived I was met by the mother, a big startled looking woman, very clean and apologetic who merely said, Is this the doctor? and let me in. In the back, she added. You must excuse us, doctor, we have her in the kitchen where it is warm. It is very damp here sometimes.

The child was fully dressed and sitting on her father's lap near the kitchen table. He tried to get up, but I motioned for him not to bother, took off my overcoat and started to look things over. I could see that they were all very nervous, eyeing me up and down distrustfully. As often, in such cases, they weren't telling me more than they had to, it was up to me to tell them; that's why they were spending three dollars on me.

The child was fairly eating me up with her cold, steady eyes, and no expression to her face whatever. She did not move and seemed inwardly, quiet; an unusually attractive little thing, and as strong as a heifer in appearance. But her face was flushed, she was breathing rapidly, and I realized that she had a high fever. She had magnificent blonde hair, in profusion. One of this picture children often reproduced in advertising leaflets and the photogravure sections of the Sunday papers.

She's had a fever for three days, began the father and we don't know what it comes from. My wife has given her things, you know, like people do, but it don't do no good. And there's been a lot of sickness around. So we tho't you'd better look her over and tell us what is the matter.

As doctors often do I took a trial shot at it as a point of departure. Has she had a sore throat?

Both parents answered me together, No . . . No, she says her throat don't hurt her.

Does your throat hurt you? added the mother to the child. But the little girl's expression didn't change nor did she move her eyes from my face.

Have you looked?

I tried to, said the mother, but I couldn't see.

As it happens we had been having a number of cases of diphtheria in the school to which this child went during that month and we were all, quite apparently, thinking of that, though no one had as yet spoken of the thing.

Well, I said, suppose we take a look at the throat first. I smiled in my best professional manner and asking for the child's first name I said, come on, Mathilda, open your mouth and let's take a look at your throat.

Nothing doing.

Aw, come on, I coaxed, just open your mouth wide and let me take a look. Look, I said opening both hands wide, I haven't anything in my hands. Just open up and let me see.

Such a nice man, put in the mother. Look how kind he is to you. Come on, do what he tells you to. He won't hurt you.

At that I ground my teeth in disgust. If only they wouldn't use the word 'hurt' I might be able to get somewhere. But I did not allow myself to be hurried or disturbed but speaking quietly and slowly I approached the child again.

As I moved my chair a little nearer suddenly with one catlike movement both her hands clawed instinctively for my eyes and she almost reached them too. In fact she knocked my glasses flying and they fell, though unbroken, several feet away from me on the kitchen floor.

Both the mother and father almost turned themselves inside out in embarrassment and apology. You bad girl, said the mother, taking her and shaking her by one arm. Look what you've done. The nice man . . .

For heaven's sake, I broke in. Don't call me a nice man to her. I'm here to look at her throat on the chance that she might have diphtheria and possibly die of it. But that's nothing to her. Look here, I said to the child, we're going to look at your throat. You're old enough to understand what I'm saying. Will you open it now by yourself or shall we have to open it for you?

Not a move. Even her expression hadn't changed. her breaths however were coming faster and faster. Then the battle began. I had to do it. I had to have a throat culture for her own protection. But first I told the parents that it was entirely up to them. I explained the danger but said that I would not insist on a throat examination so long as they would take the responsibility.

If you don't do what the doctor says you'll have to go to the hospital, the mother admonished her severely.

Oh yeah? I had to smile to myself. After all, I had already fallen in love with the savage brat, the parents were contemptible to me. In the ensuing struggle they grew more and more abject, crushed, exhausted while she surely rose to magnificent heights of insane fury of effort bred of her terror of me.

The father tried his best, and he was a big man, but the fact that she was his daughter, his shame at her behaviour and his dread of hurting her made him release her just at the critical times when I had almost achieved success, till I wanted to kill him. But his dread also that she might have diphtheria made him tell me to go on, go on though he himself was almost fainting, while the mother moved back and forth behind me raising and lowering her hands in an agony of apprehension.

Put her in front of you on your lap, I ordered, and hold both her wrists.

But as soon as he did the child let out a scream. Don't, you're hurting me. Let go of my hands. Let them go I tell you. Then she shrieked terrifyingly, hysterically. Stop it! Stop it! You're killing me!

Do you think she can stand it, doctor! said the mother.

You get out, said the husband to his wife. Do you want her to die of diphtheria?

Come on now, hold her, I said.

Then I grasped the child's head with my left hand and tried to get the wooden tongue depressor between her teeth. She fought with clenched teeth, desperately! But now I also had grown furious – at a child. I tried to hold myself down but I couldn't. I know how to expose a throat for inspection. And I did my best. When finally I got the wooden spatula behind the last teeth and just the point of it into the mouth cavity, she opened up for an instant but before I could see anything she came down again and gripping the wooden blade between her molars she reduced it to splinters before I could get it out again.

Aren't you ashamed, the mother yelled at her. Aren't you ashamed to act like that in front of the doctor?

Get me a smooth-handled spoon of some sort, I told the mother. We're going through with this. The child's mouth was already bleeding. Her tongue was cut and she was screaming in wild hysterical shrieks. Perhaps I should have desisted and come back in an hour or more. No doubt it would have been better. But I have seen at least two children lying dead in bed of neglect in such cases, and feeling that I must get a diagnosis now or never I went at it again. But the worst of it was that I too had got beyond reason. I could have torn the child apart in my own fury and enjoyed it. It was a pleasure to attack her. My face was burning with it.

The damned little brat must be protected against her own idiocy, one says to one's self at such times. Others must be protected against her. It is a social necessity. And all these things are true. But a blind fury, a feeling of adult shame, bred of longing for muscular release are the operatives. One goes on to the end.

In a final unreasoning assault I overpowered the child's neck and jaws. I forced the heavy silver spoon back of her teeth and down her throat till she gagged. And there it was – both tonsils covered with membrane. She had fought valiantly to keep me from knowing her secret. She had been hiding that sore throat for three days at least and lying to her parents in order to escape just such an outcome as this.

Now truly she was furious. She had been on the defensive before but now she attacked. Tried to get off her father's lap and fly at me while tears of defeat blinded her eyes.

William Carlos Williams

In the next story the narrator is the spectator who watches a court case
and from his distant position tells the reader what has happened.

The Case for the Defence

It was the strangest murder trial I ever attended. They named it the Peckham murder in the headlines, though Northwood Street, where the old woman was found battered to death, was not strictly speaking in Peckham. This was not one of those cases of circumstantial evidence in which you feel the jurymen's anxiety – because mistakes *have* been made – like domes of silence muting the court. No, this murderer was all but found with the body; no one present when the Crown counsel outlined his case believed that the man in the dock stood any chance at all.

He was a heavy stout man with bulging bloodshot eyes. All his muscles seemed to be in his thighs. Yes, an ugly customer, one you wouldn't forget in a hurry – and that was an important point because the Crown proposed to call four witnesses who hadn't forgotten him, who had seen him hurrying away from the little red villa in Northwood Street. The clock had just struck two in the morning.

Mrs Salmon in 15 Northwood Street had been unable to sleep; she heard a door click shut and thought it was her own gate. So she went to the window and saw Adams (that was his name) on the steps of Mrs Parker's house. He had just come out and he was wearing gloves. He had a hammer in his hand and she saw him drop it into the laurel bushes by the front gate. But before he moved away, he had looked up – at her window. The fatal instinct that tells a man when he is watched exposed him in the light of a street-lamp to her gaze – his eyes suffused with horrifying and brutal fear, like an animal's when you raise a whip. I talked afterwards to Mrs Salmon, who naturally after the astonishing verdict went in fear herself. As I imagine did all the witnesses – Henry MacDougall, who had been driving home from Benfleet late and nearly ran Adams down at the corner of Northwood Street. Adams was walking in the middle of the road looking dazed. And old Mr Wheeler, who lived next door to Mrs Parker, at No. 12, and was wakened by a noise – like a chair falling – through the thin-as-paper villa wall, and got up and looked out of the window, just as Mrs Salmon had done, saw Adams's back and, as he turned, those bulging eyes. In Laurel Avenue he had been seen by yet another witness – his luck was badly out; he might as well have committed the crime in broad daylight.

'I understand,' counsel said, 'that the defence proposes to plead mistaken identity. Adams's wife will tell you that he was with her at two in the morning on February 14, but after you have heard the witnesses for the Crown and examined carefully the features of the prisoner, I do not think you will be prepared to admit the possibility of a mistake.'

It was all over, you would have said, but the hanging.

After the formal evidence had been given by the policeman who had found the body and the surgeon who examined it, Mrs Salmon was called. She was the ideal witness, with her slight Scotch accent and her expression of honesty, care and kindness.

The counsel for the Crown brought the story gently out. She spoke very firmly. There was no malice in her, and no sense of importance at standing there in the Central Criminal Court with a judge in scarlet hanging on her words and the reporters writing them down. Yes, she said, and then she had gone downstairs and rung up the police station.

'And do you see the man here in court?'

She looked straight at the big man in the dock, who stared hard at her with his pekingese eyes without emotion.

'Yes,' she said, 'there he is.'

'You are quite certain?'

She said simply, 'I couldn't be mistaken, sir.'

It was all as easy at that.

'Thank you, Mrs Salmon.'

Counsel for the defence rose to cross-examine. If you had reported as many murder trials as I have, you would have known beforehand what line he would take. And I was right, up to a point.

'Now, Mrs Salmon, you must remember that a man's life may depend on your evidence.'

'I do remember it, sir.'

'Is your eyesight good?'

'I have never had to wear spectacles, sir.'

'You are a woman of fifty-five?'

'Fifty-six, sir.'

'And the man you saw was on the other side of the road?'

'Yes, sir.'

'And it was two o'clock in the morning. You must have remarkable eyes, Mrs Salmon?'

'No, sir. There was moonlight and when the man looked up, he had the lamplight on his face.'

'And you have no doubt whatever that the man you saw is the prisoner?'

I couldn't make out what he was at. He couldn't have expected any other answer than the one he got.

'None whatever, sir. It isn't a face one forgets.'

Counsel took a look round the court for a moment. Then he said, 'Do you mind, Mrs Salmon, examining again the people in court? No, not the prisoner. Stand up, please, Mr Adams,' and there at the back of the court with thick stout body and muscular legs and a pair of bulging eyes, was the exact image of the man in the dock. He was even dressed the same – tight blue suit and striped tie.

'Now think very carefully, Mrs Salmon. Can you still swear that the man you saw drop the hammer in Mrs Parker's garden was the prisoner – and not this man, who is his twin brother?'

Of course she couldn't. She looked from one to the other and didn't say a word.

There the big brute sat in the dock with his legs crossed, and there he stood too at the back of the court and they both stared at Mrs Salmon. She shook her head.

What we saw then was the end of the case. There wasn't a witness prepared to swear that it was the prisoner he'd seen. And the brother? He had his alibi, too; he was with his wife.

And so the man was acquitted for lack of evidence. But whether – if he did the murder and not his brother – he was punished or not, I don't know. That extraordinary day had an extraordinary end. I followed Mrs Salmon out of court and we got wedged in the crowd who were waiting, of course, for the twins. The police tried to drive the crowd away, but all they could do was keep the road-way clear for traffic. I learned later that they tried to get the twins to leave by a back way, but they wouldn't. One of them – no one knew which – said, 'I've been acquitted, haven't I?' and they walked bang out of the front entrance. Then it happened, I don't know how, though I was only six feet away. The crowd moved and somehow one of the twins got pushed on to the road right in front of a bus.

He gave a squeal like a rabbit and that was all; he was dead, his skull smashed just as Mrs Parker's had been. Divine vengeance? I wish I knew. There was the other Adams getting on his feet from beside the body and looking straight over at Mrs Salmon. He was crying, but whether he was the murderer or the innocent man nobody will ever be able to tell. But if you were Mrs Salmon, could you sleep at night?

Graham Greene

In small groups, discuss these two stories in terms of
- character
- dialogue
- setting
- plot
- symbolism
- first-person singular narration.

ASSIGNMENTS

MAKING AND PRESENTING

1 Re-read the myth of *Daedalus and Icarus*. You will notice that it is told in the **first person** and that the narrator in all but the last four lines is Icarus himself.
Now re-tell the myth of Daedalus and Icarus using first-person narrative but from Daedalus's viewpoint, or from the viewpoint of a character standing on the clifftop watching the events.

2 Look at the two pictures on page 129 and, using the first-person narrative technique, invent a story that they might have to tell, either as individuals or by linking their lives in some way. Remember that the way of telling must fit the character you have created: you must consider carefully the situations that they find themselves in; their hopes for the future; their past experiences; and the places that they know and live in. Try to bring their whole existence to life for your readers especially by inventing their own voices.

3 Keeping the first-person voice, convert the short story *The Use of Force* into a radio play.

4 Use the following story openings to create your own first-person narrative:

(a) In the darkness, I cast off the boat's line. It dropped with a splash which the silence covered as I pulled the wet rope on board. I steered a way between the night buoys. Freedom was just beginning . . .

(b) I was born into a decent and respectable, easily shocked, well-settled family. My father, a banker, kept us all, mother included, tightly and sometimes violently, under his control. On my sixteenth birthday, I began to rebel in a way which was to change our family life for evermore . . .

(c) Even as a young child, I had always scoffed at the occult; always laughed at those who believed in ghosts and ran from bogeymen, but what happened the other night is something that I still cannot explain and it all started so innocently.

5 Artists over the centuries have been fascinated with the myth of Icarus. The story has been re-written many times, and often painted and sculpted.

Find out more about this myth (it is a story involving murder, imprisonment in a maze and an escape attempt on man-made wings) and write a modern-day version. You will need to think carefully about what the story means to you and why it has remained so attractive to writers and painters across the centuries.

As a starting-point for your own writing, you might try to produce an illustration of the story as told on page 126.

RESEARCHING AND RESPONDING

1 Do some research to discover the titles of the books from which the opening paragraphs have been taken on page 130. How many of these books have you read? Who are their authors? When were they written? What are their themes?

2 Using the library, make a study, for discussion or display, of one of the following authors: Jonathan Swift, Mark Twain, Graham Greene or Susan Hill.

3 Write a short essay (about 300–400 words) on the advantages and disadvantages of the first-person narrative. You can refer to any of the stories or extracts given in this chapter; refer to books that you know well to illustrate your ideas.

Start by making a list of advantages and disadvantages, and go on to find quotations or examples to support your ideas.

4 Choose a novel that you know well and make a study of it in terms of each of the following elements:
- character
- dialogue
- setting
- plot
- manner of narration
- symbol (where appropriate).

This is a difficult undertaking if you have not done it in such detail before. It would help you, if you are not sure how or where to begin examining or exploring a complete novel in this way, if you were to look at one of the short stories in this chapter and examine that, using the same six elements.

It would certainly help to discuss your ideas on these points with a partner or in a small group before you begin, and to jot down your ideas on paper as the discussion proceeds.

13 | TELLING A STORY THROUGH LETTERS, DIARIES AND JOURNALS

Look at the following pictures. They all show dramatic moments in which a letter is either being read or composed.

Compose one of the letters so that it fits the character, situation and period of the picture.

'THE LETTER FORM OFFERED A SHORT-CUT TO THE HEART'

Telling a story by means of letters is a device which was often used by the first English novelists. This device uses first-person singular narrative but it allows **a number of characters** to tell their stories directly, and to relate to each other by exchanging letters. The plot and character develop in the continuous exchange of letters.

Of this mode of narration Thomas Hardy wrote:
> 'The advantages of the letter-system of telling a story are that, hearing what one side has to say, you are led constantly to the imagination of what the other side must be feeling, and at last are anxious to know if the other side does really feel what you imagine.'

The use of letters also allows the author to present at almost the same time inner flow of feelings and the outer world of public events.

This method of telling a story has been called **epistolary**, an epistle originally being a letter sent from one person to another.

Here are two letters that were written by individuals before their death by guillotine in the year 1793. They give us a precise sense of time and circumstance and a depth of inner feeling.

To Citizen Pontavice, living at La Branche, at Saint-Brice, near Fougères, *département* of the Isle-et-Vilaine

I have just been condemned to death, my dear, loving father, after having gone through four months of imprisonment. I spared you until now the pain that learning of my detention would have caused you, but it was my duty to inform you of this terrible event the moment it could no longer be hidden from you.

I wish to spare my unhappy wife this sorrow. I would ask you, for her sake, as my last wish, to assist her in whatever she may need. I know nothing in the world as estimable as her, she has a right to all your most tender feelings. On 26 March she brought into the world a daughter who will be some consolation to her. Your care and good heart are for me pledges that you will do the rest; do not pity me, I die not guilty and without reproach. In a few hours I shall be perfectly happy, the approach of death is not horrible to me, what follows cannot be.

I embrace my mother, my sister, my aunt. I remain worthy of their esteem and friendship.

Be so kind as to tear up the note of the money that you were good enough to lend me and do not demand payment for it from my poor wife. I do not think that what I ask is unjust. Farewell, my worthy friend, my loving friend, whose fine soul will learn of this event with all the heroism of which it is capable. I am with respect,

Your son, Louis-Anne Pontavice

To Citizen Jean-Marie Le Cam, second-hand dealer, Rue du Val-d'Or, no. 11, at Brest

This 18 June 1793

My dear Jean-Marie, when you get this letter, your friend, your former master, will be no more, his head will have fallen on the scaffold. Remember that he deserves your regrets and esteem, he was always faithful to his friends and to the Republic. He has been condemned on mere suspicion, but let us forgive, all is up with me, and I appear before the Eternal with a pure heart and one never sullied by a desire for revenge.

Tell your wife to remember me and tell your sweet little Catto to give a thought sometimes to her Uncle Motte; tell Ivon that I am always his friend, tell Agnès that I love her, tell the [illegible word] never to lose their esteem for me, I merit it.

Farewell, for the last time, my dear Jean-Marie, I am about to die. I am consoled at the thought that I take with me the regrets of all those who have known me. Farewell. Farewell.

I forget none of my friends, you know them, tell them all that I die wishing them every happiness.

Groult de La Motte

- How do you respond to these 'last letters'?
- What qualities do they possess?
- Why do you think novelists might be drawn to tell their stories through a series of letters?
- Why do you think the epistolary form of narration was most popular in the 18th century?
- What might be its equivalent now?

Another device similar to that of the single letter is that of the journal or diary. In this mode of storytelling the central character keeps a journal and so is able to tell us at first hand both what has happened (advancing the plot) and how the character feels (thus deepening the plot).

The Diary of a Nobody

WHY should I not publish my diary? I have often seen reminiscences of people I have never even heard of, and I fail to see – because I do not happen to be a 'Somebody' – why my diary should not be interesting. My only regret is that I did not commence it when I was a youth.

CHARLES POOTER

The Laurels,
Brickfield Terrace,
Holloway.

CHAPTER 1

My dear wife Carrie and I have just been a week in our new house, 'The Laurels', Brickfield Terrace, Holloway – a nice six-roomed residence, not counting basement, with a front breakfast-parlour. We have a little front garden; and there is a flight of ten steps up to the front door, which, by-the-by, we keep locked with the chain up. Cummings, Gowing, and our other intimate friends always come to the little side entrance, which saves the servant the trouble of going up to the front door, thereby taking her from her work. We have a nice little back garden which runs down to the railway. We were rather afraid of the noise of the trains at first, but the landlord said we should not notice them after a bit, and took £2 off the rent. He was certainly right; and beyond the cracking of the garden wall at the bottom, we have suffered no inconvenience.

The Laurels

Our dear friend Gowing

After my work in the City, I like to be at home. What's the good of a home, if you are never in it? 'Home, Sweet Home', that's my motto. I am always in of an evening. Our old friend Gowing may drop in without ceremony; so may Cummings, who lives opposite. My dear wife Caroline and I are pleased to see them, if they like to drop in on us. But Carrie and I can manage to pass our evenings together without friends. There is always something to be done: a tin-tack here, a Venetian blind to put straight, a fan to nail up, or part of a carpet to nail down – all of which I can do with my pipe in my mouth; while Carrie is not above putting a button on a shirt, mending a pillowcase, or practising the 'Sylvia Gavotte' on our new cottage piano (on the three years' system), manufactured by W. Bilkson (in small letters), from Collard and Collard (in very large letters). It is also a great comfort to us to know that our boy Willie is getting on so well in the Bank at Oldham. We should like to see more of him. Now for my diary:

APRIL 3. Tradesmen called for custom, and I promised Farmerson, the ironmonger, to give him a turn if I wanted any nails or tools. By-the-by, that reminds me there is no key to our bedroom door, and the bells must be seen to. The parlour bell is broken, and the front door rings up in the servant's bedroom, which is ridiculous. Dear friend Gowing dropped in, but wouldn't stay, saying there was an infernal smell of paint.

APRIL 4. Tradesmen still calling: Carrie being out, I arranged to deal with Horwin, who seemed a civil butcher with a nice clean shop. Ordered a shoulder of mutton for tomorrow, to give him a trial. Carrie arranged with Borset, the butterman, and ordered a pound of fresh butter, and a pound and a half of salt ditto for kitchen, and a shilling's worth of eggs. In the evening, Cummings unexpectedly dropped in to show me a meerschaum pipe he had won in a raffle in the City, and told me to handle it carefully, as it would spoil the colouring if the hand was moist. He said he wouldn't stay, as he didn't care

much for the smell of the paint, and fell over the scraper as he went out. Must get the scraper removed, or else I shall get into a *scrape*. I don't often make jokes.

APRIL 5. Two shoulders of mutton arrived, Carrie having arranged with another butcher without consulting me. Gowing called, and fell over scraper coming in. *Must* get that scraper removed.

APRIL 6. Eggs for breakfast simply shocking; sent them back to Borset with my compliments, and he needn't call any more for orders. Couldn't find umbrella, and though it was pouring with rain, had to go without it. Sarah said Mr Gowing must have took it by mistake last night, as there was a stick in the 'all that didn't belong to nobody. In the evening, hearing someone talking in a loud voice to the servant in the downstairs hall, I went out to see who it was, and was surprised to find it was Borset, the butterman, who was both drunk and offensive. Borset, on seeing me, said he would be hanged if he would ever serve City clerks any more – the game wasn't worth the candle. I restrained my feelings, and quietly remarked that I thought it was possible for a City clerk to be a *gentleman*. He replied he was very glad to hear it, and wanted to

Our dear friend Cummings

know whether I had ever come across one, for *he* hadn't. He left the house, slamming the door after him, which nearly broke the fanlight; and I heard him fall over the scraper, which made me feel glad I hadn't removed it. When he had gone, I thought of a splendid answer I ought to have given him. However, I will keep it for another occasion.

APRIL 7. Being Saturday, I looked forward to being home early, and putting a few things straight; but two of our principals at the office were absent through illness, and I did not get home till seven. Found Borset waiting. He had been three times during the day to apologize for his conduct last night. He said he was unable to take his Bank Holiday last Monday, and took it last night instead. He begged me to accept his apology, and a pound of fresh butter. He seems, after all, a decent sort of fellow; so I gave him an order for some fresh eggs, with a request that on this occasion they *should* be fresh. I am afraid we shall have to get some new stair-carpets after all; our old ones are not quite wide enough to meet the paint on either side. Carrie suggests that we might ourselves broaden the paint. I will see if we can match the colour (dark chocolate) on Monday.

APRIL 8. SUNDAY. After Church, the Curate came back with us. I sent Carrie in to open the front door, which we do not use except on special occasions. She could not get it open, and after all my display, I had to take the Curate (whose name, by-the-by, I did not catch) round the side entrance. He caught his foot in the scraper, and tore the bottom of his trousers. Most annoying, as Carrie could not well offer to repair them on a Sunday. After dinner, went to sleep. Took a walk round the garden, and discovered a beautiful spot for sowing mustard-and-cress and radishes. Went to Church again in the evening: walked back with the Curate. Carrie noticed he had got on the same pair of trousers, only repaired. He wants me to take round the plate, which I think a great compliment.

- What can you tell from the title of the book?
- What can you tell about the nature of the central character from his diary entries?
- What do you learn about the world he lives in?
- In what period do you think the work is set?
- What do the illustrations add?
- How do you think the diary entries might develop?

Here is a letter from an 18th-century novel *Humphry Clinker,*
by Tobias Smollett.

To Mrs. Gwyllim, house-keeper at Brambleton-hall.   Glostar, April 2.

MRS. GWYLLIM,

When this cums to hand, be sure to pack up in the trunk male that stands in my closet, to be sent me in the Bristol waggon without loss of time, the following articles, viz. my rose collard neglejay, with green robins, my yellow damask, and my black velvet suit, with the short hoop; my bloo quilted petticot, my green manteel, my laced apron, my French commode, Macklin head and lappets, and the litel box with my jowls. Williams may bring over my bum-daffee, and the viol with the easings of Dr. Hill's dock-water, and Chowder's lacksitif. The poor creature has been terribly constuprated ever since we left huom. Pray take particular care of the house while the family is absent. Let there be a fire constantly kept in my brother's chamber and mine. The maids, having nothing to do, may be sat a spinning. I desire you'll clap a pad-luck on the wind-seller, and let none of the men have excess to the strong bear. Don't forget to have the gate shut every evening before dark. The gardnir and the hind may lie below in the landry, to partake the house, with the blunderbuss and the great dog; and I hope you'll have a watchfull eye over the maids. I know that hussy, Mary Jones, loves to be rumping with the men. Let me know if Alderney's calf be sould yet, and what he fought; if the ould goose be sitting; and if the cobler has cut Dicky, and how the pore anemil bore the operation. No more at present, but rests,

Yours,
TABITHA BRAMBLE

Here is a letter from a 20th-century novel, *The Color Purple*
by Alice Walker.

Dear God,

Harpo no better at fighting his daddy back than me. Every day his daddy git up, sit on the porch, look out at nothing. Sometime look at the trees out front the house. Look at a butterfly if light on the rail. Drink a little water in the day. A little wine in the evening. But mostly never move.

Harpo complain bout all the plowing he have to do.

His daddy say, You gonna do it.

Harpo nearly big as his daddy. He strong in body but weak in will. He scared.

Me and him out in the field all day. Us sweat, chopping and plowing. I'm roasted coffee bean color now. He black as the inside of a chimney. His eyes be sad and thoughtful. His face begin to look like a woman face.

Why you don't work no more? he ast his daddy.

No reason for me to. His daddy say. You here, ain't you? He say this nasty. Harpos feeling be hurt.

Plus, he still in love.

- What can you tell about the characters of the authors of these two letters?
- What background does each have?
- What do we learn about their lives?
- How much do we learn about the narrative and plot of the whole book?
- Why do you think a character might address a series of letters to God?

It is possible to use just one letter to create a sense of story and character. The following complete story is constructed as one simple letter written by Mary to a friend called Sadie.

Mary ❧

Dear Sadie

I am in the toilet as it's the only place I get a bit of peace. She is calling me down to do the dinner as I am a good cook and she is not. He raised ructions yesterday about cabbage water and I got red and you won't believe it but he smiled straight into my face. He never smiles at her. If I tell you a secret don't tell anyone. She sees another man. Didn't I walk straight into them the night I was to meet Tom Dooley and he never came. Next day she gave me a frock of hers, I suppose so's I'd keep my mouth shut. And now I am in a fix because she expects me to wear it when I go dancing and I want to wear a frock of my own. It is brushed wool, mine is, and I know it is brushed wool but I am not telling her.

Tom Dooley came the next night. He got the nights mixed up, a good job I was there. We went for a walk in the park opposite this house – there's a park, I told you that, didn't I? It's nice in the summer because there's a pavilion where they sell icecream and stuff but dead boring in the winter. Anyhow we had a walking race through the woods and he beat me blind and I got so winded I had to sit down and he sat next to me and put his arm around me. Then he kissed me and all of a sudden he raised the subject of SEX and I nearly died. I got such a fright that I took one leap off the seat and tore across the field and he tore after me and put his arms around me and then I burst out crying, I don't know why. And I had to come in home and when I did he was here by himself. She's always out. Goes to pubs on her own or wandering around the road gathering bits of branches saying how sad and how beautiful they are. Did you ever hear such nonsense in all your life. She wouldn't darn a sock. Anyhow he was here listening to music. He always is. And he called me in to warm my feet and sat me down and we hardly said one word except that he asked me was I all right and I had to say

something, so I said I got a smut in my eye. Didn't he get an eye-glass and was poking away at it with a little paint brush and didn't she come in real quiet in her crêpe-soled shoes.

'Oh, togetherness,' she said in her waspy voice and you wouldn't see me flying up the stairs to bed. Next morning – and you mustn't breathe this to a soul – she was up at cock-crow. Said she had heartburn and went out to do some weeding. It's winter and there's nothing in those flower beds only clay. Guess what, wasn't she waiting for the postman and no sooner had he come than she was all smiles and making coffee and asking me what kind of dancing did I like, and didn't the phone ring and when she tripped off to answer it I had a gawk at the letter she got. I could only scan it. Real slop. It was from a man. It said darling be brave. See you a.m. Now I haven't told you this but I love their child. He has eyelashes as long as daisies and lovely and black. Like silk. I admired them one day and he wanted to pull one out for me. I'd do anything for that kid.

Anyhow I discovered where she keeps the letters – under the hall carpet. She presses flowers there too. Of course if I wanted to, I could show them to hubby, find them, pretend I didn't know what they were. I'm not sure whether I will or not. I heard him telling her once that he'd take the kid and go to Australia. I'd love to go. The kid has a pet name – he's called Buck – and he loves bread and jam and I think he prefers me to her. I have to go now as she's calling me. Not a word to my mother about this. I'll let you know developments.
Your fond friend
Mary

PS I am thinking of changing my name. How do you like the sound of Myrtle?

Edna O'Brien

- What do you learn about Mary from this letter?
- What kind of style is the letter written in?
- What background do you think Mary comes from?
- How many characters are introduced in the letter?
- What is her relationship to the different members of the family she works for?
- How complete is this short story, in your view?
- How do you think a story using letters could develop out of this one letter?

THE NOVEL AS JOURNAL, FROM THE 18th CENTURY TO THE 20th CENTURY

The journal can be used to tell a story in a similar manner to the letter.
The following is from Daniel Defoe's 18th-century *Robinson Crusoe*,
which is written in the form of a journal by a shipwrecked survivor.

The Journal

September 30, 1659. I poor miserable *Robinson Crusoe*, being shipwreck'd, during a dreadful Storm, in the offing, came on Shore on this dismal unfortunate Island, which I call'd *the Island of Despair*, all the rest of the Ship's Company being drown'd, and my self almost dead.

All the rest of the Day I spent in afflicting my self at the dismal Circumstance I was brought to, *viz.* I had neither Food, House, Clothes, Weapon, or Place to fly to, and in Despair of any Relief, saw nothing but Death before me, either that I should be devour'd by wild Beasts, murther'd by Savages, or starv'd to Death for Want of Food. At the Approach of Night, I slept in a Tree for fear of wild Creatures, but slept soundly tho' it rain'd all Night.

October 1. In the Morning I saw to my great Surprise the Ship had floated with the high Tide, and was driven on Shore again much nearer the Island, which as it was some Comfort on one hand, for seeing her sit upright, and not broken to Pieces, I hop'd, if the Wind abated, I might get on board, and get some Food and Necessaries out of her for my Relief; so on the other hand, it renew'd my Grief at the Loss of my Comrades, who I imagin'd if we had all staid on board might have sav'd the Ship, or at least that they would not have been all drown'd as they were; and that had the Men been sav'd, we might perhaps have built us a Boat out of the Ruins of the Ship, to have carried us to some other Part of the World. I spent great Part of this Day in perplexing my self on these things; but at length seeing the Ship almost dry, I went upon the Sand as near as I could, and then swam on board; this Day also it continu'd raining, tho' with no Wind at all.

From the 1st of *October*, to the 24th. All these Days entirely spent in many several Voyages to get all I could out of the Ship, which I brought on Shore, every Tide of Flood, upon Rafts. Much Rain also in these Days, tho' with some Intervals of fair Weather: But, it seems, this was the rainy Season.

Oct. 20. I overset my Raft, and all the Goods I had got upon it, but being in shoal Water, and the things being chiefly heavy, I recover'd many of them when the Tide was out.

Oct. 25. It rain'd all Night and all Day, with some Gusts of Wind, during which time the Ship broke in Pieces, the Wind blowing a little harder than before, and was no more to be seen, except the Wreck of her, and that only at low Water. I spent this Day in covering and securing the Goods which I had sav'd, that the Rain might not spoil them.

Oct. 26. I walk'd about the Shore almost all Day to find out a place to fix my Habitation, greatly concern'd to secure my self from an Attack in the Night, either from wild Beasts or Men. Towards Night I fix'd upon a proper Place under a Rock, and mark'd out a Semi-Circle for my Encampment, which I resolv'd to strengthen with a Work, Wall, or Fortification made of double Piles, lin'd within with Cables, and without with Turf.

From the 26th. to the 30th. I work'd very hard in carrying all my Goods to my new Habitation, tho' some Part of the time it rain'd exceeding hard.

The 31st. in the Morning I went out into the Island with my Gun to see for some Food, and discover the Country, when I kill'd a She-Goat, and her Kid follow'd me home, which I afterwards kill'd also because it would not feed.

November 1. I set up my Tent under a Rock, and lay there for the first Night, making it as large as I could with Stakes driven in to swing my Hammock upon.

Nov. 2. I set up all my Chests and Boards, and the pieces of Timber which made my Rafts, and with them form'd a Fence round me, a little within the Place I had mark'd out for my Fortification.

Nov. 3. I went out with my Gun and kill'd two Fowls like Ducks, which were very good Food. In the Afternoon went to work to make me a Table.

The next passage is from Robert O'Brien's 20th-century novel *Z for Zachariah*, which is about the survivor of a nuclear holocaust.

May 20th

I am afraid.

Someone is coming.

That is, I think someone is coming, though I am not sure, and I pray that I am wrong. I went into the church and prayed all this morning. I sprinkled water in front of the altar, and put some flowers on it, violets and dogwood.

But there is smoke. For three days there has been smoke, not like the time before. That time, last year, it rose in a great cloud a long way away, and stayed in the sky for two weeks. A forest fire in the dead woods, and then it rained and the smoke stopped. But this time it is a thin column, like a pole, not very high.

And the column has come three times, each time in the late afternoon. At night I cannot see it, and in the morning, it is gone. But each afternoon it comes again, and it is nearer. At first it was behind Claypole Ridge, and I could see only the top of it, the smallest smudge. I thought it was a cloud, except that it was too grey, the wrong colour, and then I thought: there are no clouds anywhere else. I got the binoculars and saw that it was narrow and straight; it was smoke from a small fire. When we used to go in the truck, Claypole Ridge was fifteen miles, though it looks closer, and the smoke was coming from behind that.

Beyond Claypole Ridge there is Ogdentown, about ten miles further. But there is no one left alive in Ogdentown.

I know, because after the war ended, and all the telephones went dead, my father, my brother Joseph and cousin David went in the truck to find out what was happening, and the first place they went was Ogdentown. They went early in the morning; Joseph and David were really excited, but Father looked serious.

When they came back it was dark. Mother had been worrying – they took so long – so we were glad to see the truck lights finally coming over Burden Hill; six miles away. They looked like beacons. They were the only lights anywhere, except in the house – no other cars had come down all day. We knew it was the truck because one of the lights, the left one, always blinked when it went over a bump. It came up to the house and they got out; the boys weren't excited any more. They looked scared, and my father looked sick. Maybe he was beginning to be sick, but mainly I think he was distressed.

My mother looked up at him as he climbed down.

'What did you find?'

He said, 'Bodies. Just dead bodies. They're all dead.'

'All?'

We went inside the house where the lamps were lit, the two boys following, not saying anything. My father sat down. 'Terrible,' he said, and again, 'terrible, terrible. We drove around, looking. We blew the horn. Then we went to the church and rang the bell. You can hear it five miles away. We waited for two hours, but nobody came. I went into a couple of houses – the Johnsons', the Peters' – they were all in there, all dead. There were dead birds all over the streets.'

My brother Joseph began to cry. He was fourteen. I think I had not heard him cry for six years.

May 21st

It is coming closer. Today it was almost on top of the ridge, though not quite, because when I looked with the binoculars I could not see the flame, but still only the smoke – rising very fast, not far above the fire. I know where it is: at the crossroads. Just on the other side of the ridge, the east–west highway, the Dean Town road, crosses our road. It is Route number nine, a State highway, bigger than our road, which is County road 793. He has stopped there and is deciding whether to follow number nine or come over the ridge. I say *he* because that is what I think of, though it could be *they* or even *she*. But I think it is he. If he decides to follow the highway he will go away, and everything will be all right again. Why would he come back? But if he comes to the top of the ridge, he is sure to come down here, because he will see the green leaves. On the other side of the ridge, even on the other side of Burden Hill, there are no leaves; everything is dead.

There are some things I need to explain. One is why I am afraid. Another is why I am writing in this composition book, which I got from Klein's store a mile up the road.

I took the book and a supply of ballpoint pens back in February. By then the last radio station, a very faint one that I could hear only at night, had stopped broadcasting. It has been dead for about three or four months. I say *about*, and that is one reason I got the book: because I discovered I was forgetting when things happened, and sometimes even *whether* things happened or not. Another reason I got it is that I thought writing in it might be like having someone to talk to, and if I read it back later it would be like someone talking to me. But the truth is I haven't written in it much after all, because there isn't much to write about.

Sometimes I would put in what the weather was like, if there was a storm or something unusual. I put in when I planted the garden because I thought that would be useful to know next year. But most of the time I didn't write, because one day was just like the day before, and sometimes I thought – what's the use of writing anyway, when nobody is ever going to read it? Then I would remind myself: some time, years from now, *you're* going to read it. I was pretty sure I was the only person left in the world.

But now I have something to write about. I was wrong. I am not the only person left in the world. I am both excited and afraid.

- What can we tell about the central character from these journal entries?
- What can we tell about the character's predicament?
- What can we tell about the place he or she inhabits?
- How do you think the narratives of these two stories will develop?
- What would you say were the main differences (in style and content) between the two passages?
- How does the use of the journal to tell a story differ from that of the letter?

A S S I G N M E N T S

MAKING AND PRESENTING

1. Compose the letter that Sadie writes back to Mary, the characters in Edna O'Brien's short story. This will require a very close reading of Mary's letter on page 144.

2. Write a further letter in the same style as that written **either** by Tabitha Bramble in *Humphry Clinker* or by the character writing to God in *The Color Purple*.

3. Re-read the letters from condemned prisoners on page 139. Imagine that those letters are part of an exchange of letters between the prisoners and their families. Compose the letters addressed to the condemned person by a family relative.

4. Imagine a character who, for some reason, is facing imminent death. Compose the last letter that such a person would write, remembering that there may now be nothing left to conceal.

5. At the back of an old cupboard which you have been told to clean out, you find a series of letters, hidden there by someone who obviously wanted to keep the contents a secret. Invent a selection of the letters so as to bring out their story.

6 Three friends plan a weekend away from home together. In the course of the weekend, they become separated in some way and one is left out of everything. After the weekend they each write a letter to the others and try to explain what happened on that weekend trip . . . but they all have a different version of the events.

Write the letters that passed between them as a result of the weekend trip. Try to show how they might be deceiving each other; or how, perhaps, some events were carefully planned beforehand by two of the group without informing the third. This will give you a good opportunity to get inside the minds of three very different characters and to present three completely separate views of the same happenings. It should also lead you to consider whether the narrator (in this case the letter-writers) must always tell the 'truth' to the reader and especially whether, even in novels, the 'truth' exists.

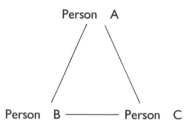

7 Here is the final page from the diary of a missing person. Work out for yourself what led up to this desperate last entry and write a series of diary entries from the weeks leading up to this one.

July

24 Sunday

Tonight I am definitely leaving. I haven't told anyone here yet. I cannot trust anyone. I cannot stand it any more...the pain and the torment. I meet M— at mid-night on X bridge. I can't wait...

You could develop this into a full-length short story told wholly or in part in the diary form of narrative.

RESEARCHING AND RESPONDING

1 Read the letter written by Tabitha Bramble in *Humphry Clinker*, and the letter to God from *The Color Purple*, on page 143. What can you tell about the characters of the authors of these two letters and about their backgrounds? Write a brief account of what you think the reader learns about their lives from these letters.

2 Using the library (and asking other readers), make a list of other novels and stories which make use of letters, diaries, journals and log-books. Make a note of their titles and authors and of how they are used. This material could be used for both classroom discussion and and a display.

3 Read the novel *Robinson Crusoe* by Daniel Defoe, or *Z for Zachariah* by Robert O'Brien, or *The Secret Diary of Adrian Mole aged 13¾* by Sue Townsend, and discuss the theme and method of narration of the book you have chosen.

4 Make a dramatic recording on cassette or video to show the use of letters and journal entries in the writing of fiction.

5 *The Tenant of Wildfell Hall* (1848) by Anne Brontë has been called 'a feminist book'. What do you think this description means?
Do some research into feminism and women writers. Either write an essay on what you discover, or report back, using notes, to your class.

6 Using all that you have discovered in this chapter, write an essay on the advantages and disadvantages of telling a story through letters or journal entries. Quote some actual examples in your work and refer to as many writers as you can.

14 | DRAMATIC MONOLOGUE

In real life we talk to ourselves. A conversation goes on inside our minds most of the time. We often say: 'I keep telling myself' . . . 'I talked myself into it' . . . 'I keep going over it in my mind' . . . There is a hidden daily conversation in our lives which nobody else can hear or even know about.

Many authors wanting to tell the story through their characters have tried to represent this continuous hidden conversation. In novels and stories this device is called **dramatic monologue**. Because at times we all talk to ourselves, it is very easy for us to recognise dramatic monologue in fiction and to understand it.

In the following excerpt from *The Adventures of Tin-Tin*, all the conversation, except in the first frame, is **monologue**. The character Calculus is talking to himself as he walks through the wood. What we read is the flow of his inner conversation.

Now look at the following excerpt from the Welsh writer John Gwilym Jones's story *The Wedding*. In it the public question: 'Wilt thou take this man to be thy wedded husband?' is followed by **the private monologue** of Lizzie, the woman about to be married.

'Lizzie Mary Jones, wilt thou have this man to be thy wedded husband?'

'I will.' There: I have spoken the words simply, coolly, feeling nothing more than the reasonable excitement of any bride. This is not how I imagined my wedding. There was a time when I saw myself as the young man's fancy. I wandered with him through the white wheat and sauntered along the paths of the sheep till we reached the green blade of grass. But at last, after many tribulations, after bearing the cruelty of father and mother, after writing with blood from my own arm, I was forced to stand beside Maddocks in church, wretched as a faded lily. Behind me sat my proud family; beside me, haughtily, Maddocks was marrying my body while outside, somewhere, breaking his heart, was Wil. Don't break your heart, Wil. Soon the Maid of Cefn Ydfa will lie still in her grave and Wales will be singing your idyll . . .

There was a time when I imagined myself saying 'I will', trembling with a consuming passion. Beside me stood a powerful he-man, a man among men, not unlike Clarke Gable in *I Adored Her*. He had one of those haggard attractive faces with wavy, brilliantined hair and a cheeky little twist to the corner of his mouth. I felt exhilarated at having humiliated him and bewitched him into saying 'I will' with such humble gratitude; yet the touch of his hand on mine as he placed the ring made me flush, every inch of me. I stood there brazen, abstractions like morality and chastity and temperance having ceased to be, even quite tangible things like my father's frown and my mother's smack and the tongue of Betsan Jones next door having become as nothing in the world to me . . .

Another time I would marry above my station. Behind me would sit my mother. 'A Triplex grate, wooden bedsteads, a three-piece suite and a carpet,' she would say to herself. 'I'm taking a fortnight's holiday this year,' my father would say to the quarry steward, 'to stay with my daughter at Bumford Hall.' 'I'm off to Paris,' my sister Gwen would say. 'To Paris?' 'Yes, with Lady Elizabeth.' 'Lady Elizabeth?' 'My sister, Lady Elizabeth Bumford, you know . . .' But here's what happens. I am marrying one of my own kind, not forced and not feeling anything other than the ordinary thrill of any girl on her wedding day. I say 'I will' quite simply, seemingly unconcerned, perfectly satisfied and perfectly happy because I know I am doing the right and the wise thing to do.

The dramatic monologue in the next passage takes us into the main character's mind as he sits in a restaurant ordering his food.

THE MENU. Let's see; fish, sole . . . yes, a sole. *Entrées*, mutton cutlets . . . no. Chicken . . . yes.

— Sole. Then some chicken, with watercress.

— Yes, sir. Sole, chicken, and cress.

So I'm going to dine, and a very good idea too. Now that's a pretty woman over there; neither fair nor dark; a high-stepper, by gad; tallish, probably; must be the wife of that bald man with his back to me; more likely his mistress; somehow she hasn't just the married air; quite a pretty girl, really. She might look this way; almost exactly opposite me she is; what shall I? Oh, what's the good? There, she's spotted me. Really a pretty woman, and the man looks a bore; a pity I can only see his back; I'd like to have a look at his face too; lawyer, I should say, a family solicitor up from the country. Absurd I am! How about the soup? The glass in front of me reflects the gilded frame; the gilded frame behind me of course; those arabesques in bright vermillion, all scarlet flashes; but the light is pale yellow; walls, napery, mirrors, wine-glasses, all yellowed by the gaslight. It's comfortable here, well-appointed place. Here's the soup, piping hot; waiter might splash some, better keep an eye on him. All's well; let's begin. Too hot, this soup; wait, try again. Not half bad. I lunched a bit too late, no appetite left. All the same I must eat some dinner. Soup finished. That woman looked this way again; expressive eyes she has and the man with her seems a dull bird; I might get to know her by some fluke; queerer things happen; why not? If I keep on looking at her, it might lead to something; but they've reached the joint already; never mind, if I choose I can catch them up at the post. Where's that waiter gone to? Slow as a funeral they are, these restaurant dinners; I might fix up to have my meals at home; the concierge could do the cooking, and it would be cheaper too. He'd make a mess of it, for a certainty. I'm a fool; deadly dull it would be, and how about the days when I don't come back? At least in a restaurant one isn't bored. What's that waiter up to?

Edouard Dujardin, *We'll to the Woods No More*

- How well do you think these passages capture the inner flow of thought?
- How difficult are they to follow?
- What do they tell us about the main characters?
- How could a story be built up using dramatic monologue of this kind?

Using the same device as these authors, create your own dramatic monologue. Concentrate on one of the figures in the images on the following two pages. Study the character and situation carefully. Then in your own writing try to bring out the inner flow of thoughts and feelings.

WORKING FROM IMAGES

Henri Rousseau: *The Sleeping Gypsy*, 1897

Some well-known novels and stories have been written through the use of dramatic monologue. Here is one complete chapter from Dorothy Richardson's *Pilgrimage*.

CHAPTER VII

Why must I always think of her in this place? . . . It is always worst just along here . . . Why do I always forget there's this piece . . . always be hurrying along seeing nothing and then, suddenly, Teetgen's Teas and this row of shops? I can't bear it. I don't know what it is. It's always the same. I always feel the same. It is sending me mad. One day it will be worse. If it gets any worse I shall be mad. Just here. Certainly. Something is wearing out of me. I am meant to go mad. If not, I should not always be coming along this piece without knowing it, whichever street I take. Other people would know the streets apart. I don't know where this bit is or how I get to it. I come every day because I am meant to go mad here. Something that knows brings me here and is making me go mad because I am myself and nothing changes me.

- What do you imagine to be the point of such a short chapter?
- What do we learn about the particular character?
- What do you notice about the style of writing?
- How is this chapter different from most other chapters in fiction?

This is the opening of the novel *Female Friends* by Fay Weldon. It reports the inner thoughts of the character Chloe before she falls asleep.

I

Understand, and forgive. It is what my mother taught me to do, poor patient gentle Christian soul, and the discipline she herself practised, and the reason she died in poverty, alone and neglected. The soles of her poor slippers, which I took out from under the bed and threw away so as not to shame her in front of the undertaker, were quite worn through by dutiful shuffling. Flip-flop. Slipper-slop. Drifting and dusting a life away.

There is a birth certificate in Somerset House – where all our lives and deaths are listed, and all our marriages and our divorces too – which describes me as Evans, Chloe, born to Evans, Gwyneth, *née* Jones, and Evans, David, housepainter, of 10 Albert Villas, Caledonian Road, London, N1, on February 20th, 1930. Evans, Chloe, female. There is as yet, no death certificate there for me, though looking through the files which now crowd those once seemingly endless Georgian rooms, I shocked myself by half expecting to find it there.

Sooner or later, of course, that certificate will be added.

Understand, and forgive, my mother said, and the effort has quite exhausted me. I could do with some anger to energize me, and bring me back to life again. But where can I find that anger? Who is to help me? My friends? I have been understanding and forgiving my friends, my female friends, for as long as I can remember.

Marjorie, Grace and me.

Such were Chloe's thoughts, before she slept.

- How much do we learn about Chloe from the reported monologue?
- What kind of background does she come from?
- What kind of character does she have?
- What other characters are introduced?
- What kind of themes are being established?
- How do you think the novel might develop after this opening chapter?

Some modern writers, like Virginia Woolf and James Joyce, wanted to go even further than the dramatic monologue. They wanted to suggest that the mind has many conversations going on within it – streams of memory, thought, feeling and association. To show this stream they even took out all form of punctuation. Strangely it is not difficult to read. Here, for example, are two short passages from James Joyce's *Ulysses*. The first passage, presenting the inner conversation of Leopold Bloom, uses conventional punctuation. The second, presenting the inner conversation of Mollie Bloom, uses no punctuation at all.

Leopold Bloom's Monologue

He crossed at Nassau street corner and stood before the window of Yeates and Son, pricing the field glasses. Or will I drop into old Harris's and have a chat with young Sinclair? Wellmannered fellow. Probably at his lunch. Must get those old glasses of mine set right. Goerz lenses, six guineas. Germans making their way everywhere. Sell on easy terms to capture trade. Undercutting. Might chance on a pair in the railway lost property office. Astonishing the things people leave behind them in trains and cloak rooms. What do they be thinking about? Women too. Incredible. Last year travelling to Ennis had to pick up that farmer's daughter's bag and hand it to her at Limerick junction. Unclaimed money too. There's a little watch up there on the roof of the bank to test those glasses by.

Mollie Bloom's Monologue

Yes because he never did a thing like that before as ask to get his breakfast in bed with a couple of eggs since the *City Arms* hotel when he used to be pretending to be laid up with a sick voice doing his highness to make himself interesting to that old faggot Mrs Riordan that he thought he had a great leg of and she never left us a farthing all for masses for herself and her soul greatest miser ever was actually afraid to lay out 4d for her methylated spirit telling me all her ailments she had too much old chat in her about politics and earthquakes and the end of the world let us have a bit of fun first God help the world if all the women were her sort down on bathingsuits and lownecks of course nobody wanted her wear I suppose she was pious because no man would look at her twice I hope Ill never be like her

- How easy do you find these passages to follow?
- Is Mollie's monologue more difficult than Leopold's?
- What is the point of taking out punctuation? Does it work?

In the following passage, which uses third-person narrative and dramatic monologue, Dorothy Richardson brings out Miriam's pleasure in having a room of her own in London at the age of 21.

Miriam's Room

She closed the door and stood just inside it looking at the room. It was smaller than her memory of it. When she had stood in the middle of the floor with Mrs Bailey, she had looked at nothing but Mrs Bailey, waiting for the moment to ask about the rent. Coming upstairs she had felt the room was hers and barely glanced at it when Mrs Bailey opened the door. From the moment of waiting on the stone steps outside the front door, everything had opened to the movement of her impulse. She was surprised now at her familiarity with the detail of the room . . . that idea of visiting places in dreams. It was something more than that . . . all the real part of your life has a real dream in it; some of the real dream part of you coming true. You know in advance when you are really following your life. These things are familiar because reality is here. Coming events cast *light*. It is like dropping everything and walking backwards to something you know is there. However far you go out, you come back . . . I am back now where I was before I began trying to do things like other people. I left home to get here. None of those things can touch me here . . .

A light had come in the dormer on the other side of the street. It remained unscreened. Watching carefully she could see only a dim figure moving amongst motionless shapes. No need to trouble about the blind. London could come freely in day and night through the unscreened happy little panes; light and darkness and darkness and light.

London, just outside all the time, coming in with the light, coming in with the darkness, always present in the depths of the air in the room.

The carpet is awful, faded and worn almost to bits. But it is right, in this room . . . This is the furnished room; one room. I have come to it. 'You could get a furnished room at about seven shillings rental.' The awful feeling, no tennis, no dancing, no house to move in, no society. The relief at first when Bennett found those people . . . maddening endless roads of little houses in the east wind . . . their kind way of giving more than they had undertaken, and smiling and waiting for smiles and dying all the time in some dark way without knowing it; filling the rooms and the piano and the fern on the serge table-cloth and the broken soap-dish in the bathroom until it was impossible to read or think or play because of them, the feeling of them stronger and stronger till there was nothing but crying over the trays of meals and wanting to scream.

The thought of the five turnings to the stations, all into long little roads looking alike and making you forget which was which and lose your way, was still full of pain . . . the *relief* of moving to Granville Place still a relief, though it felt a mistake from the first. Mrs Corrie's old teacher liking only certain sorts of people knew it was a mistake, with her peevish silky old face and her antique brooch. But it has been the beginning of London . . .

Following advice is certain to be wrong. When you don't follow advice there may be awful things. But they are not arranged beforehand. And when they come you do not know that they are awful until you have half got hold of something else. Then they change into something that has not been awful. Things that remain awful are in some way not finished. . . . Those women are awful. They will get more and more awful, still disliking and disapproving till they die. I shall not see them again . . . I will never again be at the mercy of such women or at all in the places where they are. That means keeping free of all groups. In groups sooner or later one of them appears, dead and sightless and bringing blindness and death . . . although they seem to like brightness and children and the young people they approve of. I run away from them because I must. They kill me. The thought of their death is awful. Even in heaven no one could explain anything to them, if they remain as they are. Wherever people advise you to go there is in the end one of those women . . .

When she turned out the gas the window spaces remained faintly alight with a soft light like moonlight. At the window she found a soft bluish radiance cast up from below upon the opposite walls and windows. It went up into the clear blue darkness of the sky.

When she lay down the bed smelt faintly of dust. The air about her head under the sharply sloping ceiling was still a little warm with the gas. It was full of her untrammelled thoughts. Her luggage was lying about, quite near. She thought of washing in the morning in the bright light on the other side of the room . . . leaves crowding all round the lattice and here and there a pink rose . . . *several pink roses* . . . the lovely air chilling the water . . . the basin quite up against the lattice . . . dew splashing off the rose bushes in the little garden almost dark with trellises and trees, crowding with Harriett through the little damp stiff gate, the sudden liney smell of Harriett's pinafore and the thought of Harriett in it, feeling the same, sudden bright sunshine, two shouts, great cornfields going up and up with a little track between them . . . up over Blewburton . . . *Whittenham Clumps*. Before I saw Whittenham Clumps I had always known them. But we saw them before we knew they were called Whittenham Clumps. It was a surprise to know anybody who had seen them and that they had a name.

St Pancras bells were clamouring in the rooms; rapid scales, beginning at the top, coming with a loud full thump on to the fourth note and finishing with a rush to the lowest which was hardly touched before the top note hung again in the air, sounding outdoors clean and clear while all the other notes still jangled together in her room. Nothing had changed. The night was like a moment added to the day; like years going backwards to the beginning; and in the brilliant sunshine the unchanging things began again, perfectly new. She leaped out of bed into the clamorous stillness and stood in the window rolling up the warm hair that felt like a shawl round her shoulders. A cup of tea and then the bus to Harriett's. A bus somewhere just out there beyond the morning stillness of the street. What an *adventure* to go out and take a bus without having to face anybody. They were all out there, away somewhere, the very thought and sight of them, disapproving and deploring her surroundings. She listened. There they were. There were their very voices, coming plaintive and reproachful with a held-in indignation, intonations

that she knew inside and out, coming on bells from somewhere beyond the squares – another church. She withdrew the coloured cover and set her spirit lamp on the inkstained table. Strong bright light was standing outside the window. The clamour of the bells had ceased. From far away down in the street a loud hoarse voice came thinly up. *'Referee–Lloyd's–Sunday Times–People–*pypa . . .' A front door opened with a loud crackle of paint. The voice dropped to speaking tones that echoed clearly down the street and came up clear and soft and confidential. *'Referee? Lloyd's?'* The door closed with a large firm wooden sound and the harsh voice went on down the street.

St Pancras bells burst forth again. Faintly interwoven with their bright headlong scale were the clear sweet delicate contralto of the more distant bells playing very swiftly and reproachfully a five-finger exercise in a minor key. That must be a very high-Anglican church; with light coming through painted windows on to carvings and decorations.

As she began on her solid slice of bread and butter, St Pancras bells stopped again. In the stillness she could hear the sound of her own munching. She stared at the surface of the table that held her plate and cup. It was like sitting up to the nursery table. 'How frightfully happy I am,' she thought with bent head. Happiness streamed along her arms and from her head.

Dorothy Richardson, *Pilgrimage* Vol. II

STREAM OF CONSCIOUSNESS

Neons

light me bright me match me cigarette me bright city turn on be loud tell everybody switch yes sing red pencil tick me to on centre mid town go go glow sky lit lines wire buzz me to see ring on me in neon on heady excite me thrill me hold me to tight rush rush be big loud go right through now leap nerve me beat drums loud louder fast run fast right now once go places all the time eat more restaurant flash me show me lively dance put lipstick on neons all colour zap me power lines shine letter light big n me blow me put high fast see me watch zing my string best bouncy tube glow in me get ready do it now don't wait hurry get it right first time do it once no again switch me on i travel fast light switch me on pink candy say words loudspeaker my microphone leap high as can big city centre city big very buildings whole wide world hot lights on stage line my eyes breathe deep all revved up fast car go fast car go fast good kill somebody dress to top fashion struct get them wiggle pink face daze me amaze me shine me neons on sweet buzz meter front room seat skip dance non stop favour-

ite flower colour allans sweets on river shine thrill me thrill me rise in a loop get up early do lots the more better fast faster lit light on me in such show glow me ania it's now don't wait hurry up top tip they clap they whistle stomp yell out aloud more on high want more and more fresh new dare do do new do now very it just here spot lit wear shiny glistony get tight tonight darling neon electric buy me eat sweets almonds go places every day get money work now just right dare do do new flash me up bow come out lit shine me coca cola i don't sleep seven up fun city pin ball parlour amusements ride sky mid night click throw me bright lines whirlwind wake up little susy break dark venture: fling adventure red bulbs around my lights stage mirror my name bright around and around light up found this does me out aloud each letter after neon thrill lights wonderful to wonderful stop my breath split thrill me delight move me collect thrills one be brave live now don't go back again have ones big thrills lights above red town break out fast do once twice glow shine me see me what's what glow colour in dark tyger put sugar gold eyes on bright lights lively now lively up fix me up lips dance all night loud band hot pepper bit me on the highway lights jewel see get to glow just do did it cinema lit flash sign best form top push you can see me now shake spout give me a thrill burst aureole spangles boots with spurs lips ruby glass red fluorescent lit light tubes shine me vinyl head on neon high city red fingernails look at me curve shine lines easy to see me show gas blow me light up shine up shape up pull my socks all up me neon can't miss spiv can't take my eyes curve arc shine me night best in dark stick me up stand out sparkling fresh hit triple whisky pink angle centre lights dance dancing can do anything switch me on zag zig sky glow bulb ready whole sky shine get on up

Ania Walwicz

A S S I G N M E N T S

MAKING AND PRESENTING

1 Choose a character and a situation from the grid below and write the inner conversation or dramatic monologue that might go on in the character's mind as he or she approaches the situation that you have chosen. It might help you if you re-read Leopold and Mollie Bloom's internal monologues before you start.

Character	Situation
A teenager	Suddenly faced by a large and hostile gang in a lonely place
A parent	Waiting for news from a doctor about a serious matter
An old man or woman	On hearing that he or she has won an immense amount of money
A 'down-and-out'	In the minutes before or immediately after a car accident

2 Here are some more situations to give you practice in writing dramatic monologues. Think of your own imaginary character being asked one of the following questions, and then write a short piece of monologue.

'Did you or did you not take the handbag from the table?'

'Do you really love me?'

'You won't grass on me, will you?'

'Do you take this woman/man to be your lawfully wedded wife/ husband?'

3 Work on one of the situations below to present the inner thoughts of the character concerned:

A 16-year-old preparing to go to a friend's late-night party . . .

A famous boxer walking into the ring . . .

A child in a dentist's waiting-room . . .

Someone, out of work for a long time, waiting to be interviewed for a job . . .

4 Look at the monologue of Mollie Bloom on page 157 and then experiment by writing for yourself a passage of internal thinking without any punctuation. It could perhaps take as its theme thoughts on the way to work or to school . . .

5 In small groups, record on cassette a selection of interior monologues. Give an introduction to the readings (saying why you have chosen them and where they have been taken from) and a brief commentary to each monologue.

6 Design your own cover for any stream-of-consciousness monologue. Try and bring out in the picture for the cover some of the main images in the writing.

RESEARCHING AND RESPONDING

1 Using the library and with the help of a dictionary of literary terms, do some research on stream-of-consciousness writing. Look up some of the work of the novelists James Joyce and Virginia Woolf. Prepare materials either for classroom discussion **or** for a display on stream-of-consciousness writing.

2 Write an account of the strengths and limitations of stream-of-consciousness writing, giving examples both from your own work and from that of any other author.

15 | THIRD-PERSON NARRATIVE

Here are your two main characters.

Here is your setting.

- How might the story begin?
- How might the plot develop?
- What might be the theme of the story?

Here is one possible opening.

Mrs Chevalier is ageing rapidly. Once she seemed tall and boasted a thin waist – but now, now, she is small and withered. She regularly hides her hair under a large silk scarf and hopes that no one will look too closely at the wrinkles under her blue eyes or the heavy furrows that line her brow.

Mr Chevalier also likes to wear something on his head. Generally, a large boater. He doesn't place it there to hide anything, but rather to show that he considers himself still young, still something of a sport, one of the boys.

Mr and Mrs Chevalier, after thirty-five years of marriage, still share one interest. The circus! They love circuses; they are in love with everything to do with the circus: with the clowns, with the animal tamers, with the trapeze artists, with the manager in his black top hat – even with the animals.

And so it was on 22nd February 1942, with little money, after a silly argument about growing old, they came by chance upon a circus in the side street of their own town.

'Look,' he said.

'Yes,' she said.

'At last!' he said.

'We must see it'.

'Whatever it costs'.

'Of course,' she said.

They crossed the road, not even noticing the traffic that roared past them on each side, and found themselves peering through the tiny cracks in the high wooden boards. They felt like small children again.

'Can you see?' he said.

''Course I can,' she said, laughing.

- How could this story be developed?
- How does the method of telling it differ from the methods of narration we have already considered?

'ONCE UPON A TIME THERE WAS...'

This way of telling a story remains the oldest and most common method of telling a story. It is called **third-person narration**. The author presents the story but remains invisible. The characters are 'out there'. We are introduced to them and learn about them as the narrative unfolds. In our childhood we all listened to stories which began, 'Once upon a time there was . . .'. That is third-person narrative.

Here is the opening of a traditional fairytale about a husband and wife which uses third-person narrative.

*T*he Fisherman and his Wife

 HERE was once a fisherman and his wife who lived together in a hovel by the sea-shore, and the fisherman went out every day with his hook and line to catch fish, and he angled and angled.

One day he was sitting with his rod and looking into the clear water, and he sat and sat.

At last down went the line to the bottom of the water, and when he drew it up he found a great flounder on the hook. And the flounder said to him,

'Fisherman, listen to me; let me go, I am not a real fish but an enchanted prince. What good shall I be to you if you land me? I shall not taste well; so put me back into the water again, and let me swim away.'

'Well,' said the fisherman, 'no need of so many words about the matter, as you can speak I had much rather let you swim away.'

Then he put him back into the clear water, and the flounder sank to the bottom, leaving a long streak of blood behind him. Then the fisherman got up and went home to his wife in their hovel.

'Well, husband,' said the wife, 'have you caught nothing to-day?'

'No,' said the man – 'that is, I did catch a flounder, but as he said he was an enchanted prince, I let him go again.'

'Then, did you wish for nothing?' said the wife.

'No,' said the man; 'what should I wish for?'

'Oh dear!' said the wife; 'and it is so dreadful always to live in this evil-smelling hovel; you might as well have wished for a little cottage; go again and call him; tell him we want a little cottage, I daresay he will give it us; go, and be quick.'

And when he went back, the sea was green and yellow, and not nearly so clear. So he stood and said,

> 'O man, O man! – if man you be
> Or flounder, flounder, in the sea –
> Such a tiresome wife I've got,
> For she wants what I do not.'

Then the flounder came swimming up, and said,

'Now then, what does she want?'

'Oh,' said the man, 'you know when I caught you my wife says I ought to have wished for something. She does not want to live any longer in the hovel, and would rather have a cottage.'

'Go home with you,' said the flounder, 'she has it already.'

So the man went home, and found, instead of the hovel, a little cottage, and his wife was sitting on a bench before the door. And she took him by the hand, and said to him,

'Come in and see if this is not a great improvement.'

So they went in, and there was a little house-place and a beautiful little bedroom, a kitchen and larder, with all sorts of furniture, and iron and brass ware of the very best. And at the back was a little yard with fowls and ducks, and a little garden full of green vegetables and fruit.

'Look,' said the wife, 'is not that nice?'

'Yes,' said the man, 'if this can only last we shall be very well contented.'

'We will see about that,' said the wife. And after a meal they went to bed.

So all went well for a week or fortnight, when the wife said,

'Look here, husband, the cottage is really too confined, and the yard and garden are so small.' . . .

Here is the opening of a modern novel, *The Bell,* about a wife and husband. It uses the same method, introducing the two main characters and telling us about them from a distance.

DORA GREENFIELD left her husband because she was afraid of him. She decided six months later to return to him for the same reason. The absent Paul, haunting her with letters and telephone bells and imagined footsteps on the stairs had begun to be the greater torment. Dora suffered from guilt, and with guilt came fear. She decided at last that the persecution of his presence was to be preferred to the persecution of his absence.

Dora was still very young, though she vaguely thought of herself as past her prime. She came of a lower middle-class London family. Her father had died when she was nine years old, and her mother, with whom she had never got on very well, had married again. When Dora was eighteen she entered the Slade school of art with a scholarship, and had been there two years when she encountered Paul. The rôle of an art student suited Dora. It was indeed the only rôle she had ever been able whole-heartedly to play. She had been an ugly and wretched schoolgirl. As a student she grew plump and peach-like and had a little pocket money of her own, which she spent on big multi-coloured skirts and jazz records and sandals. At that time, which although it was only three years ago now seemed unimaginably remote, she had been happy. Dora, who had so lately discovered in herself a talent for happiness, was the more dismayed to find that she could be happy neither with her husband nor without him.

Paul Greenfield, who was thirteen years older than his wife, was an art historian connected with the Courtauld Institute. He came of an old family of German bankers and had money of his own. He had been born in England and attended an English public school, and preferred not to remember the distinction of his ancestors. Although his assets were never idle, he did not speak of stocks and shares . . .

Iris Murdoch

- How do you imagine these stories will continue?
- Who is telling the story?
- What is the relationship of the person telling the story to the characters?

In most third-person narratives the author writes as though he or she knows everything about the characters. This has been called 'the omniscient author'. (The French novelist Flaubert compared such an author to God.) The author knows the feelings and thoughts of everyone, what has happened in the past (as Iris Murdoch knows about the past of Dora and Paul Greenfield), and what will happen in the future. The author stands back and presents the story rather like the unseen camera which makes the film.

The novelist Patricia Highsmith, in *Plotting and Writing Suspense Fiction*, has explained why she likes the device of third-person narration and why she uses it for most of her crime stories.

THE FIRST-PERSON SINGULAR is the most difficult form in which to write a novel; on this writers seem to be agreed, even if they agree on no other matter in regard to point of view. I have bogged down twice in first-person-singular books, so emphatically that I abandoned any idea of writing the books. I don't know what was the matter, except that I got sick and tired of writing the pronoun 'I', and I was plagued with an idiotic feeling that the person telling the story was sitting at a desk writing it. Fatal! Also, I have quite a bit of introspection in my heroes, and to write all this in the first person makes them sound like nasty schemers, which of course they are, but they seem less so if some all-knowing author is telling what is going on in their heads.

Perhaps because it is all round easier for me, I prefer the point of view of the main character, written in the third-person-singular, and I might add masculine, as I have a feeling which I suppose is quite unfounded that women are not so active as men, and not so daring. I realize that their activities need not be physical ones and that as motivating forces they may well be ahead of the men, but I tend to think of women as being pushed by people and circumstances instead of pushing, and more apt to say, 'I can't' than 'I will' or 'I'm going to.'

The very easiest point of view, I hardly dare to remark, might be that of a non-criminal person in a story in which he or she is pitted against the criminal. Obviously, the writer must identify with the person through whose eyes the story is being told, for it is that person's feelings, thoughts, and reactions that will be the lifeblood of the story. This is not the same as saying that this character will be the *action* of the story. I can easily imagine a suspense story told through the eyes of an old man or woman confined to a sickbed, merely an observer of what goes on. But even a suspense novel is, like all novels, an emotional thing; it is the five senses, plus the intellect which judges and makes decisions, that count and form the real book.

Suspense novelists are apt to choose the point of view of an active person – a man able to fight, run, and use a gun, if need be. This can also become boring both to readers and to the writer, if constantly repeated. It has crossed my mind to write a suspense book from the corpse's point of view. 'This is the corpse speaking.' And then he or she proceeds to tell the story preceding his or her death, the details of dying, death, and then what is going on afterward. Never mind asking how a corpse can do all this. In fiction, it is not always necessary to answer logical questions. But I am hardly original in this idea. It has been used by more than half a dozen crime novelists, according to critic Anthony Boucher, and he adds, 'It keeps recurring to people, always as a new and striking idea . . .'

- Why does Patricia Highsmith dislike first-person forms of narration?
- What form of telling does she prefer?
- Why does she choose a masculine main character for her stories?
- What does she regard as the 'easiest point of view' for telling a story?
- What is the most common viewpoint of suspense writers?
- What does Patricia Highsmith see as the danger of this method?
- What do you think she means by 'in fiction it is not always necessary to answer logical questions'? Do you agree?

THIRD-PERSON NARRATIVE WITH ONE MAIN VIEWPOINT

In some stories the author using the third person takes the reader into the narrative through one main character. Look, for example, at the following story where we are invited to experience the execution of Charles I through the viewpoint of an ordinary apprentice.

The Apprentice

29th January (or, as we should say, 10th February) 1649.

Charles I was executed on this day, upon a scaffold outside the second window on the north of Whitehall Banqueting hall, at four in the afternoon.

MEN WERE WELL into the working week; it was a Tuesday and apprentices were under the hard eyes of their masters throughout the City of London and in the rarer business places that elbowed the great palaces along the Strand. The sky was overcast and the air distastefully cold, nor did anything in the landscape seem colder than the dark band of the river under those colourless and lifeless January clouds.

Whether it were an illusion or a reality, one could have sworn that there was a sort of silence over the houses and on the families of the people; one could have sworn that men spoke in lower tones than was their custom, and that the streets were emptier. The trial and the sentence of the King had put all that great concourse of men into the very presence of Death.

The day wore on; the noise of the workmen could be heard at the scaffold by Whitehall; one hour was guessed at and then another; rumours and flat assertions were busy everywhere, especially among the young, and an apprentice to a harness-maker in the Water Lane, near Essex House, knew not what to believe. But he was determined to choose his moment and to slip away lest he should miss so great a sight. The tyranny of the army kept all the city in doubt all day long, and allowed no news; none the less, from before noon there had begun a little gathering of people in Whitehall, round the scaffold at which men were still giving the last strokes of the hammer. Somewhat after noon a horseshoe of cavalry assembled in their long cloaks and curious tall civilian hats; they stood ranked, with swords drawn, all round the platform. Their horses shifted uneasily in the cold.

The harness-maker's apprentice found his opportunity; his master was called to the door for an order from Arundel House, and the lad left his bench quickly, just as he was, without hat or coat, in the bitter weather, and darting through the side door ran down through the Water Gate and down its steps to the river. The tide was at the flood and his master's boat lay moored. He cast her off and pulled rapidly up the line of gardens, backing water when he came to the public stairs just beyond Whitehall. Here he quickly tied the painter and ran up breathless to Whitehall Gate, fearing he might have missed his great expectation. He was in ample time.

It was perhaps half-past three o'clock when he got through the gate and found himself in the press of people. Far off to the left, among the soldiery that lined the avenue from the park to the Mall, and so to St James's, a continuous roll of drums burdened the still air.

The crowd was not very large, but it filled the space from the gate to the scaffold and a little beyond, save where it was pressed outward by the ring of cavalry. It did not overflow into the wide spaces of the park, though these lay open to Whitehall, nor did it run up towards Charing Cross beyond the Banqueting Hall.

The apprentice was not so tall as the men about him; he strained and elbowed a little to see, and he was sworn at. He could make out the low scaffold, a large platform all draped in black, with iron staples, and a railing round it; it covered the last three blank windows of Whitehall, running from the central casement until it met the brick house at the north end of the stonework; there the brickwork beneath one of the windows had been taken out so as to give access through it from the floor within to the scaffold on the same level without; and whispers round told the apprentice, though he did not know how much to trust them, that it was through this hasty egress that the King would appear. Upon the scaffold itself stood a group of men, two of them masked, and one of the masked ones, of great stature and strong, leant upon the axe with his arms crossed upon the haft of it. A little block, barely raised above the floor of the platform, he could only see by leaping on tiptoe, catching it by glimpses between the heads of his neighbours or the shoulders of the cavalry guard; but he noticed in those glimpses how very low it was, and saw, ominous upon it, two staples driven as though to contain the struggler. Before it, so that one kneeling would have his face toward the palace and away from the crowd, was a broad footstool covered with red velvet, and making a startling patch upon all that expanse of black baize.

It was cold waiting; the motionless twigs of the small bare trees in the park made it seem colder still. The three-quarters struck in the new clock behind him upon Whitehall Gate, but as yet no one had appeared.

In a few moments, however, there was a movement in the crowd, heads turning to the right, and a corresponding backing of the mounted men to contain the first beginnings of a rush, for the commanders of the army feared, while they despised, the popular majority of London; and the wealthy merchants, the allies of the army, had not joined this common lot. This turning of faces towards the great blank stone wall of the palace was caused by a sound of many footsteps within. The only window not masked with stone, the middle window, was that upon which their gaze universally turned. They saw, passing it very rapidly, a group of men within; they were walking very sharply along the floor (which was here raised above the level of the window itself and cut the lower panes of it); they were hurrying towards the northern end of the great Banqueting Hall. It was but a moment's vision, and again they appeared in the open air through the broken brickwork at the far end of the stone façade.

For a moment the apprentice saw clearly the tall King, his face grown old, his pointed beard left full, his long features not moved. The great cloak that covered him, with the Great Star of the Garter upon the left shoulder, he drew off quickly and let fall into the hands of Herbert. He wore no hat; he stepped forward with precision towards the group of executioners, and a little murmur ran through the crowd.

The old bishop, moving his limbs with difficulty, but suppliant and attendant upon his friend, stood by in an agony. He helped the King to pull off his inner coat until he stood conspicuous in the sky-blue vest beneath it, and round his neck a ribbon and one ornament upon it, a George carved in onyx. This also he removed and gave to the bishop, while he took from his hands a little white silken cap and fixed it firmly upon his long and beautiful hair. From beneath the sky-blue of his garment, at the neck and at the wrists, appeared frills of exquisite linen and the adornment of lace. He stood for a few moments praying, then turned and spoke as though he were addressing them all. But the apprentice, though he held his breath, and strained to hear, as did all others about him, could catch no separate word, but only the general sound of the King's voice speaking. The movement of the horses, the occasional striking of a hoof upon the setts of the street, the distance, covered that voice. Next, Charles was saying something to the masked man, and a moment later he was kneeling upon the footstool. The apprentice saw him turn a moment and spread his arms out as an example of what he next should do; he bent him toward the block – it was too low; he lay at full length, and the crowd lifted and craned to see him in this posture.

The four heavy strokes of the hour struck and boomed in the silence. The hands of the lying figure were stretched out again, this time as a final signal, and right up in the air above them all the axe swung, white against the grey sky, flashed and fell.

In a moment the group upon the scaffold had closed round, a cloth was thrown, the body was raised, and among the hands stretched out to it were the eager and enfeebled hands of the bishop, trembling and still grasping the George.

A long moan or wail, very strange and dreadful, not very loud, rose from the people now that their tension was slackened by the accomplishment of the deed. And at once from the north and from the south, with such ceremony as is used to the conquered, the cavalry charged right through, hacking and dispersing these Londoners and driving them every way.

The apprentice dodged and ran, his head full of the tragedy and bewildered, his body in active fear of the horses that pursued flying packets of the crowd down the alley-ways of the offices and palace buildings.

He went off by a circuitous way to find, not his master's house after such an escapade, but his mother's, where she lived beyond St Martin's.

The dusk did not long tarry; as it gathered and turned to night small flakes of snow began to fall and lie upon the frozen ground.

Hilaire Belloc

- How much of this story is told through the viewpoint of the apprentice?
- How much of it is told by the author, outside the apprentice?
- Find examples in the story of when we see
  (a) what the apprentice saw, and
  (b) when we see other incidents that the author wants us to see.
- How would the story have us respond to the death of Charles I?
- In your view, how successful is the telling of this story?
- Why do you think the author has chosen third-person narrative to tell it?
- What might be other ways of telling the story?
- How might an author who supports the execution tell the story?

THIRD-PERSON NARRATIVE WITH CHANGING VIEWPOINTS

In other stories and in most novels the author using third-person narration takes the reader into a number of different characters. In this way we are able to move in and out of the differing viewpoints of the characters and to see why they behave as they do.

Look now at the story *Red Letter Day* by Joyce Cary.

Red Letter Day

The old man, the well-off uncle, arrived early to tea – it was the first of the month, his regular day. But just before his coming the young couple had themselves been invited to a party for that same afternoon – a 'good' party. They stood now in the hall wondering how it would be possible, even at this late hour, to escape from their guest.

'After all, any afternoon does for him,' said the wife, laying her hand on the drawing-room door.

'But, darling, do remember – this is quite a red letter day for the old boy, he gets out so seldom.'

'Exactly,' that's what I say, it's all the same to him when he comes.'

'It would be idiotic to offend him.'

'It would be idiotic to refuse the Goodwins – it's just luck our being asked at all, and if we refuse they'll never think of us again. They have such hundreds of friends already.'

'But it's four o'clock *now*. What excuse can we give? And you know how touchy and suspicious these old men are. They get so wrapped up in themselves. He'll see in half a second that you're putting him off and never forgive it. I shouldn't blame him. I shouldn't exactly enjoy it myself.'

They argued savagely, nose to nose, in furious whispers which sounded like the hissing of snakes roused from a summer nap in some warm garden heap.

In the drawing-room, sunk in the deepest armchair, the old man waited, gazing absently through the open glass door at a freshly watered lawn. His ears were good except in a crowd – he heard the whispering but gave it no attention. It was none of his business, and he was too old and tired to waste time on other people's business. So he continued to look at the garden. And it seemed to him now that the smell of the wet grass was coming to him – and perhaps a whiff of sweet-briar from the hedge. His wide thin nostrils twitched. Yes, no doubt of it. And a faint but distinct current of pleasure vibrated in his old dry nerves. How nice that was. He'd forgotten how nice – something he missed in that flat of his. How easy it was to lose touch with simple ordinary enjoyments, and how precious they were.

He had hesitated about his visit today – his nurse had been all against it, she had kept on reminding him of his bad nights, and that last attack which had so nearly finished him – she was certainly an excellent woman, most devoted and reliable. But he had insisted that he had family duties. He was expected. He must go. How glad he was now that he had taken the trouble and the risk.

Suddenly his grand-niece, aged six, dashed into the room from the garden. She was carrying an immense doll of black stuff with a round face, goggle-eyes made of pearl shirt buttons, and enormous teeth. At the sight of the visitor, she stopped abruptly, stared and blushed. She was startled by his thin, yellow cheeks and deep wrinkles.

The old man moved only his large pale eyes towards the child. He could not afford to waste energy.

At last, aware of the child's silence and supposing her embarrassed, he murmured, 'Is that your best dolly?' But the question expected no answer, the glance had that appreciation seen only in the very young and the very old whose pleasure is unmixed with reflection, without any overtone of idea. The old man did not seek even to placate the child, he enjoyed her as he had enjoyed the garden, that whiff of grass and briar brought to him by an accident of time and place.

The child ignored a remark which, as she perceived at once, was merely polite. She put the doll behind her back, and walked slowly up to the old man, staring at him with an intent piercing curiosity. Then she said, 'Are you *very* old?'

He looked at her with the permanently raised eyebrows of his age, and echoed placidly: 'Very old.'

'Very, very old?'

'Very, very old.'

'You're going to die soon.'

'Yes, I suppose so.' His eyes, bright with pleasure in spite of the eyebrows fixed in their record of old griefs, gazed at her with absent-minded wonder. He was thinking 'Yes, how charming they are, children – how nice she is.'

'You only have two years more.'

'Two years?'

'That's what it says in the almanack.'

'Two years.' He repeated the phrase as a child turns over words without troubling to consider them. 'The almanack.'

'Yes, Mummy's almanack.'

'Your mother's almanack,' he murmured. It did not interest him to discover in this way that his niece had been looking into *Whitaker* to calculate his expectation of life. He had no time for such boring considerations. He said dreamily, as if the words were prompted by some part of his brain which, being set in motion, continued in the same direction quite apart from his thoughts, 'And what is dolly's name?'

The whispering outside had come to an end. The young couple entered the room from the side door behind his chair. They both had that air of hardly restrained impatience which belongs to young healthy creatures everywhere: colts, kittens; the girl, buxom and a little too rosy, the man lean, with a soft thick mouth. Their bodies seemed to bring with them that atmosphere of a snug private room, over-curtained and rather stuffy, which belongs to happily married couples in the youth of their pleasure.

And like others who enjoy much happiness, they hated the least interruption of it. They hated and resented this quarrel. As they came towards the old man, their faces expressed the highest degree of exasperation.

When he turned his eyes towards them and made a gesture as if to get up, both smiled the same smile, one that did not even affect pleasure but only politeness.

'Don't, don't get up,' the woman cried, and kissed his forehead, gently pushing him back into the chair. 'Uncle dear, it's such a nuisance –' and she began an elaborate story, plainly a construction of lies, about a telephone call from a friend who was suddenly taken ill. But if he would not mind amusing himself for half an hour – an hour at the very most – they would hurry back. Or perhaps he would rather come another day when they would be free to enjoy his visit.

The old man seemed to reflect, and said, 'Thank you.' Then, after another pause, as if for deeper reflection, he added, 'I'm afraid I'm rather early, aren't I?'

The couple exchanged furious glances. What enraged them was that he did not trouble even to examine their

hint. He was too vague, too gaga. The woman tried again – 'The only thing that worries us, Uncle, is that we might be kept – it's always so uncertain, when people are ill.'

'Don't trouble about me, my dear – I'll be quite all right.'

They looked inquiry at each other. The wife pushed out her cupid's mouth, too small for her round cheeks, and half closed her eyes as if to say, 'You see – I told you he was going to spoil everything.' The husband frowned from her to the uncle, unable to decide which was the chief cause of his enormous disgust.

'Two years,' the little girl exclaimed loudly. She had never taken her eyes off the visitor. 'In two years you'll be dead.' She gave a little skip. 'In two years.'

The couple were horrified. They looked blank, senseless, shocked – as if someone had let off a bomb and blown out all the windows. The husband, very red, said in a voice of foolish surprise: 'Really – that's hardly – ah . . .'

The young woman took the child by the arm and said, 'That's enough, Susan. Come, it's time for you to go upstairs.' At the same moment she gave the uncle a glance full of guilty anger, which meant, 'Yes, I'm wicked, but it's all your fault.'

Susan jerked away from her mother and said angrily, 'No, I don't want to –' The old man slowly unfolded his long, thin arm towards her as if in sympathy. He murmured, 'I haven't seen the dolly, have I?'

The little girl gazed at him. She was still fascinated by the idea of his age. She said, 'Two years, and then you'll be dead.'

'Susan, be quiet.'

The little girl's eyelids flickered. She was feeling what death meant. Suddenly she went to her mother and put her arms round her skirts, as if for protection. The old man's eyebrows rose a little more; a colour, almost youthful, came into his cheeks, and he smiled. He was charmed by this picture, so spontaneous, so unexpected. He thought, 'How pretty that is. How nice they are.'

Joyce Cary

This story depends on our moving between the characters so that we see them now on the inside, now on the outside.

■ Find those places in the story where we are inside the viewpoint of each character.

■ What would you say was the main theme of the story?

ASSIGNMENTS

MAKING AND PRESENTING

1. Write your own story in the third person, based on the photograph on page 162.

2. There might be other ways of presenting the story of the execution of Charles I. How would an author who actually supported the execution present the story? Re-write the story as a third-person narrative presenting the view of one of the King's enemies.

3. Describe an execution, not necessarily that of Charles I, in first-person or third-person narrative, from the point of view of a supporter **and** of an opponent. When it is complete, record it on cassette.

4. Write your own suspense story in the third person from the corpse's point of view. (Before starting the story, re-read Patricia Highsmith's comments on page 166.)

5. Tell the story *Red Letter Day* from the child's point of view, in first-person narrative. If you think that the re-telling is successful, go on to make a tape-recording of it.

RESEARCHING AND RESPONDING

1. Read the story *The Apprentice* once more and try to explain why the author chose third-person narrative as the way of telling it. It will help you to try to work out how the author wants us to respond to the story. Are we meant to feel pleased or sorry that Charles I is being executed? It might help you here to see how much of the story is told through the viewpoint of the apprentice and how much is told by the author, outside the apprentice.
   Find examples in the story when
   (a) we see what the apprentice saw,
   (b) we are shown other incidents that the author wants us to see.
   How successfully has the author presented this story as far as you as a reader are concerned? Jot down your responses and write an account of how the story works.

2. *Red Letter Day* has a more complex narrative style. Although it is still a third-person narrative, the story depends for its effect on the reader moving between the characters, so that we see them now on the outside, now on the inside.
   Find the places where we are taken 'inside' each character. Discuss your findings with a partner. How easy was it at first to understand what was going on? Do you think that this technique of moving inside and

outside characters gives an author more scope in writing a story? What has been gained here by doing it this way? What, for example, is the main theme of the story? Write your own critical study.

3 Using the library, see if you can find out more about the life and writing of **either** Joyce Cary **or** Iris Murdoch.

4 Make a list of a number of stories and novels that you have read. Divide them according to whether they have used first-person or third-person narrative. Make notes on how the stories have been constructed and which ones you prefer. Write an account of your discoveries about the form of the stories and defend your preferences. This work could be developed into a classroom display.

■ What kind of story would you expect from these titles and covers?

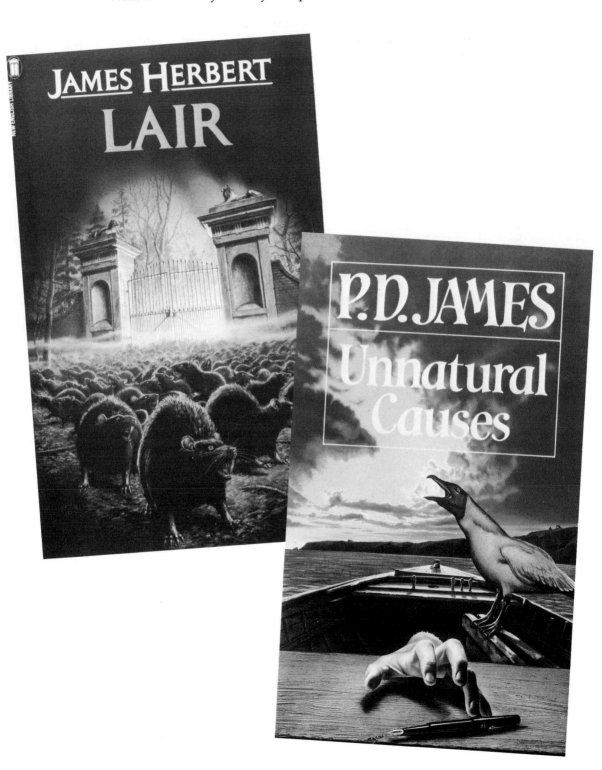

Christina Compson, the beautiful, spirited woman who inherited Henzel's glasshouse, has always flouted convention: running the business herself, bearing a child out of wedlock and then marrying one of her gaffers. And the mistakes of the past, and the long-running, bitter feud with the rival side of the Henzel family, inevitably overshadow the lives of Christina's and Joe's children.

The two eldest, Emily and Paul, raised as brother and sister, are drawn closer together when they learn of their own illegitimacy. As children they are inseparable; as adults only Paul's love of glass could part them. Paul finds that he has inherited his natural father's delicate talent as an engraver, and determines to go to France – home of some of the best glassmakers, and of his family. But Emily is fiercely opposed to the idea; she knows that if he goes, she will lose her dearest friend, the man she has grown to love more than as a brother . . .

Also in The Glassmakers Saga by Donna Baker from Headline
CRYSTAL

HEADLINE
Fiction/Saga

The Glassmakers Saga

BLACK CAMEO

DONNA BAKER

HEADLINE

BLACK CAMEO

DONNA BAKER

There are many different kinds of fiction. Here are some of them:

Western	Crime
Humour	War
Horror	Fantasy
Supernatural	Science Fiction
Adventure	

- Can you add to the list?
- Often we can tell the kind of narrative merely from the cover and from the title. What kind of story would you expect from the following titles? Group them according to the kind of **genre** you think they belong to:

Coral Island	*The Case of Dr A.D. Hunter*
The Demon Lover	*The Document in the Case*
The Arabian Nights	*History of Miss Betsy*
Women in Love	*Thoughtless*
War and Peace	*The Time Machine*
Typhoon	*Crime and Punishment*
The French Lieutenant's	*Sons and Lovers*
Woman	*A Tale of Two Cities*
Pride and Prejudice	*Frankenstein*
Masterman Ready	*Cold Blood*
A Jealous Ghost	*Mad Monkton*

Consider now the following seven openings of some novels. What kind of story would you expect? Can you say why?

AS GREGOR SAMSA awoke one morning from a troubled dream, he found himself changed in his bed to some monstrous kind of vermin.

He lay on his back, which was as hard as armour-plate, and, raising his head a little, he could see the arch of his great brown belly, divided by bowed corrugations. The bed-cover was slipping helplessly off the summit of the curve, and Gregor's legs, pitiably thin compared with their former size, fluttered helplessly before his eyes.

'What has happened?' he thought. It was no dream.

Franz Kafka, *The Metamorphosis*

IN SOME NATURES there are no half-tones; nothing but raw primary colours. John Bodman was a man who was always at one extreme or the other. This probably would have mattered little had he not married a wife whose nature was an exact duplicate of his own.

Robert Barr, *An Alpine Divorce*

TRUE! – nervous, – very, very dreadfully nervous I had been and am! But why *will* you say that I am mad? The disease had sharpened my senses – not destroyed – not dulled them. Above all was the sense of hearing acute. I heard all things in the heaven and in the earth. I heard many things in hell. How, then, am I mad? Hearken! and observe how healthily – how calmly I can tell you the whole story.

It is impossible to tell how first the idea entered my brain, but once conceived, it haunted me day and night. Object there was none. Passion there was none. I loved the old man.

Edgar Allan Poe, *The Tell-tale Heart*

IT IS a truth universally acknowledged, that a single man in possession of a good fortune must be in want of a wife.

Jane Austen, *Pride and Prejudice*

NOT that horse, mister. Not that big slab-sided brute. Take any or all of the rest, I'm selling the whole string. But not that one. By rights I should. He's no damn good to me. The best horse either one of us'll likely ever see and he's no damn good to me. Or me to him. But I'll not sell him . . .

Try something, mister. Speak to him. The name's Mark . . . There. See how his ears came up? See how he swung to check you and what you were doing? The way any horse would. Any horse that likes living and knows his name. But did you notice how he wouldn't look at me? Used to perk those ears and swing that head whenever he heard my voice. Not any more. Knows I'm talking about him right now and won't look at me. Almost ten months it is and he still won't look at me . . .

Jack Schaefer, *That Mark Horse*

THE BODIES were discovered at eight forty-five on the morning of Wednesday 18 September by Miss Emily Wharton, a 65-year-old spinster of the parish of St Matthew's in Paddington, London, and Darren Wilkes, aged 10, of no particular parish as far as he knew or cared. This unlikely pair of companions had left Miss Wharton's flat in Crowhurst Gardens just before half past eight to walk the half-mile stretch of the Grand Union Canal to St Matthew's church. Here Miss Wharton, as was her custom each Wednesday and Friday, would weed out the dead flowers from the vase in front of the statue of the Virgin, scrape the wax and candle stubs from the brass holders, dust the two rows of chairs in the Lady Chapel, which would be adequate for the small congregation expected at that morning's early Mass, and make everything ready for the arrival at nine twenty of Father Barnes.

P. D. James, *A Taste for Death*

CALL me Ishmael. Some years ago — never mind how long precisely — having little or no money in my purse, and nothing particular to interest me on shore, I thought I would sail about a little and see the watery part of the world. It is a way I have of driving off the spleen, and regulating the circulation. Whenever I find myself growing grim about the mouth; whenever it is damp, drizzly November in my soul; whenever I find myself involuntarily pausing before coffin ware-houses, and bringing up the rear of every funeral I meet; and especially whenever my hypos get such an upper hand of me, that it requires a strong moral principle to prevent me from deliberately stepping into the street, and methodically knocking people's hats off — then, I account it high time to get to sea as soon as I can. This is my substitute for pistol and ball. With a philosophical flourish Cato throws himself upon his sword; I quietly take to the ship. There is nothing surprising in this. If they but knew it, almost all men in their degree, some time or other, cherish very nearly the same feelings towards the ocean with me.

Herman Melville, *Moby Dick*

All the different genres merit our interest and study, but here we concentrate our attention on one popular genre: science fiction, or SF.

- How would you describe science fiction?
- What are its main concerns?
- When and where would you expect the action to take place?
- What kind of characters will be developed?
- What will be the main themes?

  Make your own list of SF titles: from novels, stories, films, television and comics.

- Which of these do you regard as the best?
- What makes for good science fiction?

Science fiction is often considered a modern genre, but in many ways it is a very old one. Whenever authors have placed their plots in the future and wondered what people might be like in different conditions, they have structured their work in the manner of SF. They have imagined another world in future time and explored its nature. As early as A.D.150 an author called Lucian wrote a story called *True History* in which his hero visited the sun and moon and took part in interplanetary warfare. It all sounds very modern! To take another example, Mary Shelley wrote science fiction in 1816. In the Preface to her novel *Frankenstein* she tells the reader how the story started, partly in some conversations about the re-animation of corpses, and partly in her imagination as she lay in bed.

THEY talked of the experiments of Dr Darwin (I speak not of what the doctor really did or said that he did, but, as more to my purpose, of what was then spoken of as having been done by him), who preserved a piece of vermicelli in a glass case till by some extraordinary means it began to move with voluntary motion. Not thus, after all, would life be given. Perhaps a corpse would be reanimated; galvanism had given token of such things: perhaps the component parts of a creature might be manufactured, brought together, and endued with vital warmth.

Night waned upon this talk, and even the witching hour had gone by before we retired to rest. When I placed my head on my pillow, I did not sleep, nor could I be said to think. My imagination, unbidden, possessed and guided me, gifting the successive images that arose in my mind with a vividness far beyond the usual bounds of reverie. I saw – with shut eyes, but acute mental vision – I saw the pale student of unhallowed arts kneeling beside the thing he had put together. I saw the hideous phantasm of a man stretched out, and then, on the working of some powerful engine, show signs of life and stir with an uneasy, half-vital motion. Frightful must it be, for supremely frightful would be the effect of any human endeavour to mock the stupendous mechanism of the Creator of the world. His success would terrify the artist; he would rush away from his odious handi-work, horror-stricken. He would hope that, left to itself, the slight spark of life which he had communi-cated would fade, that this thing which had received such imperfect animation would subside into dead matter, and he might sleep in the belief that the silence of the grave would quench forever the tran-sient existence of the hideous corpse which he had looked upon as the cradle of life. He sleeps; but he is awakened; he opens his eyes; behold, the horrid thing stands at his bedside, opening his curtains and look-ing on him with yellow, watery, but speculative eyes.

I opened mine in terror.

The story, depending on the relationship between the author's imagination and the possibilities of technology, is one that we could well classify as science fiction, although Mary Shelley called it a ghost story.

The genre of science fiction became popular at the beginning of the 20th century with the novels of Jules Verne and H.G. Wells, and is now one of the most popular forms of fiction (with romance and crime).

A recent account of the genre has argued that SF has changed since the 1920s in a number of important ways.

IN THE 1920s and 1930s science fiction dealt primarily with the exploits of the individual or adventurer, often in battle for the existence of mankind, against inimical inhabitants of other worlds, and the background was dimly seen. In the 1940s and 1950s, it dealt chiefly with the scientific aspect of the background, with the foreground serving only as the immediate excuse for the story. In the 1960s, it deals with all aspects of the background, with the total society of the future; the scientific content merely accounts for differences in detail from our own day. It may be that science fiction, as such, is therefore dying; or, rather, that all fiction is becoming science fiction. As scientific advance becomes more rapid, as it fills life more completely, it will be difficult to write any significant work of fiction set in the present that does not take science into its account. Thus, while the earlier sorts survive in magazines and TV serials, the best science fiction and the best general fiction tend to merge.

A Dictionary of Literary Terms

'The best science fiction and the best general fiction tend to merge.'

■ What do you think is meant by this? Do you agree?

■ Does this mean that it is now difficult to isolate science fiction from other genres?

Here is a story written by a journalist responding to world news: Russia and the US discussing the withdrawal of all medium-range missiles. It moves quickly into science fiction. The last chapter, Chapter Twelve, has not been included. It is left for you to conclude the narrative.

MILES KINGTON

Russia and the US discussed the withdrawal of all medium-range insects

(YESTERDAY we brought you the first half of a new thriller, When We are Gone. Story so far. America and Russia are making secret joint plans, in case a nuclear war wipes out mankind, to ease the succession of the next top species. Unfortunately, Russia favours ants and America supports cockroaches. Who will win? Now read on.)

Chapter Seven

"I'm not a scientist," said the new young President of the USA, "But as I understand it, the position is this, and correct me if I'm wrong. We are developing a strain of super-cockroach and the Russians are developing a strain of super-ant, to take over after the war."

"Yes and no," said the scientist. "We are also developing our cockroach to attack and destroy ants. Unfortunately, our spies tell us that the Russians are working on a cockroach-eating ant."

"What happens if one of these creatures breaks out and takes over the world *before* we have a nuclear war?"

The scientist hesitated.

"It's difficult to see inside an insect's mind, Sir, but all the information we have indicates that ants think they are already the top species. Roaches, too. Of course, there may be some other species entirely different which really is the most likely to take over."

Unnoticed by either scientist or President, down on the carpet, a small spider nodded to himself and ran off.

Chapter Eight

By the second year of his presidency, America was spending 10 per cent of its defence budget on the cock-roach programme, and public rumours about the super-roach were rife. What the spiders thought is not known.

"I've seen these roaches, Sir," said the Defence Secretary, "and boy, are they huge. They are frightening. They scare me rigid."

"Do they scare ants?"

"In our tests they do, yes. But we can't get hold of any Russian ants to test. Now, if you could let me have a few billion dollars to capture some Russian ants . . ."

Chapter Nine

"By the way, do your cockroaches scare dolphins?" asked the President.

"Not to my knowledge," said the Secretary for Defence. "We think the battle for domination should be fought on land. Why?"

"Because our intelligence tells us that the Japanese are developing a super-dolphin in secret, for world domination after the next war."

Chapter Ten

In 1994, escalation of species development was getting so out of hand that a test ban treaty was proposed. The Americans and Russians met at Geneva to discuss the end of underground testing of ants and cockroaches, and a possible withdrawal of all medium-range insects. The talks were indecisive, and were hailed as a breakthrough.

The spiders were not invited, but they attended anyway. What they thought is not known, and they issued no communique.

Chapter Eleven

Halfway through his second term, the scientist came to see the President again.

"Bad news, Sir. A whole bunch of super-roaches has broken out of the test grounds in Nevada, gone on the rampage, then gone to ground."

"Destroy them."

"Can't, Sir. We've bred them to be indestructible. Even nuking them wouldn't help. And I don't think the public would stand for a nuclear attack on a bunch of insects. There's only one thing . . ."

"Uh huh?"

"The Russians have been training their ants to defeat cockroaches. Why don't we ask for their help? Fly some of their super-ants over to deal with our super-roaches?"

Down at floor level, a spider permitted himself a small smile.

Chapter Twelve

Science fiction has used all the devices of the traditional novel. Here, for example, are the openings to two SF stories using the device of the journal.

progris riport 1 – martch 5 1965

Dr Strauss says I shud rite down what I think and evrey thing that happins to me from now on. I dont know why but he says its importint so they will see if they will use me. I hope they use me. Miss Kinnian says maybe they can make me smart. I want to be smart. My name is Charlie Gordon. I am 37 years old and 2 weeks ago was my birthday. I have nuthing more to rite now so I will close for today.

progris riport 2 – martch 6

I had a test today. I think I faled it. and I think that maybe now they wont use me. What happind is a nice young man was in the room and he had some white cards with ink spillled all over them. He sed Charlie what do you see on this card. I was very skared even tho I had my rabits foot in my pockit because when I was a kid I always faled tests in school and I spilled ink to.

I told him I saw a inkblot. He said yes and it made me feel good. I thot that was all but when I got up to go he stopped me. He said now sit down Charlie we are not thru yet. Then I dont remember so good but he wantid me to say what was in the ink. I dint see nuthing in the ink but he said there was picturs there other pepul saw some picturs. I cudnt see any picturs. I reely tryed to see. I held the card close up and then far away. Then I said if I had my glases I coud see better I usally only ware my glases in the movies or TV but I said they are in the closit in the hall. I got them. Then I said let me see that card agen I bet Ill find it now.

I tryed hard but I still coudnt find the picturs I only saw the ink. I told him maybe I need new glases. He rote something down on a paper and I got skared of faling the test. I told him it was a very nice inkblot with littel points all around the eges. He looked very sad so that wasnt it. I said please let me try agen. Ill get it in a few minits becaus Im not so fast sometimes. Im a slow reeder too in Miss Kinnians class for slow adults but Im trying very hard.

He gave me a chance with another card that had 2 kinds of ink spilled on it red and blue.

He was very nice and talked slow like Miss Kinnian does and he explaned it to me that it was a *raw shok.* He said pepul see things in the ink. I said show me where. He said think. I told him I think a inkblot but that wasnt rite eather. He said what does it remind you – pretend somthing. I closd my eyes for a long time to pretend. I told him I pretend a fowntan pen with ink leeking all over a table cloth. Then he got up and went out.

I dont think I passd the *raw shok* test.

progris report 3 – martch 7

Dr Strauss and Dr Nemur say it dont matter about the inkblots. I told them I dint spill the ink on the cards and I couldnt see anything in the ink. They said that maybe they will still use me. I said Miss Kinnian never gave me tests like that one only spelling and reading. They said Miss Kinnian told that I was her bestist pupil in the adult nite school becaus I tryed the hardist and I reely wantid to lern. They said how come you went to the adult nite scool all by yourself Charlie. How did you find it. I said I askd pepul and sumbody told me where I shud go to lern to read and spell good. They said why did you want to. I told them becaus all my life I wanted to be smart and not dumb. But its very hard to be smart. They said you know it will probly be tempirery. I said yes. Miss Kinnian told me. I dont care if it herts.

Later I had more crazy tests today.

Daniel Keyes, *Flowers for Algernon*

30 August

Dr Nades recommends that I keep a diary of my work. She says that if you keep it carefully, when you reread it you can remind yourself of observations you made, notice errors and learn from them, and observe progress in or deviations from positive thinking, and so keep correcting the course of your work by a feedback process.

I promise to write in this notebook every night, and reread it at the end of each week.

I wish I had done it while I was an assistant, but it is even more important now that I have patients of my own.

As of yesterday I have six patients, a full load for a scopist, but four of them are the autistic children I have been working with all year for Dr Nades's study for the Nat'l Psych. Bureau (my notes on them are in the cli psy files). The other two are new admissions:

Ana Jest, 46, bakery packager, md., no children, diag. depression, referral from city police (suicide attempt).

Flores Sorde, 36, Engineer, unmd., no diag., referral from TRTU (Psychopathic behaviour – Violent).

Dr Nades says it is important that I write things down each night just as they occurred to me at work: it is the spontaneity that is most informative in self-examination (just as in autopsychoscopy). She says it is better to write it, not dictate onto tape, and keep it quite private, so that I won't be self-conscious. It is hard. I never wrote anything that was private before. I keep feeling as if I was really writing it for Dr Nades! Perhaps if the diary is useful I can show her some of it, later, and get her advice.

My guess is that Ana Jest is in menopausal depression and hormone therapy will be sufficient. There! Now let's see how bad a prognostician I am.

Will work with both patients under scope tomorrow. It is exciting to have my own patients, I am impatient to begin. Though of course teamwork was very educational.

31 August

Half-hour scope session with Ana J. at 8:00. Analyzed scope material, 11:00–17:00. N.B.: Adjust right-brain pickup next session! Weak visual Concrete. Very little aural, weak sensory, erratic body image. Will get lab analyses tomorrow of hormone balance.

Ursula Le Guin, *The Diary of the Rose*

- What can you tell about the characters from their diary entries?
- What do you notice about the language being used?
- What can you tell about the setting?
- How do you imagine the plot will develop?
- What are the possible advantages of this method of narration for SF?

Here are two complete science fiction stories.

The Fun They Had

Margie even wrote about it that night in her diary. On the page headed May 17, 2155, she wrote, 'Today Tommy found a real book!'

It was a very old book. Margie's grandfather once said that when he was a little boy *his* grandfather told him that there was a time when all stories were printed on paper.

They turned the pages, which were yellow and crinkly, and it was awfully funny to read words that stood still instead of moving the way they were supposed to – on a screen, you know. And then, when they turned back to the page before, it had the same words on it that it had had when they read it the first time.

'Gee,' said Tommy, 'what a waste. When you're through with the book, you just throw it away, I guess. Our television screen must have had a million books on it and it's good for plenty more. I wouldn't throw *it* away.'

'Same with mine,' said Margie. She was eleven and hadn't seen as many telebooks as Tommy had. He was thirteen.

She said, 'Where did you find it?'

'In my house.' He pointed without looking, because he was busy reading. 'In the attic.'

'What's it about?'

'School.'

Margie was scornful. 'School? What's there to write about school? I hate school.' Margie always hated school, but now she hated it more than ever. The mechanical teacher had been giving her test after test in geography and she had been doing it worse and worse

until her mother had shaken her head sorrowfully and sent for the County Inspector.

He was a round little man with a red face and a whole box of tools with dials and wires. He smiled at her and gave her an apple, then took the teacher apart. Margie had hoped he wouldn't know how to put it together again, but he knew how all right and after an hour or so, there it was again, large and black and ugly with a big screen on which all lessons were shown and the questions were asked. That wasn't so bad. The part she hated most was the slot where she had to put homework and test papers. She always had to write them out in a punch code they made her learn when she was six years old, and the mechanical teacher calculated the mark in no time.

The Inspector had smiled after he had finished and patted her head. He said to her mother, 'It's not the little girl's fault, Mrs Jones. I think the geography sector was geared a little too quick. These things happen sometimes. I've slowed it up to an average ten-year level. Actually, the overall pattern of her progress is quite satisfactory.' And he patted Margie's head again.

Margie was disappointed. She had been hoping they would take the teacher away altogether. They had once taken Tommy's teacher away for nearly a month because the history sector had blanked out completely.

So she said to Tommy, 'Why would anyone write about school?'

Tommy looked at her with very superior eyes. 'Because it's not our kind of school, stupid. This is the old kind of school that they had hundreds and hundreds of years ago.' He added loftily, pronouncing the word carefully, 'Centuries ago.'

Margie was hurt. 'Well, I don't know what kind of school they had all that time ago.' She read the book over his shoulder for a while, then said, 'Anyway, they had a teacher.'

'Sure they had a teacher, but it wasn't a *regular* teacher. It was a man.'

'A man? How could a man be a teacher?'

'Well, he just told the boys and girls things and gave them homework and asked them questions.'

'A man isn't smart enough.'

'Sure he is. My father knows as much as my teacher.'

'He can't. A man can't know as much as a teacher.'

'He knows almost as much I betcha.'

Margie wasn't prepared to dispute that. She said, 'I wouldn't want a strange man in my house to teach me.'

Tommy screamed with laughter. 'You don't know much, Margie. The teachers didn't live in the house. They had a special building and all the kids went there.'

'And all the kids learned the same thing?'

'Sure, if they were the same age.'

'But my mother says a teacher has to be adjusted to fit the mind of each boy and girl it teaches and that each kid has to be taught differently.'

'Just the same they didn't do it that way then. If you don't like it, you don't have to read the book.'

'I didn't say I didn't like it,' Margie said quickly. She wanted to read about those funny schools.

They weren't even half finished when Margie's mother called, 'Margie! School!'

Margie looked up. 'Not yet, mamma.'

'Now,' said Mrs Jones. 'And it's probably time for Tommy, too.'

Margie said to Tommy, 'Can I read the book some more with you after school?'

'Maybe,' he said nonchalantly. He walked away whistling, the dusty old book tucked beneath his arm.

Margie went into the schoolroom. It was right next to her bedroom, and the mechanical teacher was on and waiting for her. It was always on at the same time every day except Saturday and Sunday, because her mother said little girls learned better if they learned at regular hours.

The screen was lit up, and it said: 'Today's arithmetic lesson is on the addition of proper fractions. Please insert yesterday's homework in the proper slot.'

Margie did so with a sigh. She was thinking about the old schools they had when her grandfather's grandfather was a little boy. All the kids from the whole neighbourhood came, laughing and shouting in the school yard, sitting together in the schoolroom, going home together at the end of the day. They learned the same things so they could help one another on the homework and talk about it.

And the teachers were people.

The mechanical teacher was flashing on the screen: 'When we add the fractions ½ and ¼ –'

Margie was thinking about how the kids must have loved it in the old days. She was thinking about the fun they had.

Isaac Asimov

The Pedestrian

To enter out into that silence that was the city at eight o'clock on a misty evening in November, to put your feet upon that buckling concrete walk, to step over grassy seams and make your way, hands in pockets, through the silences, that was what Mr Leonard Mead most dearly loved to do. He would stand upon the corner of an intersection and peer down long moonlit avenues of side-walk in four directions, deciding which way to go, but it really made no difference; he was alone in this world of AD 2052, or as good as alone, and with a final decision made, a path selected, he would stride off, sending patterns of frosty air before him like the smoke of a cigar.

Sometimes he would walk for hours and miles and return only at midnight to his house. And on his way he would see the cottages and homes with their dark windows, and it was not unlike walking through a graveyard where only the faintest glimmers of firefly light appeared in flickers behind the windows. Sudden grey phantoms seemed to manifest upon inner room walls where a curtain was still undrawn against the night, or there were whisperings and murmurs where a window in a tomb-like building was still open.

Mr Leonard Mead would pause, cock his head, listen, look, and march on, his feet making no noise on the lumpy walk. For long ago he had wisely changed to sneakers when strolling at night, because the dogs in intermittent squads would parallel his journey with barkings if he wore hard heels, and lights might click on and faces appear and an entire street would be startled by the passing of a lone figure, himself, in the early November evening.

On this particular evening he began his journey in a westerly direction, towards the hidden sea. There was a good crystal frost in the air; it cut the nose and made the lungs blaze like a Christmas tree inside; you could feel the cold light going on and off, all the branches filled with invisible snow. He listened to the faint push of his soft shoes through autumn leaves with satisfaction, and whistled a cold quiet whistle between his teeth, occasionally picking up a leaf as he passed, examining its skeletal pattern in the infrequent lamplights as he went on, smelling its rusty smell.

'Hello, in there,' he whispered to every house on every side as he moved. 'What's up to-night on Channel 4, Channel 7, Channel 9? Where are the cowboys rushing, and do I see the United States Cavalry over the next hill to the rescue?'

The street was silent and long and empty, with only his shadow moving like the shadow of a hawk in mid-country. If he closed his eyes and stood very still, frozen, he could imagine himself upon the centre of a plain, a wintry, windless Arizona desert with no house in a thousand miles, and only dry river beds, the streets, for company.

'What is it now?' he asked the houses, noticing his wrist watch. 'Eight-thirty p.m.? Time for a dozen assorted murders? A quiz? A revue? A comedian falling off the stage?'

Was that a murmur of laughter from within a moon-white house? He hesitated, but went on when nothing more happened. He stumbled over a particularly uneven section of side-walk. The cement was vanishing under flowers and grass. In ten years of walking by night or day, for thousands of miles, he had never met another person walking, not one in all that time.

He came to a cloverleaf intersection which stood silent where two main highways crossed the town. During the day it was a thunderous surge of cars, the gas stations open, a great insect rustling and a ceaseless jockeying for position as the scarab-beetles, a faint incense puttering from their exhausts, skimmed homeward to the far directions. But now these highways, too, were like streams in a dry season, all stone and bed and moon radiance.

He turned back on a side street, circling around towards his home. He was within a block of his destination when the lone car turned a corner quite suddenly and flashed a fierce white cone of light upon him. He stood entranced, not unlike a night moth, stunned by the illumination, and then drawn towards it.

A metallic voice called to him:

'Stand still. Stay where you are! Don't move!'

He halted.

'Put up your hands!'

'But –' he said.

'Your hands up! Or we'll shoot!'

The police, of course, but what a rare, incredible thing; in a city of three million, there was only *one* police car left, wasn't that correct? Ever since a year ago, 2051, the election year, the force had been cut down from three cars to one. Crime was ebbing; there was no need now for the police, save for this one lone car wandering and wandering the empty streets.

'Your name?' said the police car in a metallic whisper. He couldn't see the men in it for the bright light in his eyes.

'Leonard Mead,' he said.

'Speak up!'

'Leonard Mead!'

'Business or profession?'

'I guess you'd call me a writer.'

'No profession,' said the police car, as if talking to itself. The light held him fixed, like a museum specimen, needle thrust through chest.

'You might say that,' said Mr Mead. He hadn't written in years. Magazines and books didn't sell any more. Everything went on in the tomblike houses at night now, he thought, continuing his fancy. The tombs, ill-lit by television light, where the people sat like the dead, the grey or multicoloured lights touching their faces, but never really touching *them*.

'No profession,' said the phonograph voice, hissing. 'What are you doing out?'

'Walking,' said Leonard Mead.

'Walking!'

'Just walking,' he said simply, but his face felt cold.

'Walking, just walking, walking?'

'Yes, sir.'

'Walking where? For what?'

'Walking for air. Walking to *see*.'

'Your address!'

'Eleven South Saint James Street.'

'And there is air *in* your house, you have an air *conditioner*, Mr Mead?'

'Yes.'

'And you have a viewing screen in your house to see with?'

'No.'

'No?' There was a crackling quiet that in itself was an accusation.

'Are you married, Mr Mead?'

'No.'

'Not married,' said the police voice behind the fiery beam. The moon was high and clear among the stars and the houses were grey and silent.

'Nobody wanted me,' said Leonard Mead with a smile.

'Don't speak unless you're spoken to!'

Leonard Mead waited in the cold night.

'Just *walking*, Mr Mead?'

'Yes.'

'But you haven't explained for what purpose.'

'I explained; for air, and to see, and just to walk.'

'Have you done this often?'

'Every night for years.'

The police car sat in the centre of the street with its radio throat faintly humming.

'Well, Mr Mead,' it said.

'Is that all?' he asked politely.

'Yes,' said the voice. 'Here.' There was a sigh, a pop. The back door of the police car sprang wide. 'Get in.'

'Wait a minute, I haven't done anything!'

'Get in.'

'I protest!'

'Mr Mead.'

He walked like a man suddenly drunk. As he passed the front window of the car he looked in. As he had expected, there was no one in the front seat, no one in the car at all.

'Get in.'

He put his hand to the door and peered into the back seat, which was a little cell, a little black jail with bars. It smelled of riveted steel. It smelled of harsh antiseptic; it smelled too clear and hard and metallic. There was nothing soft there.

'Now if you had a wife to give you an alibi,' said the voice. 'But –'

'Where are you taking me?'

The car hesitated, or rather gave a faint whirring click, as if information, somewhere, was dripping card by punch-slotted card under electric eyes. 'To the Psychiatric Centre for Research on Regressive Tendencies.'

He got in. The door shut with a soft thud. The police car rolled through the night avenues, flashing its dim lights ahead.

They passed one house on one street a moment later, one house in an entire city of houses that were dark, but this one particular house had all of its electric lights brightly lit, every window a loud yellow illumination, square and warm in the cool darkness.

'That's *my* house,' said Leonard Mead.

No one answered him.

The car moved down the empty river bed streets and off away, leaving the empty streets with the empty side-walks, and no sound and no motion all the rest of the chill November night.

Ray Bradbury

ASSIGNMENTS

MAKING AND PRESENTING

1   **Continuing stories**   Look back over the two story openings, to *Flowers for Algernon* and *The Diary of the Rose,* and add another ten or twelve diary entries so as to complete one of these stories. Try to catch something of the tone and narrative style of the original piece.

2   Take any of the openings to stores on pages 175–6 and continue the story in the same style (as you imagine it).

3   Using an experimental approach, write a science fiction short story entitled *Lost in Time.* Before you start you might like to consider your approaches to the following:

(a) **Characters**
How can you make your characters original? Are you going to have a central character . . . a hero? Is the central character a human, a fictional creation of your own . . . a robot . . . or something that you alone have invented, something unique?
Will it help you to draw, sketch or doodle the characters before you start writing?
Would it help you to think of the setting or landscape, or even spacescape, before you begin? How does this affect your characters?

(b) **Telling the story**
What sort of language are you going to use to tell the story? Are you going to be the storyteller or is it going to be some other person, a 'third person', who is going to do it? Are you going to use standard English or are you going to invent a new form of English to suit your purpose? What languages are your characters going to speak? Is there room for you to introduce some type of code system?

What form is the story going to take: a simple account; a diary; part of a spacecraft's log-book? Is it going to be told from the point of view of one character only or of more than one? If you want to use more than one character as a storyteller, you need to think of ways of identifying each narrator . . . by using different-coloured inks, for example, or by working out completely different voices for your storytellers.

(c) **Putting the story together**
Experiment with the way you put your story together. Work out any different, new and original 'futuristic' ways that you can find to give your story a different structure.

–Is it going to involve a journey? How do you record it?

–Are you including an element of mystery and suspense? Will this mean a series of cliff-hangers or false trails?

–Is there going to be a chase or a final confrontation? Will you need to think about building up to a climax?

–Are you thinking of moving around in time? Will you need to write in flashbacks or to give glimpses of the future of the story?

4 Use one of the following openings to write your own SF story:

(a) The sun was getting smaller each day and the earth was getting colder . . . we had to do something and do it quickly if we were to survive . . .

(b) They stood there frozen with fear, staring at the solid, silvery object which had just appeared before their eyes not twenty yards away. Then, slowly, some internal mechanism whirred and a panel, which they had not previously noticed, began to slide open . . .

(c) I thought that an afternoon out picking blackberries would be the perfect relaxation until I saw that small cylinder hidden in the brambles, radiating a bright green luminous light . . .

5 Design a book-jacket; include an account of the author and a brief summary of the story, for any science fiction novel or story which you like.

6 Using music (for example, Holst's *The Planets*, Vaughan Williams's *Antarctica*, Strauss's *Thus Spake Zarathustra*, or various pieces of electronic music), record on video or cassette the opening scene of a science fiction story, either invented by yourself or adapted from an established story.

RESEARCHING AND RESPONDING

1 **'The Book Programme – year 2050'**   Assuming that there **are** books in the year 2050, write and perform the script of a radio or television show (or the equivalent entertainment medium for the year 2050) which looks back at some of the favourite science fiction books of this century. Talk about how far the visions of the future described in these books actually came true.

You will probably have some favourite books in mind for this purpose, but if you want to read some others, these titles will make good reading and help you:

H.G. Wells, *The Time Machine*
John Christopher, *Death of Grass*
(or any book from the *Tripods* trilogy)
Aldous Huxley, *Brave New World*
Bruce Swindells, *Brother in the Land*
Louise Lawrence, *Children of the Dust*
Isaac Asimov, *2001*

There are many SF books by Ray Bradbury and Nicholas Fisk, and, of course, the vision of the future that George Orwell presents in *1984*.

2 Find out more about two of the following science-fiction writers and prepare a five-minute talk about **one** book by each writer: H.G. Wells, Jules Verne, Isaac Asimov, Doris Lessing, Arthur C. Clarke, John Wyndham, Kurt Vonnegut, John Christopher, Ursula Le Guin.

3 Science-fiction stories have become one of the most popular genres for the comic-strip style of presentation. In this form, they usually rely upon a strong 'heroic' central character who possesses superhuman powers. The names of these characters have almost become part of modern folklore: Superman . . . Wonderwoman . . . Batman . . . Spiderman . . ., and so on.
Collect a number of the adventures of these characters together and try to work out what it is that makes them so popular. What character qualities do they represent? What are their special powers and how do they use them? What sort of people or creatures are their opponents? Can you pick out a pattern or structure in the stories? What can you say about the style of the illustrations – the colours, the quality of line drawing, about how action is presented and exaggerated? Make a series of notes for classroom discussion.

4 From your research and reading, prepare a classroom display on 'The Development of Science Fiction'.

5 **Exploring genre**   Make a study of your own library (school library or local library) and see how the books (fiction as well as non-fiction) are divided according to genre. You may have to ask the librarian for some help. Make a list of the classifications and report back to the class.

6 Make a study of the reading habits of a group of people. For example:
(a) the road in which you live.
(b) a class in your school
(c) a group of old-age pensioners
(d) a random group using the local library on one afternoon.
Find out what genres are preferred and why.

7 Drawing on your own reading (and making use of the library), make notes on the different kinds of genre in fiction. Give as many examples as you can. Also jot down your own preferences as a reader. What is it that draws you to some stories and not to others? Write up your notes as an essay entitled 'Genre in Fiction'.

GLOSSARY
OF
TERMS

allegory   a story in which the characters and setting represent moral or spiritual ideas.

anti-hero   the central character in a story or novel who contrasts with the traditional hero in being human, ordinary, uncertain, etc.

autobiography   a narrative in which the author tells the story of his or her own life or some part of it. See chapter 2.

biography   a narrative in which the author tells the story of somebody else's life.

collage   any art created by bringing together words or images from different sources.

confession   an account of very personal experience, originally a form of spiritual autobiography in which the author describes his or her conversion to faith.

dialect   a language or manner of speaking peculiar to an individual, class or region.

dialogue   the actual speech used by the characters in any narrative. See chapter 8.

documentary   a narrative kept very close to actual life, often using evidence from newspapers, reports, letters, etc.

epistolary fiction   a novel or story constructed through an exchange of letters between the characters. See chapter 13.

fable   a short story which generally uses animals and is designed to make a moral point.

fairy story   narrations in the oral tradition about the fortunes and misfortunes of various heroes or heroines.

first-person narrative   a story told using the 'I' or 'we' voice. See chapter 12.

flash-back   a term used to describe any scene in a narrative to show past events.

genre   a type or kind of writing, e.g. autobiography, novel, story, poem. See chapter 16.

hero   main male character in the narrative, generally seen as possessing good human qualities.

heroine   main female character in the narrative, generally seen as possessing good human qualities.

interior monologue   a device for showing the immediate inner thoughts of a character in fiction. See **stream of consciousness.** See also chapter 14.

irony   a form of expression, often satirical, where the words used **say** one thing and **mean** another.

legend   the heroic story of people who once lived or may have lived, e.g. Robin Hood.

memoir   a form of autobiography in which the author concentrates mainly on public events.

monologue   the narration of a novel or story through the mind of a character, following the flow of that character's thoughts and feelings. See chapter 14.

myth   narratives which, unlike legend, involve divine heroes and heroines.

narrative   a connected account of events, fictional or real. See chapter 1.

narrator   the person telling the story.

novella   a long short story.

oral tradition   the tradition of stories, sayings, poems, which are handed down through speech and not writing. See chapter 5.

parable   a simple short story which makes a moral point.

plot   the plan and sequence of events in fiction often designed to create suspense and curiosity in the reader. See chapter 10.

protagonist   the central character in narrative. See chapter 7.

re-telling   the practice of taking an old story and telling it in a new way. See chapter 6.

satire   a kind of protest against the state of things through ridicule.

setting   the place where the events happen in a story or novel. See chapter 9.

stream of consciousness   a style of writing which seeks to capture the changing flow of inner experience. See chapter 14.

style   the distinctive manner of expression in any writing.

sub-plot   a subsidiary plot in a narrative which works in with the main plot.

symbol   an object which stands for something else, e.g. a pair of scales can symbolise justice. See chapter 11.

theme   the central idea of the narrative.

third-person narrative   the most common way of telling a story where the author tells the story at a distance from his or her characters. See **first-person narrative.** See also chapter 15.

INDEX OF AUTHORS

ACKNOWLEDGEMENTS

The authors and publisher would like to thank the following for permission to reproduce from copyright material:

Childhood by Nathalie Sarraute, translated by Barbara Wright by permission of John Calder (Publishers) Ltd. *As I Walked Out One Midsummer Morning* by Laurie Lee, by permission of Andre Deutsch Ltd, 1969. *I Know Why the Caged Bird Sings* copyright © Maya Angelou, published by Virago Press. *Writing a Novel* by John Braine, by permission of Methuen London. 'At Sea' from *Boule de Suif and other stories* by Guy de Maupassant, translated by H.N.P. Sloman, © H.N.P. Sloman 1946, reproduced by permission of Penguin Books Ltd. *The Lost Diaries of Albert Smith* by Robert Muller, by permission of the author. *Riddley Walker* by Russell Hoban published by Jonathan Cape, by permission of David Higham Associates Ltd. *A Family Supper* by permission of Rogers, Coleridge and White Ltd. "Brian 'Squizzy' Taylor" by Moya Costello, by permission of the author. 'The Fury' from *The Desperadoes* © Stan Barstow 1966, published by Michael Joseph Ltd. 'Annie Luker's Ghost' from *Folktales Told Around the World*, ed. Dorson, © 1975 by The University of Chicago. All rights reserved. 'Give and Take' by Robert Henry and 'Journey by Night' by Undine Guiseppi from *Backfire* by permission of U. Guiseppi. 'The Triumph of Jessie Jones' by Daphne Glazer by permission of the author. 'The Poison Ladies' from *The Watercress Girl and other stories* by H.E. Bates published by Michael Joseph Ltd, by permission of the Estate of H.E. Bates. 'The Vulture' from *Great Wall of China* and 'The Home-Coming' from *Description of a Struggle* by Franz Kafka © 1933 Copyright 1958 by Schocken Books Inc. Martin Secker and Warburg Ltd. 'Town Mouse and Country Mouse' from *Fables of Aesop* translated by S.A. Handford, © S.A. Handford 1954, reproduced by permission of Penguin Books Ltd. 'The Mouse Who Went to the Country' by James Thurber, by permission of Hamish Hamilton. *The Songlines* by Bruce Chatwin published by Jonathan Cape, by permission of the Estate of Bruce Chatwin. 'Cameron 44.40' from *In Watermelon Sugar* by Richard Brautigan published by Jonathan Cape, by permission of the Estate of Richard Brautigan. 'Seen in the Canteen' from *Adam, One Afternoon* by Italo Calvino reprinted by permission of Martin Secker and Warburg Ltd. *The Graduate* by Charles Webb by permission of Constable Publishers. *The Craft of Novel Writing* by Dianne Doubtfire, by permission of Allison and Busby. 'Yellow Trains' by Penelope Lively © 1978 from *Pack of Cards* © 1986 by permission of William Heinemann Ltd. 'Lost in the Unreality of Docklands' by Penelope Lively from the *Guardian* by permission of Murray Pollinger. 'The De Wets Come to Kloof Grange' from *This Was the Old Chief's Country* copyright 1951 Doris Lessing, reprinted by permission of Jonathan Clowes Ltd, London, on behalf of Doris Lessing.

Unleaving by Jill Paton-Walsh published by The Bodley Head, by permission of David Higham Associates Ltd. *A Passage to India* by E.M. Forster published by Edward Arnold. *Waterland* by Graham Swift © 1983 reprinted by permission of William Heinemann Ltd. *Out of Africa* by Karen Blixen published by Jonathan Cape, by permission of the Estate of Karen Blixen. *The Brothers Rico* by Georges Simenon, by permission of the author. 'The Flowers' from *In Love and Trouble*, and *The Color Purple* by Alice Walker published by The Women's Press, by permission of David Higham Associates Ltd. *The Pumpkin Eater* by Penelope Mortimer, by permission of Century Hutchinson Ltd. 'A Message from the Emperor' by Franz Kafka, by permission of Macdonald and Co. Ltd. *Lanterns Across the Snow* © Susan Hill 1987, reproduced by permission of Michael Joseph Ltd. *Gorilla, My Love* by Toni Cade Bambara, by permission of The Women's Press Ltd. *The Progress of Love* by Alice Munro published by Chatto and Windus. *The Magus* by John Fowles published by Jonathan Cape, by permission of the author and Anthony Sheil Associates Ltd. 'The Use of Force' reprinted by permission of Faber and Faber Ltd from *The Doctor Stories* by William Carlos Williams. 'The Case for the Defence' from *Collected Stories* by Graham Greene published by William Heinemann Ltd and The Bodley Head Ltd by permission of Laurence Pollinger. *Last Letters* by Oliver Blanc, by permission of Andre Deutsch Ltd. 'Mary' from *Mrs Reinhardt and other stories* by Edna O'Brien, published by Weidenfeld and Nicholson Ltd. *Z for Zachariah* by Robert O'Brien published by Victor Gollancz Ltd. *The Wedding* by John Gwyilym Jones published by Gomer Press. *We'll to the Woods No More* by Edouard Dujardin published by Libris by permission of New Directions Publishing Corporation. *Pilgrimage* by Dorothy Richardson copyright © 1967 by Rose Odle, published by Virago Press. *Female Friends* copyright © Fay Weldon 1975 first published by Heinemann, by permission of the author and Anthony Sheil Associates Ltd. *Ulysses* by James Joyce published by The Bodley Head, by permission of the Executors of the James Joyce Estate. 'Neons' from *Boat* by Ania Walwicz published by Angus and Robertson. *The Bell* by Iris Murdoch published by Chatto and Windus. 'The Apprentice' by Hilaire Belloc reprinted by permission of the Peters Fraser and Dunlop Group Ltd. 'Red Letter Day' from *Spring Song* by Joyce Cary by permission of the Cary Estate. *A Dictionary of Literary Terms* by Barnett, Berman and Burto published by Constable Publishers. Extract from *The Independent* by Miles Kington by permission of the author and *The Independent*. *The Compass Rose* by Ursula Le Guin, by permission of A.P. Watt Ltd on behalf of the author. "The Fun They Had" from *Earth is Room Enough* by Isaac Asimov, copyright © 1957 by Isaac Asimov. Used by permission of Doubleday, a division of Bantam, Doubleday, Dell Publishing Group, Inc.

Illustrations

p.8 Claire Bretecher: *More Frustration*; Methuen, London   p.9 George Grosz: *The Owners*, 1920 © DACS 1990   p.10 From *Women's Review*, by permission of the Syndics of Cambridge University Library   p.11 From Gustav Dore: *The Adventures of Baron Munchausen*; by permission of the Syndics of Cambridge University Library   p.12 From Phillips: *The New Inferno*, 1911   p.15 By courtesy of Badedas   p.15 By courtesy of Heineken; Lowe Howard-Spink   p.18 Cambridgeshire Collection, Cambridgeshire Libraries   p.18 Michael Brooke   p.18 Kay Saunders   p.19 Ursula Powys-Lybbe   p.20 Collection Fundacion Robert Brady, A.C., Cuernavaca, Morelos, Mexico; reproduccion autorizada por El Instituto Nacional de Bellas Artes y Literatura   p.20 © The Imogen Cunningham Trust   p.20 'The Little Deer' by Frida Kahlo from the collection of Mr Espinosa Ulloa, Mexico City. Photo by Raul Salinar. Taken from A Biography of Frida Kahlo by Hayden Herrera published by Bloomsbury   p.28 Courtesy of the Dorothea Lange Collection. © The City of Oakland, The Oakland Museum, 1964, 1938   pp.29/120 Oslo

Kommunes Kunstamlinger, Munch-Museet; Munchforlaget a/s   p.42 Evelyn Waugh: *Scoop*; by courtesy of Penguin Books Ltd.   p.41 Lewis Carroll: *Alice in Wonderland and Through the Looking Glass*; by courtesy of Bantam Press   p.41 Maureen O'Donoghue: *Winner*; by courtesy of Penguin Books Ltd.   p.41 Mervyn Peake: *Titus Groan*; by courtesy of Methuen London Ltd.   p.51 Hutchinson Library   p.52 The Raymond Mander and Joe Mitchenson Theatre Collection Ltd.   p.60 Edward Hicks: *The Peaceable Kingdom*, The Brooklyn Museum, 40.340, Dick S. Ramsay Fund   p.61 Picasso: *Minotauromacia*, 1936 © DACS 1990; Cliche des Musees Nationaux, Paris. © Photo RMN – SPADEM   p.62 Charles Keeping: *Prometheus*; B.L. Kearley Ltd.   p.70 Michael Brooke   p.71 Paul Strand: *Blind Woman, New York, 1916*. Copyright © 1971, Aperture Foundation, Inc., Paul Strand Archive   p.75 Weintraub Entertainment   p.75 © 1967 United Artists Corporation. All Rights Reserved.   p.76 By permission of the Syndics of Cambridge University Library   pp.82–3 Raymond Briggs: *When the Wind Blows*, London, 1982; © Raymond Briggs. Reproduced by permission of Hamish Hamilton Ltd. p.84 M4218 *Une discussion litteraire a la deuxieme Galerie Honore Daumier*, France, 1808 – 1879, Lithograph 238 × 220 mm from Babock Bequest, courtesy, Museum of Fine Arts, Boston   p.91 Courtesy of the Dorothea Lange Collection. © The City of Oakland, The Oakland Museum, 1938   p.92 Topham   pp.96/122 From Manguel and Guadalupi: *Dictionary of Imaginary Places*; by permission of the Syndics of Cambridge University Library   pp.97/109 Reproduced by permission of Shuckburgh Reynolds Ltd from *Whodunnit?*, edited by H.R.F. Keating, 1982; by permission of the Syndics of the Cambridge University Library   p.104 M.

Tursi/Sygma; from John Hillelson Agency   p.116 Alice Walker: *In Love and Trouble*, Harcourt Brace Jovanovich   p.117 James Thurber: *The Thurber Carnival*, © Hamish Hamilton Ltd.   p.117 By courtesy of Esso Petroleum Co. Ltd.   p.121 From Bunyan: *Pilgrim's Progress*; by permission of the Syndics of Cambridge University Library   p.129 International Museum of Photography at George Eastman House   p.137 Rijks museum – Stichting, Amsterdam   p.138 Soldat d'une garrison autrichienne ecrivant une lettre, A. Kertesz; © Ministere de la Culture – France.   p.140 From Grossmith: *Diary of a Nobody*; by permission of the Syndics of Cambridge University Library   p.145 From Daniel Defoe: *Robinson Crusoe*, J.M. Dent 1974   pp.150-1 Translation © Methuen Children's Books   p.153 Brian Harris: *The Independent*   p.154 Henri Rousseau: *The Sleeping Gypsy*, 1897; oil on canvas (129.5 × 200.7 GM) Collection, The Museum of Modern Art, New York, Gift of Mrs Simon Guggenheim.   p.155 Marc Riboud from the John Hillelson Agency   p.162 Le Cirque, A. Kertesz; © Ministere de la Culture, France   p.173 P.D. James: *Unnatural Causes*, artist Mark Harrison, by courtesy of Sphere Books Ltd   p.173 James Herbert: *Lair*; artist Gerald Grace; by courtesy of New English Library Ltd.   p.174 Donna Baker: *Black Cameo*; by courtesy of Headline Book Publishing PLC   p.177 Robert Heinlain: *Friday*; by courtesy of New English Library Ltd.

Every attempt has been made to locate copyright holders for all material in this book. The publisher would be glad to hear from anyone whose copyright has been unwittingly infringed.